LOSING AND FUSING
Borderline Transitional Object and Self Relations

**Roger A. Lewin, M.D., and
Clarence G. Schulz, M.D.**

JASON ARONSON INC.
Northvale, New Jersey
London

The author gratefully acknowledges permission to quote from the following:

COLLECTED POEMS by Wallace Stevens. Copyright © 1936 by Wallace Stevens and renewed © 1964 by Holly Stevens. Reprinted by permission of Alfred A. Knopf, Inc.

FULLY EMPOWERED by Pablo Neruda. Translation copyright © 1967, 1969, 1970, 1975 by Alastair Reid. Reprinted by permission of Farrar, Straus and Giroux, Inc.

An earlier version of Chapter 9 appeared in *Psychiatry*, February 1992, volume 55, pages 16–21.

Production Editor: Leslie Block

This book was set in 11½ on 13½ Garamond by Lind Graphics of Upper Saddle River, New Jersey, and printed and bound by Haddon Craftsmen of Scranton, Pennsylvania.

Library of Congress Cataloging-in-Publication Data

Lewin, Roger A.
    Losing and fusing : borderline transitional object and self relations / by Roger A. Lewin and Clarence G. Schulz.
        p. cm.
    Includes bibliographical references and index.
    ISBN 0-87668-490-8 (hard cover)
    1. Borderline personality disorder—Treatment. 2. Self psychology. 3. Object relations (Psychoanalysis) I. Schulz, Clarence G. II. Title.
    [DNLM: 1. Borderline Personality Disorder—therapy. 2. Psychotherapy—methods. WM 190 L672s]
RC569.5.B67L48 1992
616.85′8520651—dc20
DNLM/DLC
for Library of Congress   92-6219

Manufactured in the United States of America. Jason Aronson Inc. offers books and cassettes. For information and catalog write to Jason Aronson Inc., 230 Livingston Street, Northvale, New Jersey 07647.

Contents

Acknowledgment

Acknowledgments are redundant, for any deeply felt work is itself an acknowledgment of a whole lifetime's worth of people, both of those who gave us life and those who have and are sharing it with us. The most sincere acknowledgment is in the work we do.

This particular book came to be during a period of my life that was at the same time undeniably sad, even tragic, and yet also undeniably fruitful and satisfying. The memory of my first wife, the late Julia Vandivort Lewin, and of her special sensitivity and care for the deeply vulnerable, wounded, and diffident, was with me throughout its writing. Mrs. Erna Furman and Dr. Jerome Styrt have both taught me and cared for me over extended periods. Their practical human examples have been instruction, inspiration, and solace.

My wife Joan has been generous and feelingful in her support of this book, especially at times when I doubted the worth of the project. Her contributions have been both personal and professional. It is through her and her work that I first was able to glimpse the profundity of what movement therapy has to offer. My daughter Rachel has accepted the work of writing as yet another inhabitant of our household with good grace at a difficult time.

Under the auspices of Sheppard Pratt, Steve Sharfstein has provided both moral and financial support. Without his confidence in it, I am not sure this book would have been written. One of the great pleasures of this book has been the opportunity for continued and deepening dialogue with Clarence Schulz, who has been a true friend as well as a remarkable teacher and colleague. I can only hope that we have been able to give back to a rich tradition a measure of what it has given us. Certainly, we owe a debt to the vision of Moses Sheppard and the countless individuals who have helped keep it alive.

Roger A. Lewin, M.D.

Creativity requires a holding environment. My concentric series of supports were in place during the evolution of this book. Thanks are due to my patients, coauthor, family, residents, colleagues, publisher, teachers, friends, opponents, hospital staff, and the profession.

They were all there for me, for us.

Clarence G. Schulz, M.D.

Everything Helped A Little, But Not Enough

Twenty-year-old Mona's five years of illness and treatment had already included virtually everything in the way of symptoms and virtually everything in the way of treatment. In a remarkable and all-too-common feat of repression and denial, she and her family insisted that she had had no troubles until middle adolescence. They might as well have said that she had had nothing but trouble, so frail was her sense of self.

Since that time she had had an unending series of crises featuring cutting, burning, suicide attempts, anxiety attacks, mood disturbances, somatic disturbances, pseudoseizures, alcohol and drug abuse, anorexia and some suggestion of dissociative episodes. Needless to say, the trouble went back much farther than middle adolescence, probably preceding the dawn of any linguistically organized memory.

A range of treatments had been tried. She had had four short-term hospitalizations, outpatient psychotherapies ranging from one to four times a week, family interventions, psychopharmacological treatment with antidepressants, lithium, neuroleptics, anticonvulsants, stimulants, and even a series of electroconvulsive treatments.

Mona's summary of this extended and painful adventure was as concise as it was arresting. "Everything helped a little," she said, "but not enough." When asked what she looked forward to for herself, she said, "I want to go to school and to be happy." She betrayed no sense that any of her quandary was internal. Nor did she seem to have the least inkling of what the content of this happiness that she said she sought might be. It sounded more like a state of unfeeling than a state of feeling. It was not so much that she was convinced that solutions had to come from the outside, as that the question had never been posed for internal debate. She took it as much for granted that it was all up to others as fish take for granted the water in which they swim. She had hardly a glimmer of a sense of herself as a self-reflective person.

Mona helps us to focus our attention very quickly and very directly on the problem of *enough*. What is it that makes it possible for something to be enough? All forms of sufficiency are relative. Whether what we have and get is enough for us depends on our capacity to cherish it, to appreciate it, and to perform that most commonplace and yet complicated of human functions, namely, to enjoy.

Whenever we talk about satisfaction, we are talking about making something be enough. This notion of an active process is built into the history of the word, which is derived from the Latin *satis*, meaning "enough," and *facere*, meaning "to make or to do." In a suggestive linguistic twist, the word *satis* seems to emerge from the same network of roots that has given rise to sad and to "asset." (Asset is related to the French word *assez,* which means "enough.")

Psychologically, since there is no experience that cannot be spoiled, the capacity to experience any internal asset depends crucially on the capability for being sad. It is as if the history of the language has anticipated some of Melanie

Klein's (1955) ideas about movement toward the depressive position. Containment and the capacity to maintain separateness and tolerate separation, loss, and reunion are very closely related. To contain our own experiences, we must be separate. We must not be so fused with others as to be too confused with them and by them. We must be able to remain with ourselves through stresses, even when important others are not literally present.

Any satisfaction, any experience of enough, involves a making do. It involves the acceptance of limits. For experience to have shape and form, it must be bounded. Viewed against the background of primordial human wishing, there is already something sad about this. Enough means neither too much nor too little. It has to do with the capacity to locate experience in a middle range, which most borderline patients are not able to do.

The middle range, that area in which it is possible for an experience to be enough or satisfactory, remains to be constructed. Nor is the construction of this internal psychological space a simple project. Borderline patients exist at the limit, always in tension, as if they need the tension to produce an edge that convinces them that they exist. Borderline patients can test limits. What they cannot do is to limit the testing.

In much of what follows, our focus is on what makes it possible for something to be experienced as enough, that is, neither "too much" nor "too little." We try to understand what advantages borderline patients derive from oscillating as they do between the two poles of "too much" and "too little," experiencing themselves as alternately overwhelmed and deprived, intruded upon and abandoned, compelled to acquiesce and compelled to revolt, but always at intolerable levels of tension.

Why do they need to be stuck where they are stuck? Why do pain and interpersonal tensions seem to have a constitutive, if not constitutional role for them? What is it about their fragile and fragmentary sense of self that requires this kind of propping up? Why are separation experiences so threatening? Why do they need to be so negativistic? Why is any move forward so fraught with regressive dangers? What is the trouble with getting better?

We also try to relate our understanding to various strategies for therapeutic intervention. In other words, we try to develop a framework for understanding the borderline patient's predicament that renders it more familiar and more readable and therefore is a help in stabilizing the therapist's own self as this predicament impacts on him. This does not mean that we have in mind particular concrete prescriptions for the treatment of individual patients or individual symptoms. In general, we see borderline patients as being stuck with more concrete levels of understanding, more concrete devices for promoting self-continuity and self-coherence, and handicapped in moving toward gentler and more abstract ways of soothing themselves and keeping themselves in stable relationships with themselves—a problem that we all confront. To a lesser or greater degree, we all have the kinds of problems with borders that borderline patients have.

In keeping with our emphasis on the less concrete, the more general, the more heuristic, and the more integrative, what we are trying to do is to sketch an approach that, far from generating algorithmic procedures, serves the goal of enriching thought about treatments that are handcrafted over long periods of time. Our approach is more process oriented than product oriented, more collaborative than didactic, more interested in uncertainty as the prelude to seriously playful inventiveness than bent on asserting dubious certainties.

We want to help the therapist with the difficult task of keeping his mind open to the borderline experience as it presents itself across a sometimes stupefyingly wide range of clinical predicaments. We want to help the therapist become intrigued with what bothers him about treating borderline patients and bothered about why it is so hard to help these patients share that intrigue.

BREADTH OF CONCEPTION OF PSYCHIATRIC ILLNESS AND TREATMENT

A fundamental influence on the kind of treatment that a psychiatric patient receives for his disorder is the breadth or narrowness of the view of psychiatric illness that the treating person holds. For example, a person who presents with a phobia of spiders may be regarded as having a rather circumscribed, limited disorder. It may be taken, so to speak, at face value. The disorder, in this view, consists in certain reactions to spiders and consequent behaviors. Treatment would consist in influencing these reactions and behaviors. Desensitization procedures might be recommended. Efforts to link the phobia to inferences about a general personality system or dynamic organization and developmental history could be regarded as extraneous and uneconomic.

This kind of a view does not go looking for trouble.Problems are stated in terms of observable behavior. Inferences are kept to a minimum. What you see is what you get. Treatment goals are clearly bounded. An operational criterion for cure is that the patient will not manifest this fear and avoidance of spiders. A simple and lucid standard for judging efficacy of treatment results. Treatment can be rather straightforwardly described, standardized, taught, and tested in protocols. It lends itself more readily to mass production, a significant economic advantage. All those who have phobia of spiders are thought of as having the same disorder. The function and significance of the symptom is not referred to wider social, personal, and developmental contexts.

The patient may well be satisfied with this kind of an approach, as opposed to one that attempts to elicit the significances and functions of the symptom, to survey with the patient the whole field of his dynamic functioning and adaptation. Why should he reassess his style of relating to others, become invested in understanding the vicissitudes of his conflicts over aggression and intimacy, when the impact on his functioning does not seem so large to him? Why not limit the scope of the repairs to be undertaken?

Whichever approach is selected, there are opportunity costs. While the more circumscribed approach may minimize capitalizing on developmental promptings encapsulated in the symptom, the broader one may drain time and energy from other important pursuits in order to support the more elaborate therapeutic enterprise. It is often overlooked that the major investment in psychotherapy is the patient's time and trouble, only partially represented by money. Psychotherapy is an extremely taxing undertaking, not least because it involves a personal venture into the unknown and, at a minimum, provisional trust of another human being.

As the severity of illness and the complexity and diversity of symptomatic manifestations increase, a broader view of illness may come to impose itself. Consider a patient who not only has a phobia of spiders but also cuts and burns herself, abuses drugs, has made numerous suicide attempts, starves herself to the point of emaciation, often experiences sleep disturbance, complains of constant boredom, believes that she is a purely bad person, has managed totally to alienate her family, and has been unable to live outside of a hospital for longer than nine months at a stretch over a seven-year period.

If we try to describe her illness in purely behavioral terms, the clutter is quickly apparent. Treatment remedies can become cumbersome. For example, we could well have a set of prescriptions about how to manage cutting and another about how to manage burning, yet another about how to manage drugs and another about how to manage alcohol, still another about how to manage eating behavior. With all this, we might have no way of addressing the problem of occasional serious suicidal actions. We might even hear the argument that since the patient is not currently suicidal, this is not currently a problem. This last may be akin to arguing that, if a person is *not* falling over the cliff, the cliff is not there.

When the patient responds to the treatment program designed in this fashion, either with highly invested negativism or docile compliance, without any real engagement or allegiance, new quandaries are exposed. We are more likely to be driven to start making more complicated inferences, to engage in more abstract thinking about the illness, to question whether symptoms can be taken at their face values. We are more likely to think in terms of personality systems, developmental factors, constitutional constraints and vulnerabilities, and current social influences. There may be a push toward a more exploratory dimension to the treatment, a sense of the need to find a combination of approaches to the problems and to enlist the patient's active participation in the exploring and the combining. Instead of the conviction of knowing, we may find ourselves moving onto the softer ground of exploration with the conviction of not yet knowing and not knowing if we will ever get to know enough.

Where the treatment of the simple phobia might be mass produced, might have even the characteristics of the application of an algorithmic procedure, the treatment of a patient such as this one is more likely to require custom crafting, a capacity to tolerate uncertainties and indecisions, to tinker, reflect, experiment, innovate, to follow the patient as much as to lead. The patient's individual characteristics and idiosyncrasies will tell more in the treatment. The patient's will and internal motivations will be important treatment factors. It will be less easy to think of the treatment as being validated and justified by well-controlled double-blind scientific studies. In fact, the intellectual hegemony of the idea of double-blind studies may blind us to the nuances of this kind of treatment. A more directly clinical guidance system will have to come into play in the treatment, with the patient serving as his own control in evaluating results. The subjective takes center stage.

Patients such as this one will not appear as interchangeable particles. If they have important similarities, these will appear at much higher levels of abstraction with much less direct operational implication for treatment. For example, most patients like the one described above have elements of grandiosity, use splitting defenses, tolerate separation and frustration poorly, feel intense urges to merger, have ready recourse to magical thinking, have deficient impulse control, and so on. We might say that their whole functioning is pervaded by all-or-nothing mechanisms. Having put the matter this way does not prescribe treatment behaviors. It begins to sketch part of a conceptual orientation for customizing a treatment for individual patients. Translation into practice is itself a creative process, much as the rearing of each individual child is, despite a community's agreement on certain broad approaches and values.

We have often seen borderline patients who have been thought of in different partial ways at different points in their clinical courses. For example, many borderline patients are graduates of programs for eating disorders, programs designed to treat affective instability, programs designed to address self-destructive behaviors, and programs designed to address substance abuse. When patients make lists of the treatments they have received, the lists are often staggering for their length and diversity. Sometimes the patients themselves are surprised by the number and diversity of the treatments they have received. It is as if they had been on a long, strange journey and never stopped to review the various points through which they had passed. A crucial faculty for synthesis and establishment of an internal sense of personal history is strikingly absent.

One patient described herself during the time she was in college as "the A student who just wasn't there." She went on to describe her immunity to a whole array of treatments in the same terms. What had been left out in her treatment was the effort to engage her in any authentic way. Her compliant defense had never been successfully addressed. Because her mistrust not only of others but of herself was so profound, her surface was as frictionless and slippery as Teflon. What was so dangerous to her about deeper engagement? Why did she have to defeat treatment after treatment? Why was she always in the position of being both unable to live without something or someone and unable to live with the same thing or person? Was there a fundamental set of problems manifested across the whole range of her troubled living? If so, how could it best be described?

Treatments conceptualized in broader and more abstract terms have a more explicitly exploratory dimension. Because it is their aim to enlist the patient's thoughtful and feelingful participation in what amounts to a basic research-type investigation of how the patient lives, they take a long time. Often they are open-ended. Such ongoing treatments may change focus as they go along. For example, where initially and for a prolonged period the focus may just be on staying alive, as time goes on the focus may turn, for example, to issues revolving around the capacity for intimacy and enterprise. "I just didn't use to think this way," remarked one patient. "I couldn't imagine talking about this stuff back then because I didn't even know it existed." Another patient said, "You know, this kind of psychotherapy is like trying to make a picture when you have no idea what you're painting." There are needs that patients have that they are not aware of having until after they have been at least partially met. One way of thinking about treatment is as a project for the transformation of the patient's needs in experience.

DOCTOR–PATIENT RELATIONSHIP

The doctor–patient relationship is the central integrative feature in any ongoing broadly conceived treatment of a borderline patient. Everything else depends on it. To state this may seem commonplace, but it is also possible that this is one of those commonplace remarks that richly repays periodic reexamination. Taking something for granted may be a sign that we need to see it in a new and unfamiliar light. When we lose our capacity for surprise about the fundamental things, we have fallen into a form of sloth that can not serve our clinical work well. Fundamental things change with us as we change.

What do we mean when we talk of the doctor–patient relationship? How does everything else in the treatment depend on it? Why is it so easy to hate a borderline patient? Why is it so exasperating to work with these patients? Why does the disorder in the patient seem to produce an attending disorder in the doctor, if not a disorder of attention? Why is it possible to get so deeply and distressingly involved with these patients? How do these patients have the effect so often of subverting our therapeutic judgment, landing us in states where we long for clarity and definition and despair of it at the same time? Why is it so appealing simply to avoid working with these patients?

A relationship is not a thing. Rather, it is a process of a high order of complexity, with many different aspects highlighted differently at different times. It changes. It rearranges. It can appear strikingly different at different times, so much so that the two people who are party to it may both find themselves wondering whether they have changed beyond recognition. Nor is this to be regarded as out of the ordinary. If the goal is to support a personality reassessment and reorganization of sufficient scope and dimension to revalue some of the patient's basic categories of experiencing, then such a dynamic *is* required. Patients repeatedly surprise not just themselves but their doctors in the context of the doctor–patient relationship. Nor is it only the patients who surprise themselves.

Some years ago, in the midst of a discussion of procedures for assuring quality care, a colleague wryly suggested the following criterion. She proposed that, if the doctor learned something in the course of treating the patient, it was likely that the patient had gotten good clinical care. A stronger version of this quality assurance criterion might run that, *unless* the treating doctor learned something new about himself in the course of treating the patient, it was not likely that the patient had gotten first-class care.[1]

We radically underestimate ourselves if we believe that we do not have a great deal to learn about ourselves, however much we may already have come to know. We may also be underestimating ourselves if we deny that there is a great deal we might learn about ourselves that would be so painful that, not only do we wish to remain ignorant, but we stand ready to execute any messenger who brings us an inkling of this kind of curriculum. Certainly, borderline patients often react with this kind of horror when we try to bring them news of some of their basic character features. Treatment of borderline patients carries us back into the landscape of preoedipal intensities with sudden radical shifts in point-of-view, affective flavor, and organizing identifications. They show us vulnerabilities that we cannot appreciate without becoming ourselves vulnerable.

If change and variation are central features in the doctor–patient relationship, what is it that is constant in this relationship? What gives it its identity, its elasticity, its capacity to endure through change, and to change to absorb

---

1. This comment by Maria Klement, M.D., did nothing to stem the proliferation of so-called "quality assurance" technology. What it did was to propose a subjective criterion of greater simplicity and abstraction that usefully calls into question the drive toward cumbersome "objectification" of therapeutic conscience. It is a highly symptomatic development that "quality assurance" should be so biased in the direction of quantitative data.

change? Sometimes the simplest things are the subtlest and the most complicated. They may be so near and so pervasive in their importance that they are relegated to the background.

When we talk of the doctor–patient relationship, we are talking of the "back and forth" between the doctor and the patient, which takes place along a variety of channels. This "back and forth" has to do with words, looks, postural sets, and a whole series of cues that are interpreted, misinterpreted, and elaborated into fantasies, ideas, and actions by both parties. It is visceral. It happens in the body as well as in the mind, in the body of the participants' experience as well as in their experience of their bodies. We will devote a considerable amount of attention to discussing these channels and cues and the processes by which the interpretation, misinterpretation, and elaboration work. We will also discuss the dangers and difficulties that beset the workings of these processes. However, it is the "back and forth" itself that is of the most fundamental importance and that serves to protect the flexibility and vitality of the treatment. Treatment without involvement is no more possible than drying oneself off with a plastic towel.

The doctor–patient relationship is in a continual state of development and is experienced throughout by both parties as a mixture of threat and promise. With borderline patients, the doctor–patient relationship can careen suddenly and harrowingly back and forth between being too little and too much, overly valued and radically devalued. It seems often to have a kind of charge on it that is different than relationships with other patients. Nothing can be taken for granted and it is difficult to settle down to take a free breath. Here again is the telltale tension that marks the world of the borderline. In the treatment of many borderline patients, the doctor–patient relationship seems to exist by reason of being always at risk, just at the edge of extinction, as if it could only come into being by asymptotically, not asymptomatically, approaching the vanishing point.

Relationship means repetitive meetings, separations, reunions. It means repetitive risks and hopes, repetitive disillusionments and despairs, repetitive repairs and doubts, but, above all, repetitions. We intend the term *repetition* in the original etymological sense of trying over and over again. Treatment is trying, in both senses of the term. No one who has made an honest effort to work with borderline patients over any length of time and at any depth will have trouble recognizing just how trying the experience can be. Why can't apparently simple things be simple? Why can it seem even after years of work that the problem is not how to go on, but how to get started?

The doctor–patient relationship means a series of interpersonal communications; it also means an ongoing internal dialogue that is carried on in the realm of illusion in each one of the participants. "I can't remember," said one patient, "whether I told you this here in the session or whether I just told you in my mind." Another patient said, "I knew just what you would say about that, even though I still disagree with you completely. I haven't changed my mind."

We have noticed that when psychiatric residents give clinical presentations concerning their work with borderline patients they often close with a statement to the effect that they will never forget the patient, illustrating the intense internal relationship between the two. Often, the wish that they could forget the patient is only thinly veiled in their declarations of mnemonic fidelity. This conflict mirrors patients' intense struggles to find some form of involvement that does not threaten them with complete engulfment and loss of self.

What is different in the residents is the subtlety and the suppleness of their transitional processes that make it possible for them to deal with this kind of struggle in symbolic fantasy, feeling and not in action. Characterizing the developmental differences in transitional processes will be a major theme in our discussion of the treatment of borderline patients. Why do borderline patients so often seem stuck with using their own bodies as transitional objects in painful ways? Why do many of them seem to use themselves as voodoo dolls to get at others? Why can't they let go and proceed to more abstract and gentle forms of illusion? Why are they so terrified that any letting go is identical to a loss that can never be made good?

The doctor–patient relationship is a stage on which a whole variety of dramatic events can be enacted and reenacted. It provides an audience for these reenactments that can play a significant part in redirecting the pieces that are being staged. The doctor–patient relationship makes a place for experience, which always has the dual character of actuality and potentiality, not just a "having been," but also a continual "coming into being." We might even say that the doctor–patient relationship makes a home for experience, by which we mean something meaningful that happens to and in a person who counts not just for others but also for himself. By making a home, we mean the provision of a living receptivity that is emotionally convincing. Of course, here, too, it is illusion that is the foundation on which further construction can come to rest.

The doctor–patient relationship is not value free. It provides the framework for an advocacy of the values of relatedness, connection, autonomy, "back and forth" among human beings, the possibility of grief, reorganization, and repair, the view of persons and experiences as being meaningful, ongoing, and capable of making certain kinds of claims, and so forth. The advocacy of values need not be made explicit to be extremely powerful. Caring, of course, always has a destructive potential as well as a creative one: "I'll kill myself and that will take care of it once and for all," said a patient. In the treatment of borderline patients, it is, as we will discuss, especially important to try to keep both poles of potentiality in view and in balancing perspective.

One patient said, "I find it shocking that anyone should listen to me or care what I feel. I didn't think it was possible." Another said, "Sometimes I really believe that the only reason that you're in this is that you like to torture other people. I think you sit up at night to think of new ways to be cruel to me." These two statements have a considerable kinship, the second representing perhaps the more negativistic version of the first.

Of course the second patient, nothing if not consistent, would have objected to such a formulation, insisting instead that the first was just a more idealized and deceptive version of the second. It is shocking sometimes how sealed and all-encompassing a patient's world view can become. In treating borderline patients there is a considerable danger of being seduced into a mirroring rigidity. With only a modicum of the right sort of provocation, we have the capacity to become every bit as obstinate as our patients.

Everything else depends on the doctor–patient relationship for a variety of reasons. There is no clinical information, no opportunity for clinical observation outside of the relationship. We cannot know what we need to know in order to be of use to a patient except in the context of the relationship. We only know what, in the poet's awesome phrase, is "proved on our pulses."[2] Participation in relationship is our essential observational device and how we collaborate with the patient to build it, maintain it and use it will determine what we are able to come to know and in what richness and depth not only we but the patient will appreciate it.

It is also the patient's essential observational device. It permits the patient a close observation of what another person does and thus provides a passport from one realm of existence to another. One of our central concerns will be to try to explain how the borderline patient can learn both in and outside of therapy. We will advocate an appreciation of

---

2. " . . . for axioms in philosophy are not axioms until they are proved upon our pulses: We read fine things but never feel them to the full until we have gone the same steps as the Author . . . " John Keats (1818).

the patient's negativism as a centrally important form of relatedness that is the vehicle for forward movement in personality development. The borderline patient's disagreeable disagreeing commonly means that he has heard more than he can bear and is struggling inside to accommodate it. It is far more related than the kind of bland compliance that often flatters therapists and seduces them into failing to notice that they and the patient are worlds apart.

Psychopharmacological treatment initiatives with borderline patients also depend crucially on the nature of the doctor–patient relationship within which they are proposed. When these fail, it is often because of the significance the patients attach to them. For example, one patient saw a proposed anti-depressant as an effort to control him along the lines that had caused him so much suffering in his relationship with his father. He refused to take the medication until he was able to recognize and communicate this concern. Another patient steadfastly resisted medication because she was afraid that, if it helped, she would have no claim to attention or care from others. Her potential gain threatened her with a loss she could not manage even in fantasy. The capacity to discuss this kind of problem in a relationship represents already an enormous gain in personality development.

The doctor–patient relationship is the nexus for new learning, new experience, and the revaluing of old ways of not learning and avoiding experience. A patient said, "I can't really say that I ever felt anything. I was long gone before there was any opportunity for me to feel anything. That was how frightened I was, although I didn't know it at the time. That's really frightened. I think I've learned how to feel here. A lot of it has to do with watching you."

The doctor–patient relationship is the crucible in which new forms of relationship, not just to others but to the self—that most significant of others—can be forged. We might also say that the new opportunities for participation and observation in the doctor–patient relationship model new ways for the patient to observe himself and to participate within himself. The doctor–patient relationship is a "back and forth" that makes a difference in how "back and forth" is carried on. It can bring organized movement, possibility, and life into an inner landscape whose subjective flavor alternates between stark immobility and deadness on the one hand and chaotic terror on the other.

THE IDEA OF DEVELOPMENT

The developmental idea has enormous integrative power in supporting treatment design. It allows for the impact of the past on the present, for the possibility that the patient may experience the present as a repetition of the past, a new "trying again." It raises the possibility that motivational and affective states and behaviors that seem to make no sense in the present context may have a logic of their own as related to previous contexts. Present conflicts and difficulties in feeling and functioning may arise from efforts to solve conflicts or confront danger situations that live on from the past. Two case examples follow.

A cognitively talented young borderline man was highly regarded by his peers. Although his opinions and judgments were widely respected and valued, he could not tolerate even mild requests for additional information or clarifications. He complained bitterly, even venomously, that no one took his word for anything and that people treated him as if he had no idea what he was saying or what he meant, as if he couldn't even perceive properly. His bitter complaining hurt and upset everyone who knew him, who saw him as being quite unfair.

In fact, his complaint that no one took his word for even the most obvious things made quite a bit of sense in terms of his life-long effort to convey to his starkly denying mother the emotional distress that he was suffering—not just at her hands, but at the hands of his sadistically belittling father. He had good reason to feel, no matter how much positive regard others professed for him, that he was stuck in a no-win situation. What was most painful to him was that he could not take his own word for anything and lived in a continuous internal state of doubt and mistrust, not just of others but of himself.

A patient professed to feel only hatred for her father. Yet, she drank as he did, shared many of the same interests that he did, and utilized the same kind of humor that he did. She would even, from time to time, literally beat herself up, as he had beaten her. What came out as the developmental history of her hatred for her father was pursued was a sad story of a little girl's love unrequited. Unable to be liked and responded to by her father, she could only be close to him by being like him. This dynamic historical investigation served to unify many different strands of her behavior and motivation, presenting her with an opportunity to reformulate for herself her feelings and goals. Behind hatred and anger were loss and hurt, the deeper vein of helplessness.

It took her six years to accommodate the first glimmer of the idea that she could feel both love and hatred for her father. This brought in its wake a threatening shift as she could begin to bear some disillusionment with her mother, whom she defensively idealized. Throughout much of the treatment she appeared as a battleground on which the long running war between her mother and father was being fought over and over again.

The developmental idea may allow for a more multifaceted view of symptoms, one in which certain symptoms may be seen to have positive adaptational and developmental value as well as representing handicaps or failures. For example, pervasive negativism may represent an effort to shore up boundaries between self and object representations. Where a nondevelopmentally informed treatment design might propose simply to stamp out negativism because it is seen as a nuisance to people interacting with the patient and, therefore, to the patient himself, an alternative, developmentally inspired strategy would be to afford the patient an opportunity to engage in negativistic relationships, to support his efforts to defend his will and separate integrity, while trying to call his attention both to the function of his negativism and to some of its associated costs.

Another example would be the understanding, based on the developmental notion of transitional phenomena, of the way in which hallucinatory voices can serve to maintain a sense of self under conditions of serious threat. A borderline patient who had lived in Burma as a young child heard voices with Burmese names. She had had Burmese caretakers when she was very little. Her return to the United States had involved great losses for her, which she had never been able to acknowledge or mourn. Instead of seeking to get rid of the voices or telling the patient to ignore them and go on about her business, a richer strategy would focus on understanding the patient's loneliness and helping her seek alternative measures for comforting herself. Voices can often be ''heard'' as part of an effort to include feelings and memories that threaten the fragile sense of integration. Voices can encapsulate part selves that contain important left-out feelings.

The developmental idea acknowledges the tremendous influence of experience and learning, particularly early learning and experience on the patterning of the functioning of people. The importance of development has a biological base in the design of the human nervous system. It is as if the human brain had been designed to be receptive to influence from environmental stimuli, especially during certain crit-

ical organizing time periods. It develops slowly over a very
long time, with many options for making connections. Each
brain is an individual, an original, with crucial differences in
functional style and emphases. A person is more than a brain,
even more complex, even more related.

When considered in the totality of their functioning,
people and their brains are probably more alike in the way
that the Roman and Chinese empires were alike, than they
are alike in the way that two molecules of methane are alike.
That is, like empires, each must cope with certain fundamental challenges, but there is room for wide variation and
creative combinatorial richness in designing particular responses. In general, it appears that the higher the function,
the more plastic the circuitry and, to use a current metaphor,
the programming on which it depends. While brainstem
reflexes, such as those underlying the rhythmicity of respi-
ration, are quite standardized and hardwired, patterns of
linguistic or melodic composition, or of approach to ethical
imperatives, or of symbolic construction of feeling states
toward other people, are not anywhere nearly so standardized or "built in." They are more subject to shaping and
reshaping by experience and learning from experience,
more subject to both regression and progression. They are
not mere epiphenomena appended to some mechanical
device.

THE SYSTEMS IDEA

While the developmental idea serves to provide a conceptual framework for linking temporal states, relating the
personal past, present, and future to each other in a sugges-
tively dynamic way, the systems idea provides a means of
conceptualizing how to organize thinking about multiple,
simultaneous impingements and influences at different
levels from the molecular up through the personal, the

familial, and the social at a given moment in time. The systems concept enables the clinician to maintain under consideration multiple levels or aspects of a disorder. Etiologies can be conceived as the resultant of the interplay of factors described in terms of different systems. For example, if studies of identical twin pairs demonstrate a genetic risk factor for schizophrenia by showing that, if one twin is schizophrenic, the other twin's chance of being schizophrenic is much higher than the risk for schizophrenia in non-twin siblings of schizophrenics in the population, the lack of complete concordance between members of twin pairs speaks also to the need to seek other risk factors, tied to other biological aspects and other psychological and social circumstances.

We think of the borderline syndrome as emerging from the interplay of multiple and variable etiological factors. These may include mood disorders based both in biological vulnerability and experiential stress, seizure disorders, family violence, abuse, pervasive emotional insensitivity on the part of parents, poor fits between parenting figures and children, and so forth. Developmental defects lead to uncertain self-constancy with heightened vulnerability to dedifferentiation, that is, loss of self, and loss of the loved object. Emerging from the interplay of many different factors at diverse levels in a systems conceptualization is an affective identity disorder of the self.

Treatments can be conceived in terms of a single system or in terms of multiple approaches simultaneously addressed to factors conceived in terms of differing systems. The systems approach helps us to remain aware that enhancement of capacities at one level may offset dysfunction at another level. For example, a borderline woman with a neurological disease learned through psychotherapy that anxiety and fatigue made her tremors much worse, causing her considerable shame and worry about how others saw her. She began to allow herself to rest in the afternoon, something she had not been able to do previously, because she had felt that to rest was to concede a degree of inadequacy that would make it impossible for anyone to respect her or care about her. This concrete achievement represented a distinct step forward in her capacity to care for herself. It depended crucially on a change in her attitude toward herself, namely, a recognition that the idea that rest was a confession of inadequacy was an old grandiose view not well-fitted to current reality.

How medication affects a patient depends on the social setting within which it is given. Certainly, we know that how an individual experiences intoxicants is strongly modified by the social setting within which he takes them as well as by his expectations concerning their effects. Appropriate use of pharmacotherapy can make possible new initiatives both in psychotherapy and in social functioning. One patient who felt better on medication began to regress seriously because she found it threatening to feel better. The medication made her feel unfamiliar to herself, a psychological "side effect" that was managed psychotherapeutically.

Nature/nurture arguments, like polarized arguments about whether to apply psychosocial or psychopharmacological treatments, often disguise claims about the superiority of conceptualizations in terms of one or another system. Treatments applied within the framework of different systems may have additive or even synergistic effects on an aspect of a patient's disorder, or they may affect different aspects of a patient's trouble, or they may have different time courses and different durations of impact. Particularly when we are dealing with severely ill psychiatric patients, either/or thinking about different treatments may be very much against the patients' best interest. These patients need all the help they can get. Nor can we afford to neglect active internal spoiling dynamics in the patient.

A comprehensive systems view in psychiatry should allow for single selective interventions when these seem sufficient, without forestalling the option of multiple clusters of effective interventions at different levels when a more complex approach is needed, as is regularly the case with significantly disturbed borderline patients. It should help in developing the capacity to assess the various levels of impairment or dysfunction and to make available corrective measures, either specifically to redress dysfunctions or by way of compensatory offsetting developments deployed at a variety of levels in the systems affecting the patient's well being. A systems approach helps stay away from all-or-nothing notions in treatment that artificially lessen treatment options. Receiving more than one kind of help often represents a very helpful challenge to a patient's grandiose magical hopes.

THE HOLDING ENVIRONMENT

We started by describing a seriously ill borderline patient's predicament. Mona had had an enormous range of treatments, many state of the art within their own orientations, responsibly administered, yet had not seemed to get much out of any of them. In her own words, "Everything helped a little, but not enough." She did not connect with any of them. Perhaps it is not correct to say that she did not get much *out* of them. It might be more accurate to say that she was not able to get much *in* to herself. Her statement of what she wanted, "I want to go to school and to be happy," had a thinness to it that is characteristic of many borderline patients. It seemed so sad precisely because it excluded any possibility of being sad and bearing sadness long enough to come to terms with losses and limitations.

It pointed to an inner emptiness that can be at once terribly poignant and terribly exasperating. Is the borderline patient's difficulty in affect containment or is it in affect attainment? Or are the two integrally interrelated? Behind the rage and despair, the boredom and isolation, is often a conviction of emptiness that lends credence to the borderline person's difficulty in attaining affects, that is to say, bounding and defining experiences enough to be able to know them and hold onto them symbolically, to serve the construction of a more flexible self.

We discussed the borderline patient's difficulty in having any experience be "enough," rather than painfully "too much" or painfully "too little." We related this to what is really the patient's fundamental quandary, namely, the lack of sufficient capacity to bound any experience so as to enjoy it. In terms of their feelings, borderline patients are more had than having. Their tyrannical and competitive drives for control testify eloquently to their abject inner convictions of helplessness. In a vicious circle, the more they struggle for control, the more out of control they often feel and act. "I think I'm just addicted to illusions of control," said one patient, noting that her addiction was out of control.

They lack the internal capacity to accommodate their experience and to settle down into any reliable patterns of satisfaction. The issue in treating borderline patients, then, is to help them find a pathway to constructing that middle range in which bounded and satisfying experiences are possible. This middle range is a project of inner construction. The construction site is located in *terra incognita* within the patient. Nor should we seek to resolve the question of whether treatment discovers it or creates it. The borderline patient's conception of the world within, or even that there is such a thing as a world within—populated by symbolic figures capable of symbolic actions and intentions, as opposed simply to an external world of action and reaction, fight and flight, hurting and being hurt—is rudimentary.

After posing the problem in this way, we discussed four interrelated issues, including the breadth of conception of psychiatric illness and treatment, the nature and importance of the doctor–patient relationship, and development and systems as ideas that make possible integrative treatment

design. Our purpose in discussing these issues was to provide the bases for envisioning the construction of holding
environments for borderline patients that are adequate, that
is to say, good enough—neither so good or stifling as to
prevent the experiences of disillusionment that are essential
to growth, nor so bad as to frustrate the kinds of illusions
essential to any meaningful disillusionment.

As Winnicott (1953) saw so clearly, the progressive
developmental impetus of a disillusionment is predicated on
the robustness of the illusion that has preceded it. It is
probably a mistake to talk of illusions and disillusionment, as
if we passed beyond illusion. When we speak of illusions and
disillusionment, what we are really talking about is the
modification of illusions in the direction of greater suppleness and flexibility. We are talking about the development of
a *faculty*.

As we will discuss at length, it is a question of trading in
one illusion for another. What we experience as the reality
of our lives is woven of the fabric of illusion. The world we
live in wears the guise we give it. For many borderline
patients, the issue is to trade in "destructive apperception"
for "creative apperception," but this process can only take
place when the patient can move beyond the need for a way
of seeing the world that keeps him isolated and at odds with
it and aware that he exists because he hurts and resents. "I'm
ashamed," said one patient, "but I know the problem is
really me. I can't like myself. It's just too dangerous. But I
hate myself for being a coward." This patient really did not
know herself except in the process of loathing herself and
shrinking from her loathing of herself.

What, then, do we mean by a holding environment? A
holding environment provides a patient with the opportunities for containment that he is not equipped to provide from
his own internal resources. We recognize that the holding
environment cannot hold the patient unless and until the
patient is able to catch hold of the holding environment. A
holding environment is a joint construction project that is

built both from the side of the patient and from the side of those attempting to provide treatment. Holding depends on illusion, and the progressive development of illusion, close kin of play, depends on holding.

The holding environment helps the patient, no matter how stressed or distressed, maintain a state of affairs where he can remain in sufficiently cooperative relationship with his surroundings (1) to use others to help him to observe what is going on and (2) to make practical efforts at understanding and managing so as to find more adaptive and satisfying responses, both internally and interpersonally. This may include expressing sorrow and anger instead of cutting, daring to try instead of retreating into the security of failure, and so forth.

The holding environment not only supports the patient but models new capacities that can be internalized. With the borderline patient it provides an impetus in the direction of symbolic communication instead of symbiotic enmeshment. It helps the patient to feel separate and separately so that he can bear the nearness of being together and, conversely, to have an experience of nearness that shores up his capacity to feel separate and separately.

The doctor–patient relationship is a central piece of the holding environment for a borderline patient. It provides for the exploration of meanings and an ongoing investigation into both the benefits and costs gained by the patient from how he lives. It models connection as opposed to disconnection, feeling as opposed to numbness, expression in words as opposed to symbolic enactments whose symbolism is not recognized, and repair as opposed to unremitting despair. Within it, psychotropic medications can be very helpful. This central and centering relationship may be complemented by other forms of treatment including family therapy, group therapy, expressive therapies like art and dance, vocational counselling, and social supports like Alcoholics Anonymous and Narcotics Anonymous, to mention only a few possibilities. The borderline patient must find a way to come to terms with himself in order to find a way in the world, but also must find a way in the world to help him come to terms with himself.

Many patients find work situations that provide significant holding. Many are also able to use family members in this way, especially once they are sufficiently invested in therapy to bring some of their more destructive merging and distancing maneuvers into slightly better focus. As borderline patients are able to make provisional modifications in some of their character patterns, to feel separate and to separate feeling from action, their involvement with others and their capacity to gain support and holding from others increase.

The patient becomes increasingly active, if in a conflicted way, in the process of constructing a holding environment to suit his own needs. The internal capacity for kindlier illusion expands hand-in-hand with the development of real interpersonal relationships that allow a space for the positive, not instead of the negative, but alongside the negative and mixed in with it to make the more complex and rewarding, if anxiety engendering, experiences that can bring stable satisfactions. It is very important for therapists to appreciate this and to support the patient's involvement outside of therapy with those people and groups that can provide holding.

In the long run, we are all held and soothed and animated by the world of internal illusions that we have constructed for ourselves in the course of our living. "I guess," a patient said after four years of treatment, "I have to turn you into the Ayatollah Khomeini when I get scared and angry enough. That's my way of protecting myself. I wonder what life would be like for me if I didn't need an Ayatollah? I'm shocked at how dependent I am. I don't want to know about it." Of course, it was too late for her. By the time it is possible for a person to *say* that she really does not want to know about something like this, she has already probably come to know enough so that there is no turning back along the road to giving the world a clearer and kindlier visage.

A related theme integral to our work is the therapist's need to remain in contact with a holding environment that can help him manage the stress of working with borderline patients. We emphasize the importance of ongoing collegial contact, cooperation with members of other disciplines, and formal consultation as means to help maintain and nurture a flexible and resilient inner exploratory attitude. We also emphasize an exploratory attitude toward what the therapist can recognize in himself and reveal of himself to the patient. Along with this, we try to highlight what the doctor can and does receive in the way of holding from the patient and the therapeutic importance of recognizing and accepting this. Ultimately, just as the doctor is not just a giver but also a taker, the patient is not just a taker, but a giver as well.

Core Pathology of the Borderline Patient

A DISORDER OF THE SELF

The psychopathology of the borderline patient is a psychopathology of the core. We think it is best understood as a disorder of the self in which the person's unstable identity makes it difficult to attain and contain modulated and differentiated affects.

The affective palette is both primitive and restricted in range and shade. Far from enriching the self and producing appealing and intriguing complexities of texture, raw and unrefined affects are experienced as threats to the tenuous stability and ongoingness of the self, leading to the employment of characteristic defenses as outlined most notably by Kernberg (1987). These defenses have the effect of impoverishing and restricting the self while distorting both the perception of self and the perception of others.

THE FUSING DANGER

The borderline patient experiences in himself a lack of a sense of his own reliable and predictable ongoingness. The assurance of the illusion of even relative self-constancy is well beyond the horizon of the borderline patient's existential world. At its most basic level, this lack manifests itself in the threat of extinction of the self when approaching emotional closeness with someone else.

This threat can burst through with sudden and overwhelming force, producing the atmosphere of a shoot out along the lines of, "this town isn't big enough for both of us," just as the unwary psychotherapist is satisfied with what he is offering the patient. What we normally imagine as a gain, a closeness to another person that makes the other person available as a source of stimulation and enrichment, is experienced not as a promise but rather as the threat of a terrible and annihilatory loss. The closeness of the other threatens to disrupt the self. It threatens to bring on the catastrophe of a loss of the self. The other cannot possibly be of use if the self does not have the cohesion and consistency to be available for the encounter, which means to be able to be both far enough and near enough at the same time.

"I'm like iron filings when a magnet comes by," said one patient. "I just can't hang on to myself." A whole host of defensive maneuvers can be called into service to defend against the threat of a closeness that might snuff the self out. Many borderline patients have elevated interpersonal distance regulation to the level of an art form. Unfortunately, they are not aware of the problem, nor able to appreciate their own efforts without a great deal of work.

One patient noted that when she was getting close to someone she would evoke anger in the other person. Through subtle and not so subtle provocations, she would ensure that the other person took an initiative to put more distance between the two. Her active passive-aggressive maneuvering was an essential part of her self-stabilization efforts. Patients who lead with the worst foot forward often are protecting themselves from the disruption of closeness that is too great and too swift. What lies behind are their own urges to merge and their terrible conflicts around dependency needs. Intrusiveness, an apparent eagerness to engage, can actually function as a negativistic device whose purpose is to drive the other off to a safe distance.

When the sense of self is so fragile, a person may have to go to considerable lengths to gain secure distance. For example, one patient regularly arranged to be away when delivery people or the cleaning woman were scheduled to arrive at her house. She saw these visits as intrusions and needed to defend her sense of autonomy by using physical means to emphasize her separateness. Chronic lateness can serve a similar function for borderline patients. Another patient described how much she resented her answering machine because of the demands that it made on her. Yet another described how he loved to pitch in baseball because he was all alone on the mound and in control. There were other people around, but he did not have to talk with them. He worried about control in all spheres of the game.

In borderline patients, negativism is a prominent defense because it helps to ward off the sense of fusion and extinction of the self. The transference style of so many borderline patients is negativistic, with most substantial dialogue carried out as disagreement in a climate of often agitated disaccord. The positive contribution of this negativism in furthering dialogue must be appreciated by the therapist. Otherwise he risks not being able to see the patient's investment in therapy. He runs the danger of seeing the patient as not ready for psychotherapy when actually it is the therapist who is not ready for the kind of involvement that the patient needs.

Negativism cannot be moderated or mitigated until the self has developed the resources, as it were, to sing an inner identifying melody that is more subtle, more flexible, and more abstract. It is a long journey toward compositional styles that are less dependent on interpersonal dissonances for self-definition. The subjective sense of the stability of the self depends on the capacity to differentiate self-representation from object representation. The process of such differentiation is conceptualized in Figure 2–1.

Attaching brings with it the risk of disruption of the self through fusing, which can be overcome by differentiating. Or to put it another way, the enriching benefits of attaching are only available to the one who can differentiate sufficiently to skirt the dangers of fusing. The child who holds on to mother's skirt and then lets go to move off and explore is already well along in this process. Differentiating is itself a complicated series of maneuvers that depend on resources of illusion and memory, which are served by the development of the capacity to use symbols to evoke and regulate internal experiences.

The use of the suffix "ing" in the labels in Figure 2–1— "attaching," "fusing," "differentiating"—is a grammatical device pressed into service to emphasize the ongoing nature

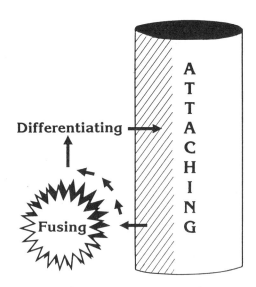

FIGURE 2–1.   The Fusing Danger

of this process in all of us. It is not simply something that is achieved once and for all. In fact, it is vital to such combinatorially enriching faculties as self-observation, empathy, and creativity that it is not. Creativity always demands at least a relative instability. Yet, the borderline patient's vulnerability in this area is dramatically heightened, as the self-representation/object representation differentiating functions have fallen far short of normal levels of consolidation.

THE LOSING DANGER

What is so devastating for borderline patients is that they face struggles they are not well equipped to manage on two fronts at once. Along with the fusion threat, there is the separation threat. The sense of the threatened loss of the object can be overwhelming. A patient felt compelled to let her clothes drop and stay just where she took them off. If she folded them up and put them away, she explained, it "would destroy my existence." "Throwing away an empty carton," she felt, "is throwing myself away." Along similar lines, another patient refused to have her conviction for a traffic violation expunged because she felt it was one of the few tangible proofs of her own existence. Another patient said, "I know you can bear it if I get mad at you. I'm the one who can't stand it. If I get mad at you, I lose you and then I crumble."

We can represent this aspect of the ongoing process in Figure 2–2, which is analogous to Figure 2–1, but a bit farther along in the stream of development.

The gloss on this diagram is that separation processes can be enriching to the self provided that adeptness in reuniting is adequate to buffer the self against the dangers of loss of the object. The problem comes when a separation involves not just the loss of a circumscribed object but

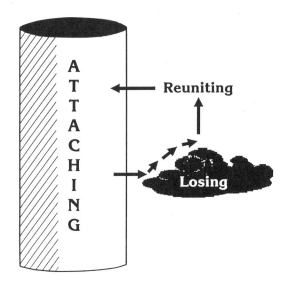

FIGURE 2–2.   The Losing Danger

disruption of all that the object is associated with inside. Every separation experience involves at least sighting the possibility of a complete loss, as is well expressed in the saying, "to leave is to die a little." The crucial element here is the qualifying "a little," the element that is intra-psychically unavailable to the borderline patient.

Lack of a secure sense of self and self-constancy, or at least self-consistency, renders a person vulnerable to separation and loss. In fact, without the capacity for reuniting, the slightest separation has the inner psychological force of abject loss: "Whenever I leave here, I'm not sure that I'll ever see you again. You don't know what it's like to walk down that hall." "You're here now. But that doesn't make any difference. Where are you when I really need you? You're not there and you don't even know it. So how can I believe you care?"

The feelings these patients experience are extremely intense. When we talk of intensity of feeling, we are really speaking of a relationship between the containing capacity of the self and the feelings potentially to be contained in that self. In much the same way, when we talk about a vessel being "full" we are describing a relationship between capacity and cargo. A thimble is filled to overflowing long before an ocean-going ship reaches its capacity. Obviously, there are a whole host of vessels whose capacities lie between these two extremes. In the borderline self, affective stimuli highlight the defects in the self.

Promptings to feel are commonly *experienced* as threatening eruptions that can shake the self to the core and demand immediate emergency mobilization. It is as if the patient felt that to contain what was knocking at the self's dwelling, it would first be necessary to knock the whole house down so that an adequate one could be built. But what would shelter the self in the meantime? The emergency mobilization against the disruptive danger determines the intense, driven, dysphoric features of borderline feeling.

Developmental deficits render the ego unable to contain anger, sadness, anxiety, grief, rage, loneliness, and other affects. The relative weakness and instability of the structure of the self make it impossible for the borderline patient to *attain* more modulated, symbolically orchestrated, differentiated, and diversified affective experience. It is as if the orchestra always played too fast and too loud, so that the effect was intense, irritating, monotonous, and overwhelming.

The "intensity" of the borderline patient's experience threatens both the self and the other. To paraphrase a formulation about hysteria, the borderline's emotionality simultaneously conceals and reveals a tremendous difficulty with emotion. It is not uncommon to hear a borderline patient after years of storm and stress say something to the effect that it is a very new experience to feel anything. What these patients are referring to is a capacity to hold on to and connect with their feelings without being so threatened.

THE FUSING–LOSING PARADIGM

All of the features of the *DSM-III-R* delineation of Borderline Personality Disorder are contained in the fusing–

losing paradigm. As a patient put it, "If I am self-confident, I will turn into somebody else. Nobody to love me anymore. Nobody to depend on." Being functional implied being alone as well as no longer existing. Two complementary unbearable dangers intertwine to close off all developmental avenues. This patient felt she was doomed either to lose her self or to lose the other, each of which form of loss could entrain the other.

We combine the two diagrams offered previously into one interconnected process, Figure 2–3. Boundary issues as well as separation issues are paramount. Attaching brings the borderline patient into a dual danger zone. Efforts to defend against one danger intensify the other, so that the patient may come to feel at the mercy of a constantly oscillating series of vicious circles.

These patients hunger for a response from others. The clinical stickiness of these patients is as prominent as their thorniness. Provocative postures along the lines of, "I'll do anything to get a response," are regularly experienced by

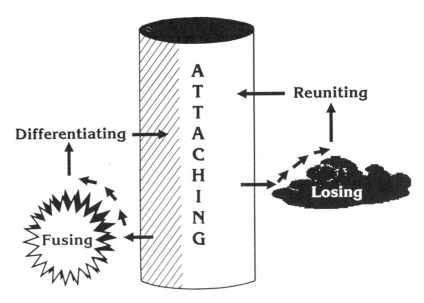

FIGURE 2–3.   Fusing and Losing

psychotherapists and other treating persons as manipulations on the part of the patients. It is all too easy to start feeling resentful, wary, even enraged at a borderline patient, because one feels the patient is taking unfair advantage by artful means. What is hard to keep in mind is just how primitive and driven the art is, just how threatened the patient feels inwardly.

Countertransference on the part of the therapist and others who work with the patient is counterpoint to the patient's need for input. At times, the patient secures this input in a very concrete way by providing for physical, afferent stimulation of the body. To name but a few of the items in the borderline repertoire, cutting, burning, fighting, binging, purging, overwork, and arguing all serve the function of providing for self-definition as well as for connection with the available others. They all engage while repulsing, often providing the other with a complicated experience of being overwhelmed that is a genuine transmission of news concerning the patient's inner state.

Projective identification as a form of countertransference response becomes a source of information about what is taking place in the patient's world. Projective identification may be thought of as a form of psychiatric ventriloquism. Often it is the therapist who is the ventriloquist's dummy, speaking lines that have been written by a borderline patient who remains aloof and untouched, quite unaware that he is the impressario of the performance. For example, a resident described how she noticed that she herself was beginning to hyperventilate as a patient described his despair in a way that was at once eerily calm and wholly chaotic.

Another therapist noticed that he had delayed telling his patient that he was going to be away in the near future. In the course of exploring this omission and the patient's responses to it, he discovered that the patient was contemplating a request to seek an increase in the number of sessions per week. The therapist was reacting to the patient's unconscious conflict over a demand for something more from the therapist. A request for more sessions, a bolster against the loss threat, brings on a fusion fear from which the patient retreats, so that while he is preoccupied with the request, he does not make it audibly so that the therapist can hear it. The magnitude of these dangers determines the patient's difficulty in becoming aware of the conflict except through the long-circuit means of projective identification, in which it is the therapist who must try to understand what has interfered with his own normal communicativeness. The therapist ends up struggling with the sense of himself as inappropriately withholding, just as the patient struggles inside with his sense of being inappropriately demanding.

Borderline patients are unable to cope with either the threat of loss of the object or the threat of the loss of the self. The contributing etiological factors are variable and can be conceptualized at different levels in a systems paradigm. Etiological elements can include depression, attention deficit disorder, temperamental extremes, sexual or physical abuse experiences, neglect, child–maternal mismatch, concurrent physical illnesses, ictal problems, and social deprivations. We want to emphasize that this list could be substantially extended. All of it is "biological" in the sense of having to do with the "logos" of living, that which gives it form and meaning. While we are not prepared to abandon this essential term to the merely molecular, we do not want to exclude conceptualizations at the level of biochemical processes. It is people who suffer and enjoy, despair and hope, love, lose, and repair, not molecules or cells.

Different levels in a systems paradigm interact. For example, a propensity to depression may render certain developmental steps very difficult, much as furthering emotional communication with congenitally blind or deaf infants requires special adaptation and devotion on the part of mothers. Severe abuse, especially combined as it regularly is with neglect in distorted parent–child relationships, is likely to have biological sequelae that present important psychological and social problems. Furman (1984) offers "the concept that a seduction is more than a developmental interference or trauma that has to be understood and mastered." "It is often," he states, "perhaps equally as important, also the symptom of a disturbed parent–child relationship that paved the way towards a seduction and/or allowed the seduction to occur."

The combination with neglect and distortions of the parent–child relationship is important, because it means that the abuse confronts an ego that already has very limited resources with a task that would be overwhelming in the best of circumstances. An out-of-control inside and an out-of-control surround collaborate to produce a chaotic world. Borderline personality disorder is a syndrome. Whatever the complex interplay of etiological factors, the result common to borderline patients is a vulnerability to loss, both of the object and of the self.

These feelings are ordinarily kept from being overwhelming by means of a panoply of defenses, which are explored in the treatment situation. As they are called into question, the feelings become more prominent. To patient and to therapist alike, it can feel as if one were in severe shock with his blood volume expanded, so that he can now be able to bleed. The work of the treatment relationship is to contain these feelings and represent them so that they become less threatening.

Another way to put this is to say that the balance between the patient's capacity to bear feeling and the stimulation to feel has to be redressed within the treatment relationship so that the patient may attain modulated, mixed, and differentiated feeling states that were previously unavailable to him. The therapist's consistent, even presence and empathically modulated interest help make it worth the patient's while to continue the struggle for increasing awareness and experience of affects. Intense feelings of rage and despair become accessible within the transference. "You don't control me yet!" exclaimed a patient vitriolically to her therapist, repeating her self-experience with her mother. Many a therapist, of course, has had the complementary experience of wondering whether a borderline patient has not taken over control of him.

In Chapter 3, we will discuss at length the ways in which transitional phenomena play an important part in representing conflicts in borderline patients. As one patient said, "I have a blanket of pain that covers me from head to foot." While his blanket was woven of different materials than the one that Linus of the *Peanuts* comic strip uses, it served many of the same functions.

THE SUNBURST DIAGRAM

Now we want to introduce what we call the *sunburst diagram*, Figure 2–4. Our initial core conflicts in the attaching process are located at the center of the diagram. We might even say that what we have described are nuclear processes of fusion and fission that fuel development in the self. Surrounding this core and deriving from it are the various flavors of affective experience encountered in the daily and nightly experience of the patient. These affects are defended against by the various mechanisms pictured in the outermost periphery of the diagram.

These defenses relate not only to the particular affects found adjacent to them in the diagram, but may be utilized in conjunction with any affect. We can picture the outer rim as being able to rotate around the ring of the affects. In the six o'clock position we have a list of healthy, adaptive, and sublimated processes. The aim of therapy is to help the patient along the way to using these in the place of more primitive maneuvers.

This diagram visually makes a number of points. The first is that affective experience arises from a relational matrix. It arises not just in us but between us. Affective

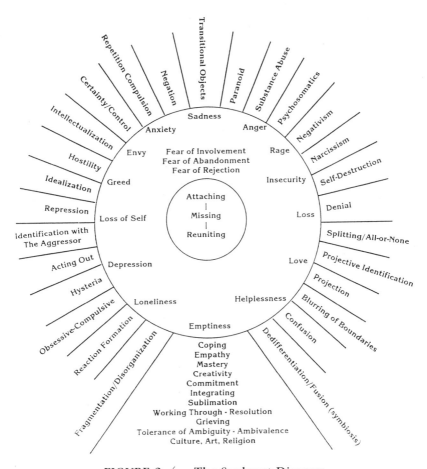

FIGURE 2–4.   The Sunburst Diagram

experience mediates the connection between us and important others. Our assigning a central place to the dynamics of attachment, differentiation, and separation picks up an evolutionary thread. A major theme in mammalian evolution is bonding between infants and their mothers and the elaboration of social groups on the basis of this attachment. The mammalian separation cry and the reaction to it are a primordial innovation with far-reaching consequences (Mac-Clean 1985).

Affective experience connects. Like any connection, it

both joins and separates. "Probably the greatest reason why we tend to rebel against our developing individual identity," writes Searles (1979a), "is because we feel it to have come between, and to be coming increasingly between, ourself, and the mother with whom we once shared a world-embracing oneness."[1] For affective experience to be modulated sufficiently to enrich the self it has to take place in the context of sufficient joining and sufficient distinguishing. It has to bridge rather than simply estrange or fuse.

The defenses can be thought of as prosthetic devices enlisted to tone down affective experience so that neither the threat of fusion nor the threat of loss becomes too great. They are frustrated and frustrating efforts at coping, mastery, recombination, working through, integration, communication, and so forth. They are inherently partial in what they have achieved. They are way stations, as we commonly recognize when we speak of maturation of defenses.

Our sunburst diagram is useful in focusing attention on the interactions between the patient and the doctor and between the patient and other figures in his world as the nexus of affect and on the problem for the patient of utilizing a variety of defenses to tone down affects that are experienced as threats to the self. For these patients, a feeling is like a bull in the china shop. Where did it come from? What is it doing here? What that is brittle and vulnerable is likely to get broken, if not shattered now that it is here?

That dangers of fusion and loss, different affective experiences, and different arrays of defenses can be bound together in a wide variety of configurations is indicated in the capacity of the middle and outer rings of the diagram to rotate not just with respect to the center but with respect to each other. This diagram can be read to suggest that any affect, not just anxiety, can have either a signal function, or

---

1. We are indebted to Dr. Sheldon Roth for bringing this passage to our attention.

a direct, raw, intrusive, and threatening valence, depending on the capacity to accommodate it.

The experience of the self is an experience of feeling. The traditional psychotherapeutic maxim that, when in doubt as to how to address a patient, the therapist should speak to the patient's affect keeps this in mind. The sunburst diagram reminds us that when we aim to help the patient with feeling, we need to keep in mind both the central importance of the patient's current position with regard to the fusing and losing dangers and the array of defenses the patient is employing to tone affective experience down so as to keep these dangers at bay.

One important conflict that often arises in therapy is between the therapist's continual urging of the good of feeling and the patient's continual urging of the good of toning down feeling or of feeling less or not at all. The sunburst diagram provides a way of viewing this issue that gives both sides their due. Feeling is a good if you can manage it and if it enriches you. Feeling is a terrible threat if you cannot tone it down to a manageable level.

In the long run, if feeling is excluded, the impoverishment of the self becomes a way of life, as far from secure as it is from satisfying. It may even become more a way of death-in-life. On the other hand, the uncritical view of feeling as a "good" leads to errors in timing and pacing that can put the therapist in the position of colluding with the patient's overwhelming himself over and over, repeating earlier unfortunate developmental disruptions. A psychotherapist cannot afford to be simply an esthesiologist who is biased in an almost Faustian manner toward the glories of feeling and experience. Instead, he must understand the claims of anesthesiology as well. Feeling opens the door not just to the pleasures and hopes of life, but also to its sorrows and tragedies.

In future chapters we will use the ideas represented in this sunburst diagram to help us take up topics as diverse as the role of transitional processes in self-experience, the negative therapeutic reaction, what we mean by "holding," how borderline patients learn, self-observation, sublimation, countertransference monitoring, self-disclosure on the therapist's part, and the therapist's own dependency. In the remaining portion of this chapter we will focus on all-or-none aspects of splitting and negativism in the defense structure of the borderline patient. We regard these as important features often overlooked by other authors, who use a more restricted concept of splitting and do not put sufficient emphasis on the fragility of the borderline patient's sense of self and the magnitude of the fusion danger. We emphasize them because we think they broaden and deepen understanding of the borderline patient's complex predicament and provide useful guidance in terms of an approach to treating borderline patients. All too often, for example, therapists are unable to maintain an appropriately ambivalent and tolerant attitude in the face of the patient's negativism. The therapist is seduced into identifying the negativistic with the wholly negative. The therapist's failure to remain in touch with the positive appreciation of and attachment to the therapist cloaked and revealed by the patient's negativism deprives the patient of a vital developmental support.

ALL-OR-NONE ATTITUDES: BROADENING THE CONCEPT OF SPLITTING

Similarly, the therapist who is not in touch with all-or-none attitudes as pervasive features of the borderline patient's thinking, feeling, and acting may not appreciate just how much support and practice and patience is required to introduce the patient to more modulated ways that go step-by-step. For example, therapists commonly assume that certain sequences that seem quite plain to the therapist are also plain to the patient. This assumption leads to a neglect of step-by-step clarifying and summarizing of sequences both in therapy and outside it. With many borderline patients, the better the therapist knows the patient, the less he can take for granted.

A borderline patient reflected years later on her hospital stay: "When I was in the hospital I hated those hall meetings. But I have to admit they helped me. It was the first time in my life I was forced to plan ahead and to go step-by-step, even if the steps were stupid and annoying. Those meetings made me do it, whether I wanted to or not. I wanted my sign outs. Now I use what I learned all the time."

All-or-none attitudes are a prominent feature of the borderline patient's approach to life. Extreme polarities surge forth regarding feelings. Gradations, intermediate steps, mixed feelings, and the emergence of emotions in partial manageable doses are not part of the borderline repertoire. Referring to herself, a patient commented, "If one part of a machine falls apart, the whole thing breaks down." Perfectionism is an important striving in all-or-nothing thinking. A patient did not want her therapist to see her as anything but perfect and wanted to destroy anything that was not perfect. Later on she was able to describe her need that her therapist be perfect himself.

Some patients will not attempt something if it can not be done perfectly. This represents an enormous handicap in learning and growing, for trying is of the very essence of development, as mistakes are of creativity. There are patients also who take the tack that, as long as they do not try anything, their perfection, a defensive notion covering their complete sense of inadequacy, cannot be called into question.

Similarly, the intensity of feelings often becomes threatening. If anger surfaces, the borderline patient believes rage and total destruction and devastation will follow. Everything inside and outside will be broken. The borderline patient experiences himself regularly in the position of the sorcerer's apprentice. Whatever he turns loose, he fears, will end up tyrannizing over him. All-or-none attitudes contribute to the sense of impatience and impulsivity in borderline behavior. "Now or never!" is the rallying cry of many a borderline patient about to throw himself off one or another precipice.

Table 2–1 summarizes a wide range of manifestations of all-or-none thinking and feeling (Schulz 1980, page 184), forms of splitting that are ubiquitous in the borderline approach to life. The manifestations of splitting enter all realms of thinking, feeling, and functioning, going far beyond the dichotomization of "good" and "bad" attitudes. The all-or-none position reflects pervasive weaknesses in the capacity of the borderline to modulate and measure responses. The advantage of this broadened concept is that it opens up a much wider range to therapeutic attention.

In supervising residents who take on very ill borderline patients, we have found the all-or-nothing concept very helpful. Among its virtues is that it is experience near, both for the therapist and for the patient. Also, it does not carry the judgmental charge that words like "good" and "bad" carry. Patients do not so readily feel devalued by discussions of their all-or-nothing approach. In addition, it is a concept broad enough to have a synthesizing thrust. It can allow the therapist and the patient to appreciate a pattern that shows across a broad array of topics, typical interactions, and life situations. "I guess I even dress borderline," joked one patient who was attired in a black skirt and a white top that day. It was true that, as treatment progressed, the stark contrasts in her dressing gave way to more complicated and patterned compositions.

When a patient says something like, "I just want to go home," or "I just want to get on with my life," or "I just want someone to understand me," or even, "I know that what I have to do is just grow up and stop whining," the word "just" expresses the implicit all-or-nothing attitude. It even, with its shrinking force, expresses an awareness on the

TABLE 2–1. TWO CONTRASTING PATIENT APPROACHES

All-or-none	Integrated
Splitting into either "good" or "bad"	Ambivalence
Rigid overcontrol vs. loss of control	Modulated expression of affects
Attack entire problem vs. avoidance of problem	Approach by breaking down into manageable parts
Now or never	Ability to tolerate delay
Murderous rage or total denial of anger	Partial expression of anger
Infatuation (crush) or denial of dependency	Mature object dependency
Either my way or your way	Shared responsibility, cooperation
Either this way or not at all	Able to consider variety of options
Perfect health vs. death	Tolerate illness or defect
Complete optimism vs. hopelessness	Realistic appraisal of limitations
Impulsivity vs. failure to act	Appropriate decision making
Extreme attachment vs. rejection of object	Stable interpersonal relationships
Harsh disapproval, self-injury vs. absent moral constraint	Fairly consistent moral regulations
Narcissistic ideal expectations vs. despair of accomplishing anything	Reasonable stable goals
Overeating vs. starvation	Moderation in caloric intake
Severe alcohol intoxication vs. abstinence	Self-control in drinking
Instant recovery vs. no progress	Improvement by small increments, working through
Special patient or feels overlooked	One individual among many

From Schulz (1980), p. 184. Reprinted by permission of Plenum Publishing Corp.

patient's part that the matter is not so simple. The use of the word "just" in this way expresses a frustrated sense of being internally overmatched that has also overtones of impatience, impulsivity, and blaming. There is always a projective pressure that intimates that the all-powerful other could and should work magic on behalf of the patient who is simultaneously and paradoxically incapable and entitled in equal measure.

"I don't want to be here. I just want to go to Hawaii and lie on the beach and soak up some rays," insisted one patient, who had tried that approach over and over again through the years, each time to more and more distressing effect. This all-or-nothing attitude tells the therapist a good deal about the state of the patient's psychological infrastructure, namely, that so many basic functions are so underdeveloped. Four and a half years later this patient said to her therapist, "You've succeeded in taking Hawaii away from me. Even if I went there, it wouldn't be there. It wouldn't be the way I used to imagine it. I can't ever have anything like that again." The pain and sorrow and the rage, as well as the considerable satisfaction, in this forward-moving renunciation were evident.

The young child who puts on a tutu and believes she is a prima ballerina or a pilot's cap and believes he is an airplane pilot engages our indulgent and sponsoring attention. We know that so much more is involved, but we are glad that the child is taking the first steps toward real achievement, with patterns of realistic efforts at mastery and satisfaction. We applaud first steps because they lead to second and third steps, to a mastery of the stepping function.

An experienced child therapist (Fiedler 1973) was once asked with some heat what she would say to a 6-year-old child who had climbed forty feet up a tree and expressed a wish to fly. Her reply was notable for its capacity to accept and speak to differing tendencies in the young and developing personality. She said, "I would empathize with the spirit of the wish, but I would tell him that, if he let go of the branch, he would be in for a long fall with a painful surprise at the end." The borderline patient is not a young child. The all-or-nothing attitude and the splitting defenses are not on the forward edge of development representing a first foray into areas that will later be more intensively colonized. They are rigid defenses used as a bulwark against what has not been mastered. Yet, it is still true that the splitting defense expresses the spirit of a set of wishes for forward movement. Mona, with whom we began the introductory chapter, was at least marginally aware of how terribly painful her life was; she wanted to go to school and to be able to make a contribution. The patient who says, "I just want to go home," is expressing her loss and loneliness, her awareness of a need to readjust her relationship to self so as to gain better access to others. The point is not to excoriate the patient for the use of primitive defenses, but rather, keeping the compromise functions of defenses in mind, to be able to deal both with the internally compromised urge to forward movement and with the contravening forces that, historically, have checkmated it. The therapist's capacity *not* to take an all-or-nothing view of even the most exasperating defenses models a portal of entry into the world of non-all-or-nothing attitudes, a world that is composed not so much of shades of gray, but, given a bit more assurance, of the variegated colors of the rainbow.

It takes repetitive pointing out of the all-or-nothing attitude before the patient begins to catch on to it. After a time, the patient may begin to say things like, "you would say that I'm being all-or-nothing about this, but . . . ." This attribution of the idea to the therapist, no matter how irritated and agitated, reflects already a first stage in internalization, for the representation of the therapist is already a component part of the patient. A tension has been set up that makes the idea of something other than an all-or-nothing attitude at least a possibility to be reckoned with.

The all-or-nothing attitude leaves out so much. This is

its virtue and its defect. A patient said, "I decided that I'd give this a chance. I decided I'd try it. But then I found myself getting so angry again. It was simpler the other way. Now, if I'm going to try, it makes everything much more confusing and that makes me angry." After the confusion and disorientation can be managed a bit better, the patient may begin to gain a sense of how much he loses out on by leaving so much out. At this stage, another patient reflected, "I have to stop seeing these guys as perfect when I start going out with them. Then they don't have any place to go but down, so I don't have anyone but myself to blame if I'm disappointed. Besides, if they're so perfect, where does that leave me? I cringe when I think how I act." The sadness is both appropriate and enriching. It is better to be able to face what we have missed than to make ourselves go on missing it because we cannot bear to look and to see our misfortune.

"I always wanted to be a fairy godmother who could make everything better with just the wave of a wand," observed a patient who was very warmhearted and sensitive to the moods and sorrows of others. What she lacked was the psychological infrastructure to accept that so much in life cannot be changed; that often she wished to hurt and harm, not just to help; that what can be helped requires a realistic sequencing of steps and budgeting of efforts; that she was so sensitive to others partly in an effort to avoid being sensitive to herself; and, perhaps hardest of all, that helping always depends on a mutual effort that links both helper and helped and puts them at each other's mercy. Behind the magic wand lurks the image of an avenging sword.

To make a more realistic set of tools is a long and painstaking process, more complex in its internal ramifications than writing and integrating the software for some feat like launching and operating a space shuttle. The patient's impatient all-or-nothing attitude is so commonly mirrored by the therapist's untherapeutic failure to appreciate the complexity and pervasiveness of the developmental revisions that are required. In a very real sense, the borderline patient has to lose his self if he is to have any chance of gaining a new self. This perception of what is involved in modifying splitting defenses leads us back onto the terrain of the fusing–losing paradigm discussed earlier.

In an intriguing contribution, "The Antithetical Meaning Of Primal Words," Freud (1910a) stressed what at first glance seems the incongruent congruency of opposed meanings. In the service of making broader links to his idea that in dreams the category of negation is simply ignored, he culled the examples that in Latin, *altus* means both "high" and "deep," *sacer* both "holy" and "accursed." He pointed out that the word *cleave* means both "to separate" and "to join," and he noted the link between the German *stumm,* meaning "dumb," and the German *stimme,* meaning "voice." He quoted a linguistic authority who was interested in the way in which ancient Egyptians used the same words for "strong" and "weak," "command" and "obey." He explored the useful notion that we think by dividing a semantic territory into opposites, each of which takes the other as a reference point. What opposites have in common is that they rely on each other for meaning. They take up a position with respect to each other. The kinship here to splitting in the broader sense of all-or-nothing attitudes emerges clearly. We establish shadings and gradations of meaning, feeling, thinking, intending, and acting on the basis of multiple sets of oppositions. Being able to establish opposition brings us out of the blur. In this sense all-or-nothing thinking is a crucial step forward.

We may think of the different poles in the all-or-nothing splitting paradigm as standing in a figure/ground relationship to each other. It is possible that we move beyond splitting by flickering back and forth fast enough to begin to see new pictures, much as the illusion of motion in motion pictures depends upon a succession of still pictures rapid enough to enlist persistence of vision to produce the subjective sense of continuity. This flickering back and forth was

termed "shimmering" by a patient who found it both interesting and enticing on the one hand and frightening on the
other. The well-known Peter–Paul Goblet figure-ground
image is included here, Figure 2–5, to remind us just how
abrupt figure–ground reversals can be and how convincing
each perceptual set is.

Moving beyond all-or-nothing attitudes requires a
change in an entire psychophysiological set. It is an inner
cultural change and, like all such cultural changes, is composed of a vast set of subsidiary changes. All too often
psychotherapeutic efforts are poorly calibrated, pushing the
patient toward changes that are beyond the scope of what he
is ready to accommodate. A patient complained, "I don't
think you know the first thing about me. I think you've made
up an idea of me that has nothing to do with me. Then you
want me to live like that." She was not simply defending her

FIGURE 2–5.   The Peter–Paul Goblet

despairing view of herself and repeating in her transference attitude what had transpired between her and her mother. She was also pointing out realistically to her therapist in the present how he had a tendency to overestimate her strengths and fail to appreciate her difficulties.

An analogy can be made to misguided efforts in the area of foreign aid. At one time in the 1960s, the United States spent a great deal of money providing tractors to underdeveloped nations. In most of these countries, spare parts were scarce, mechanical expertise even scarcer. Few people knew how to drive tractors, so mishaps were common as they tried to learn. In addition, basic agricultural practices (planting times, spacing, and weed control) were not such as to make the use of tractors an efficient or economical option. The result in some countries was that after a few years wrecked and rusting tractors could be seen abandoned in the fields at intervals of a few miles. It was a sad and discouraging sight. It reflected the lack of understanding of the step-by-step nature of successful developmental change. Planners had assumed that, since advanced American agriculture was highly mechanized, mechanization would produce advanced agriculture in developing countries.[2] Similar difficulties can be seen currently in very rich oil producing countries where the cultural underpinnings for supporting a sophisticated technological infrastructure do not exist. Perhaps similar difficulties also show in the extraordinary refractoriness to change of near desperate living conditions in Appalachia.

A major empathetic task for those treating borderline patients is to appreciate how pervasive and severe their developmental lags and lacks are. The therapist's wishing does not make it so, any more than does the patient's. A severely disturbed young borderline woman felt she had no right to exist if she could not support herself and be eco-

---

2. Based on personal observations made by Dr. Lewin in Tanzania in the late 1960s.

nomically independent. This laudable goal was manifestly unrealistic in the short term, given the depth of her disability. As part of her early efforts in this direction, she decided, with her therapist's support and encouragement, to open a bank account in her own name. She received a card from the bank and, not having yet received her confidential identifying number, tried to make a withdrawal from an automatic teller machine. The machine ate her card. Her interpretation of this event was that she had made an effort to rob a bank and been caught in the act. She retreated in terror to her apartment, fully expecting the FBI to come to arrest her. It took her two weeks before she could even tell her therapist about this experience.

Her feeling was that, if she wanted something and did not receive it, this was proof of her badness tantamount to being convicted of a crime for which the punishment would be extreme. She had a hard time accepting her therapist's explanations of how automatic teller machines worked, clinging determinedly to her own more magical and all-or-nothing view. It was more frightening to her to grasp that the world worked by rules that were independent of her volition than to feel that the FBI was after her and that her arrest was imminent.

For his part, the therapist was chastened by his recognition of how limited his understanding of the patient's view of the task had been. He had made the mistake of assuming that what would have been a simple task for him would be a correspondingly simple task for the patient. She had seen herself as approaching the source of all wealth with a magically empowering instrument. She was not making a miniscule withdrawal from the bank, but rather robbing it. This perception fit with her life-long sense of being deprived, frustrated, and forced to do without what was her due, a sense that had considerable grounding in reality. Making a withdrawal from an automatic teller machine bore a haunting resemblance to approaching her mother. The therapist realized that he, himself, shared the patient's wishful approach to her goal of achieving economic independence to a far greater degree than he had acknowledged to himself. We will come back to this kind of issue in later discussions of the progression–regression dilemma, the negative therapeutic reaction, the nature of the holding function, and the use of countertransference data.

Another borderline patient who was an adept swimmer described how strange she found it to watch other swimmers struggling in the pool. "I don't struggle. I just swim," she said. "The water holds me up." She then went on to reflect, quite accurately, that her therapist must have a similar sense of strangeness watching her struggle with things he could do easily. The comment was especially apt since he knew only too well how dismaying it was to find himself struggling up and down a swimming pool while more skilled swimmers glided by seemingly effortlessly. This patient had already taken a series of major steps out of the prison of her all-or-nothing attitudes, recognizing her lack of internal buoyancy and using observations made in an area of strength as metaphorical links to increased understanding in an area of relative weakness.

As integration takes place, with the all-or-nothing attitudes gradually replaced by more complicated and differentiated ones, the sense of sadness and remorse over what has been missed in the past gives way to a recognition of separateness and differentiated independence. The affective intensity in the transference is diminished, bringing yet another kind of sadness as the limitations on the relationship are more realistically accepted. Patients who traverse this difficult passage show more flexible and resilient approaches to their conflicts. They tolerate ambivalence and are able to forgive themselves and others without feeling that they are being betrayed or betraying themselves. They can relish complexity without feeling that it confuses them to the point of virtual extinction of the sense of self (Schulz 1984).

NEGATIVISM

Negativism creates much of the countertransference soil for therapist and staff who come in contact with borderline patients. Borderline patients, as a rule, must work long and hard before they can cooperate or collaborate in a straightforward way. When they are ready to do this, the treatment is often near its conclusion. Their oppositional tactics cannot help but be frustrating and irritating, if not enraging. No one who has worked over the long haul with borderline patients can have missed out on the experience of wondering whether it even makes sense to try, given how hard it is to establish a sense of collaborative undertaking and reliable mutuality.

At the same time that negativism provides much of the impetus to difficult countertransference experience, it is what enables the patient to continue a relationship with others without experiencing being swallowed up, extinguished, or suffering overwhelming losing danger in being with others.[3] Negativism in the child has been recognized as an important factor in constructing a sense of separateness in the individuation process. Anyone who has had to negotiate on a consistent basis with a recalcitrant 2-year-old can attest to the degree of inner mobilization and tension that is involved in this experience. It can take you very quickly back to feeling like you yourself are only 2. Parents handle this phase with varying degrees of tolerance and ease. Some try to squelch the child to teach a lesson, much as one would try to break a horse. Fearing that what they see as excessive willfulness will result in the child's taking control, a virtual overthrow of civilized government, some parents move in

---

3. A colleague was chagrined to note that he had written, "The patient has trouble distinguishing self and objection representations" when he meant to write, "The patient has trouble distinguishing self and object representations." Objection may be an essential dynamically "objectifying" movement.

too forcibly to correct the situation. This is not unlike an often observed parallel response to patients who are seen as "manipulative," "controlling," or "not yet ready for treatment." What is missed is how the treating persons have, in their turn, become manipulative and controlling, expressing their own lack of readiness to treat patients who present in a negativistic manner.

While the differentiating defensive aspects to negativism have been apparent, the connecting features have not been as readily recognized. The phrase "warmth by friction" was coined to refer to processes whereby those threatened with dedifferentiation in situations of intimacy might utilize an abrasive, distancing posture to maintain separateness and simultaneously retain a connecting link with another person. Schulz and Kilgalen (1969) give an extended development of the concept.

A patient said she was aware how she kept herself emotionally uninvolved in therapy: "I don't allow myself to get close. The closer I am the less safe I am." Another patient evoked countertransference disapproval by chronic lateness and withholding. Her father had insisted on punctuality. She would connect with him internally every time she rebelliously arrived late for her appointment. This connection was vital to her, making it hard to change her behavior before she developed more abstract and internal ways of touching base with her feelings for and against father.

More than one patient has made the observation that his or her own negativism often was so powerful an inner trend that it was beyond volitional control. "I start disagreeing with you and I can't stop myself. I can't hear what you're saying. It's even worse if part of me agrees with what you're saying. That just increases how much I argue. It's like a storm that has to blow itself out. Sometimes I have to run away because it scares me so much." Negativism can be infectious, too. A therapist noticed that, after prolonged periods of negativistic relating with a patient, he kept missing overtures from the patient. When the patient tried to draw nearer, the therapist misinterpreted the gestures as hostile or mocking, treating the patient just as he felt that the patient had been treating him. The negativism became a process that was established and maintained itself interpersonally. As the therapist and the patient began to be able to observe this process together, recognizing mutual misinterpretations, discussions of the dangers of closeness became intermittently possible. An understanding of the patient's habitual sarcasm as a way of warding off too much connection while yet ensuring a reaction in the other emerged. It became apparent that negativism shaped the patient's view of and use of words. Often she regarded words not as aids to communication but as brickbats to be tossed back and forth, to make a sharp defining line between herself and the therapist. As the negativistic defense could be recognized and discussed, the patient's loneliness and pervasive sense of sorrow and disillusionment came through more clearly, along with memories that brought the awareness of how she had come to feel this way. Her treatment followed a characteristic pattern: intense negativistic relatedness preceded the emergence of new memories and new awareness of affective correlates both to the memories and to transference repetitions of old situations. The patient used negativism to stop what was threatening at the border of the self as she struggled to begin to try to accommodate it. The negativism could be appreciated as part of a pattern of personality integration and was an important part of her repertoire.

Her therapist became comfortable with responding sometimes heatedly to the patient's negativistic postures, engaging himself in producing some warmth through friction. After the episode, he and the patient were able to discuss both features of the negativistic phases, namely how they served to frustrate, exasperate, and distance and how they promoted an intense involvement. The patient was shocked to learn, for example, that during these times of heightened tension, her therapist had a hard time getting her off his mind. Her interpretation of this, in keeping with the negativistic trend, was that he really wanted to get rid of her. She felt it was only a matter of time before he did this. Her negativistic efforts to protect against the fusion danger brought on a losing danger in her mind.

Over and over again, the therapist pointed out that it seemed to him that she pushed him away the hardest when she needed him the most. What frightened her most was her sense of her own neediness. Yet, in keeping with this terror, she saw the surrounding world as totally unavailable to meet her needs. The dialogue moved from one that was interpersonally enacted at great heat producing not much light to one where the heat and the light were in better proportion, although still very difficult to keep in proportion. Interestingly, the therapist became more attuned to how his own efforts to disown his neediness played a major part in the dialectic of negativism.

Patients can also have a negativistic response to inner promptings. For example, a patient would sabotage his own performance in academic areas where his own interests were genuine because his father, who had allowed him little rein for his own exercise of will, approved of these undertakings and valued them highly. The patient was afraid to admit his own interest and perform to the level of his ability because this blurred the line in his mind between himself and his father. When his therapist expressed an interest in a course that he was taking, his performance in that course also deteriorated rapidly, providing a more direct window into the functioning of the negativism. Like spoiling trends with which it is often closely allied, negativism can put the patient in the position of cutting off his nose to spite his face. The therapist began to appreciate just how fragile was the patient's sense of owning any of his feelings or having any say in his own decisions.

Borderline patients often lack conviction as to the authenticity of their own inner feelings and experience. Negativism serves to establish a semblance of a boundary by building a wall, behind whose confines they can start to seek the promptings of what is truly inside. It is terribly important that this wall be given a chance to develop and to be modified so that after a time it can contain windows and even doors. The great wall of negativism is created as much to keep the self in as to keep the other out. Where there is a wall, there is likely in the long run to be a way toward more inflected and differentiated communication in symbolic terms. Negativism is at once the beginning of containment and a testimony to how much needs still to be built before complex feeling states can find a secure inner home.

SUMMARY

We see the borderline syndrome as a disorder of core identity that makes the attainment of modulated affective experience extremely problematic. The borderline patient is caught between the danger of fusing with important others and the danger of losing important others. The sunburst diagram illustrates a way of thinking about the relationships among the core fusing–losing dynamics, affective experience, and a panoply of defenses. We emphasize the vulnerability of the borderline self's experience of its ongoingness to affective perturbation as the self seeks to be neither too far from nor too close to the essential other.

Of the defenses the borderline patient enlists in this struggle, we have singled out two kinds for special attention. All-or-nothing attitudes represent a broadened application of the splitting concept. The broad concept of all-or-none attitudes has the virtues of being experience near and possessing an integrative thrust, so that it is well suited to early and ongoing therapeutic discussion. Focusing on all-or-nothing attitudes can guide patient and therapist to an appreciation of the realm of the excluded middle and what the patient loses by leaving it out.

Negativism is a means of maintaining connection in the

face of the need to distance to moderate the fusing danger. By creating interpersonal warmth through friction, it produces a complex and exasperating set of countertransference pressures on the therapist. If the solidification and strengthening of the borderline's core identity processes is to occur, the therapist must learn to appreciate negativism and understand its central place in the borderline's defensive repertoire. In Chapter 3 we will focus our attention on the special nature of transitional processes in borderline patients, noting the splitting of the transitional object and the concreteness of the borderline patient's approach to transitional processes.

3

The Borderline Patient and Transitional Object Relations

TRANSITIONAL PROCESSES
AND THE ART OF LIVING

Winnicott (1953) and others following his lead have taken the transitional object concept far beyond the popular notion of the teddy bear or Linus's blanket. It is not the object by itself, but what it is endowed with that gives it important functions. Illusion with its special, at times magical properties conveys and contains the inner world for each of us. Illusion has to do with play, with inner play, which is of the very essence of the definition of the human self.

When one includes transitional phenomena—this whole realm of the work of the inner play of illusion—in addition to the transitional object, the concept develops a scope and reach that extends to vast realms of a person's existence. It is our thesis that the borderline patient's need for *tangible* transitional objects can be viewed as a fault in illusion formation contributing to a lack of creativity.

By a lack of creativity, we do not mean a deficiency in the ability to paint, sculpt, dance, or write, whether words or music. We do not mean to refer to productions that are displayed outwardly. Rather, we are, in line with a very important trend of Winnicott's thinking, referring to the inner process that weaves the garb that the world of subjective experience wears for each individual. We are referring to inner processes that give form to the individual, informing processes. We are referring to that everyday all-day-long process of creativity that gives living its special flavor for each individual. In fact, the importance of works of art is most truly in the artful working of the minds of those who interact with them. The work of art is important not in itself but for what it invokes and evokes in its audience. When we overrate the work of art and underrate the audience, we are participating in an alienating practice that verges on idolatry. It has an excessive concreteness with a focus on the external at the expense of the internal. Inner play and interplay with objects are intimately interrelated.

Borderline patients, as we see them, are deficient in their use of inner sources and resources to create illusions. For reasons that often may have to do with adverse experiences, trauma, and persistent neglect, they remain stuck at a more concrete level where the enabling and vitalizing and soothing features of more abstract illusions are not available to them. We will illustrate how the borderline patients' conflicts around attachment, loss, and fusion become represented in their transitional object relations.

ILLUSION AND DEVELOPMENT

Greenbaum (1978) comments on illusion and creativity:

Winnicott believed these earliest interactions between infant and mother contain the roots of creativity. After initial experiences of need gratification from a good enough mother, when additional needs arise, the infant develops the illusion that he "created" his object of fulfillment. Indeed, at this early stage of development, there is no ability to distinguish between need arising within the self and the object in which it finds satisfaction. . . . With the inevitable gradual disillusionment which occurs, transitional objects and phenomena appear as substitute satisfactions. They are created by the child's adaptation of a part of the external world to conform to the configurations of his need. Since our needs are never completely satisfied, we are everlastingly preoccupied with attempts to adapt outer reality to inner need and express this in such "intermediate" forms of adult activity as artistic creativity. The transitional phase of development is made possible by the mother's unchallenging adaptability to her child's need for illusion formation. [p. 195]

Transitional objects and transitional phenomena are part of a process that reflects characteristic preoedipal and oedipal developmental issues. A developmental line can be discerned that follows the development of the transitional process.

This developmental aspect has been outlined by Sugarman and Jaffe (1989). After confirming the broadened use of the concept of transitional object and transitional phenomena, they observe:

For the body, the blanket, the imaginary companion, adolescent aspirations and religion are not so disparate as they might appear at first glance. The main . . . contention is that they represent nodal points in a developmental line of transitional phenomena that are linked functionally despite their more obvious phenomenological differences. The specific nature of transitional phenomena will differ at each stage due to maturational and developmental shifts in cognitive functioning, defensive functioning, libidinal focus, affect organization, and the demands of the environment. [pp. 90–91]

The transitional process is characterized by a certain mobility and plasticity. It is a living part of the dynamic stream of rearrangement that is the growth of the personality. When the transitional process becomes rigidified and arrested in a form that does not change in keeping with changing adaptive demands both from within and without, this is the sign of a trouble. As such, it can have both diagnostic value and value in terms of framing a therapeutic approach.

Sugarman and Jaffe postulate the following four stages in transitional development: (1) the body as transitional phenomenon, (2) the object as transitional phenomenon, (3) fantasy as transitional phenomenon, and (4) idea as transitional phenomenon in adolescence. A number of observations are in order concerning this delineation of stages. The first is that these stages overlap and are intermingled. As development procedes it is a question of orchestrating them together so as to produce an organization of transitional process that draws on all four modes. The body remains important for transitional purposes throughout life, as do objects that are specially endowed for transitional purposes. But how the body is used, how objects are employed will differ as a capacity for symbolic, abstract, and generalized transitional processes emerges.

A second important observation is that transitional process focused on the body depends in a special way on sensory experience produced by self-stimulation along afferent pathways. There is a concrete quality to such experience. It is sensory experience like any other. It is also possible that painful self-stimulation, because of its special urgency and definition, may occupy a special position at this stage, especially when the stress to be accommodated is large enough to be near the threshold of what is experienced as overwhelming. Pain makes a sharp edge and provides a focus, which can help in organizing by shutting out much that is more painful. The idea that cutting or burning is soothing because it hurts less than feeling what it is like inside the self is one that many borderline patients advance.

A third observation is that the progression through the stages can be characterized in a variety of ways, each of which has something to contribute, although none entirely captures the total flavor of this extremely rich vein of development. The thrust is from the concrete to the abstract, from the literal to the metaphoric, from the particular to the general, from the body to the shape, from the local to the distant, and so forth. One of our central theses is that the borderline patient remains confined largely to the first two stages. Something has gone awry in the movement toward the transitional use of fantasy and ideas. However advanced the intellectual capacities of these patients appear to be, something in their psychological development has gone off track so that fantasies and ideas do not have the containing and shaping capacity that is required to help them soothe and organize themselves. Thus, these patients are thrown back on more primitive devices, like the use of their own bodies and concrete transitional objects.

A most dramatic example was provided by the patient who very carefully and painstakingly—in the most literal sense of this latter word—carved "I love you, Mommy" into her own flesh. Another patient, one who had long been involved in a tight and destructive symbiosis not just with her mother but with an abusive boyfriend, was contemplating driving a thumbtack into her arm, something she had quite regularly done for a long period when she was upset. She experienced her therapist's suggestion that she try hugging a stuffed animal instead as a genuinely new and useful idea, one that would not have occurred to her on her own.[1]

Here we have a model for an important kind of therapeutic intervention, one that actively supports the movement from a more concrete body-oriented transitional pro-

---

1. We are indebted to Dr. Lori Hood for this clinical vignette.

cess toward a more abstract transitional process that is open to a wider and more symbolic world. In normal development, parents and teachers are regularly intervening along these lines, so pervasively and consistently that the importance of these interventions may tend to be radically underestimated. Their importance is highlighted when they cannot be taken for granted, as in the borderline population. Winnicott (1953) emphasized the value of illusion:

> The Mother, at the beginning, by an almost 100 percent adaptation affords the infant the opportunity for the illusion that her breast is part of the infant. It is, as it were, under magical control. The same can be said of infant care in general, in the quiet times between excitements. Omnipotence is nearly a fact of experience. The mother's eventual task is gradually to disillusion the infant, but she has no hope of success unless she has been able to give sufficent opportunity for illusion. [pp. 94–95]

We regard the description of the mother's task, "to disillusion the infant," as an least partially unfortunate one. The contrast illusion/disillusion is too strong.[2] It has the dichotomizing flavor of much all-or-nothing thinking. We think it would be better to characterize the mother's task as modifying the nature and force of illusion along the lines of the sequence from concrete to abstract, external to internal, literal to metaphorical, that we have described before.

It is a question of replacing one kind and set of illusions with another. The quality of illusion persists as a necessary feature of transitional phenomena. It is a matter of extending the range and flexibility of illusion so as to make available to the individual important culturally sanctioned resources for inner self-regulation and self-definition. Illusion is the cru-

---

2. Incidentally, we have similar difficulties with the strong opposition true self/false self. Every "false self" initiative contains a grain of truth and can usefully be seen as a stymied developmental intitiative from which something of value can be reclaimed.

cial factor that makes it possible to keep an inner shape, a form of self, that can both accommodate and withstand experience.

CONNECTION WITH DEFLECTION:
THE MORTAR FACTOR

The connecting aspect of transitional phenomena is readily apparent. We will argue that the deflecting or differentiating function is equally important. Winnicott (1953) describes the not-mother aspect as well as the not-me aspect of the transitional object: "It is true that the piece of blanket (or whatever it is) is symbolical of some part-object, such as the breast. Nevertheless the point of it is not its symbolic value, so much as its actuality. Its not being the breast (or the mother) is as important as the fact that it stands for the breast (or Mother)" (pp. 91–92).

A 40-year-old divorced executive described her upcoming first date with a man in her department. As the evening approached, she became conflicted about what blouse she should wear. This issue moved very much to the forefront of her attention. She worried that the one she had in mind might be too flashy for her date. Frantically, she called her mother, who told her she should wear the blouse she had intended to wear. She debated the matter again for a long time and with considerable intensity. Finally, she concluded that she should not accept her mother's advice, because the blouse would not suit her date.

This patient presented the debate as if it were all about the blouse. It is difficult to convey the peculiar intensity with which she made the blouse her interlocutor in internal dialogue: the blouse was highlighted, anything to do with a relational worry about her date played down. After the patient had gone on at great length and with great feeling about her being torn by her indecision about the blouse, her therapist ventured that she was having considerable anxiety about whether she would be acceptable to her date and suggested that she had considerable ambivalence about going out with him. She was, as he saw it, displacing her feelings about her date and her connection or lack of connection with him onto the blouse.

The patient fantasized a negative connection with her prospective partner, involving her mother in the debate only to reject her advice, thus at once connecting with and differentiating from her as well. Self-representation/object representation differentiation is not a stationary achievement, but a continuing process. Transitional phenomena play an important part both in protecting against fusion dangers and in protecting against loss dangers in the ongoing struggle for self-representation/object-representation differentiation.

According to Hong (1978): "Thus the blanket serves as a way of maintaining the close contact with mother and at the same time meets the infant's developmental need to establish relative ego autonomy. Blanket attachment therefore represents both the child's fear of separation and the need to separate" (p. 73). It is this need for transitional support of separateness that is often crucial to borderline patients whose weak psychological infrastructures make them vulnerable to fusion upon attachment. The greater the chance of intimacy, the more the fusion terror. The transitional function of interposing something between the self and the object is often described by such words as "wedging" and "deflecting."

The problem with this usage is that the connotation of "deflecting" or "wedging" is conceptually too far removed from the connecting and linking function that occurs simultaneously. We wanted a term that, like the process being described, encapsulates in itself the sense of a "connected separateness" or a "separate connectedness." Since mortar both separates the bricks one from another and connects them, the term *mortar factor* appealed to us. The separating feature enables the binding feature, and the binding feature enables the separating feature.

We can be excused perhaps for going a bit farther with the metaphor. Mortar also suggests building. Mortar makes it possible to pile bricks one upon another to produce structures that are far more than the sum of their individual parts. Psychologically, transitional processes make an important contribution to the transformation of personality in the face of severe stresses. The transitional process may be seen as the mortar that plays a crucial role in processes of internalization that are essential to structure formation. In this connection, it is worth noting that the Sheppard and Enoch Pratt Hospital, where much of our work has been done with borderline patients both as inpatients and as outpatients, is one of the most impressive brick structures in this country. The bricks were made on the site at the time the hospital was built, in the generation after the Civil War.

Obvious distancing is present as a concomitant feature in the interpersonal operations of borderline patients. An outpatient who was having a great deal of trouble discussing her eating disorder began going to meetings of Overeaters Anonymous and describing to her therapist what was said there. She was careful to contrast what Overeaters Anonymous said with what her therapist said. On the eve of a short separation about which she was quite worried, she told her therapist that she was going "to stay here tonight to attend the OA meeting," which was being held that evening on the grounds of Sheppard Pratt. This illustrated her use of OA simultaneously to establish distance and preserve closeness.

Overt and covert disparagement may allow binding as well as separating functions on the part of both the therapist and the patient. Some of the rueful, bitter, and mordant things that therapist and patient say about each other, both face to face and behind the other's back, are important mortar for constructing the relationship. When a patient says something like, "You never change your mind. It's not clear to me you even have a mind to change," or "I saw that movie where the psychiatrist was a cannibal and he was eating his patients and I immediately thought of you," the two-way traffic across the transitional bridge is clear. Similarly, the therapist, who finds that treating a particular patient is making him wonder why he did not go into another field, would do well to pause and hear the implied compliment: "This patient is really making a psychiatrist out of me. Only a psychiatrist could or would do this."

A fetishistic or part-object focus can similarly deflect and, at the same time, enable relatedness with a whole object. A young woman regularly referred to her husband, to whom she was deeply attached, as "that jerk." Occasionally, she would express her own deepest worry, which was that she was an awful "jerk" without even knowing it. She was not explicitly aware of the striking congruence of the term.

A part of a person can be used as a transitional object. A patient recalled that, as a little girl, she would hold on to her grandmother's hand at bedtime, pretending that it was a doll. Her grandmother's fingers were the doll's hair, grandmother's palm, the doll's face, and grandmother's arm, the doll's body. Here the mortar factor allowed the simultaneous binding and separation at bedtime. This example also illustrates the complexity and difficulty of the movement from the transitional use of the body and bodily sensation to the use of an object and even fantasy. In this patient's case, the different levels were significantly intertwined. After relating this memory, the patient spoke of two books authored by psychiatrists. Bringing these authors into the consulting room served the same function of simultaneously connecting with the therapist and diluting the connection with him.

Concurrent connecting and distancing functions were illustrated by a patient who used a gift of food that she received as a transitional object. Each year at the holiday season the patient's parents sent her a parcel of food as a gift. She would allow the food to spoil. However, she was unable to dispose of the rotting result. Her parents regularly sent her food that they knew she did not like and would not want. The food had features of a transitional object in that, in its spoiled state, it represented, in part, herself as a child who had been physically abused by her father. It was a direct link to her parents, representing not only her antagonism toward them, but her awareness of their antagonism toward her. The foul odor was a reminder of their continuing pervasive presence in her life, as well as of her repudiation of her need for them.

Nothing is nearer and more powerfully moving emotionally than smell. The patient had the illusion of control in her refusal of the gift, but at the same time she re-created their control over her by not disposing of it, thereby submitting to their hold on her at the very moment that she experienced herself as struggling desperately against them. This example illustrates very well how the borderline patient seeks a concrete and tangible transitional object.

CONCRETE TRANSITIONAL PROCESS IN
BORDERLINE PATIENTS

These patients have a problem in making the shift from concrete objects to more abstract, diffuse transitional phenomena. Winnicott (1953) describes the fate of the transitional object during normal development:

> Its fate is to be gradually allowed to be decathected, so that in the course of years it becomes not so much forgotten as relegated to limbo. By this I mean that in health the transitional object does not "go inside" nor does the feeling about it necessarily undergo repression. It is not forgotten and it is not mourned. It loses meaning and this is because the transitional phenomena have become dif-

fused, have become spread out over the whole intermediate territory between "inner psychic reality" and "the
external world as perceived by two persons in common,"
that is to say, over the whole cultural field. [p. 91]

Undoubtedly, we are all normally continuously oscillating
back and forth from the concrete to the abstract. We move
back and forth between tangible icons and more abstract
value systems. One important strand in the Middle East
dilemma may by described by the fixation on tangible icons.
In that part of the world, as in many others, there is a long
history of people of many different faiths being willing to
sacrifice principles to the overriding purpose of possessing
certain religious sites that function as tangible icons.

Borderline patients appear to be fixated at the concrete
level, utilizing what we term *shelf objects*. By this we mean
objects that are available as if to be taken down from the
shelf whenever needed, much as one would use a rabbit's
foot as a good luck charm. When no longer needed, the shelf
object goes back on the shelf. What has not taken place is the
diffusion across "the whole cultural field." The movement
toward fantasy, image, symbol, value, and idea has been
blocked partway along.

In contradistinction to Winnicott, we would not see the
transitional objects as being "decathected." Rather, what we
emphasize is the change in the nature of the investment with
increased developmental capacity for abstraction, memory,
illusion formation, and conceptual linking. When this change
does not take place, an individual is left using fetishes, that is
to say, overvalued concrete objects, to ward off psychological dangers. In this connection, it is interesting to note that
Freud (1927) defined splitting in a paper on fetishism in
which he was also concerned with the distinction between
neurosis and psychosis and with issues relating to loss
through death. Splitting as a pervasive defense is often associated with a magical use of concrete objects.

The movement away from the concrete and toward the

abstract, like so much else in human development, depends crucially on the support from the outside, from what we call the holding environment, personified first in the mother and then expanding to include a number of significant others, who are both literally alive and/or culturally alive. Such support is particularly important in fitting the magnitude of the stress to be sustained to the individual's capacity to sustain stress at a particular developmental moment. With such fitting, there is always the challenge to develop and master, but the challenge does not become overwhelming and the personality is spared the need for extreme and rigid defensive maneuvers.

A clue to understanding the pervasive infantile dependency characteristic of the borderline patient may be found in Winnicott's (1953) description of illusion and disillusionment:

This problem, which undoubtedly concerns the human infant in a hidden way at the beginning, gradually becomes an obvious problem on account of the fact that the mother's main task (next to providing opportunity for illusion) is disillusionment. This is preliminary to the task of weaning, and it also continues as one of the tasks of parents and educators. In other words, this matter of illusion is one which belongs inherently to human beings and which no indivdual finally solves for himself or herself, although a theoretical understanding of it may provide a theoretical solution. If things go well in this gradual disillusionment process, the stage is set for the frustrations that we gather together under the word "weaning"; but it should be remembered that when we talk about the phenomena (which Klein has specifically illuminated) that cluster around weaning, we are assuming the underlying process, the process by which opportunity for illusion and gradual disillusionment is provided. If illusion-disillusionment has gone astray the infant cannot attain to so normal a thing as weaning, nor to a reaction to weaning at all. The mere termination of breast feeding is not a weaning. [pp. 95–96]

The borderline patient has not attained anything like a weaning that involves the possibility of substituting the more abstract for the more concrete. The borderline is still stuck at the more concrete level of transitional phenomena.

For almost six months, during much of which time she was on suicide observation because of the intensity of the suicidal ideation she was expressing, a hospitalized borderline patient slept with a razor blade clutched tight in her hand under the pillow. "I know it sounds strange," she told her therapist one day, "but I can't really tell you how comforting it feels to hold this razor blade in my hand. I don't know what I'd do without it. It's the only thing that lets me go to sleep at night. I've got others hidden around, too, in case they try to take this one away."

For this patient, the secret razor blade provided a core of autonomy around which to organize at the same time that she occupied a great deal of energy with fantasies connecting her to the staff as she worried about their taking away her most prized possession. During this period, she did very little cutting. Yet the razor blade was present with her throughout the days and the nights. In terms of constancy she contrasted it favorably with the therapist who came only once a day and with nursing staff who were available for their shifts, but then went home. The razor blade, concrete and sharp edged, filled in for a deficit in representational stability at a more abstract level.

The following episode illustrates the use of a song as a transitional object as well as a patient's shift toward the use of a fantasy-based transitional process.

An outpatient, a voice student in her 40s, seemed to lack any sense of internal sources of capability, initiative, or stability. Her father always maintained that any accomplishment was not something for which she could take credit, but rather God's doing and, therefore, to be accounted solely to His credit. She sought causes and cures for her woes outside the boundaries of her psychological self. Candidate causes included genetics, hormonal imbalances, and bad parenting. Candidate cures included medications, hypnosis, and religious and psychoanalytic gurus.

The patient wanted advice, direction, and caring from her therapist. Her therapist's being there—listening, clarifying, and even interpreting—were not enough for her. In fact, they did not seem to mean anything to her. She wanted something more concrete—to be held, to be hugged, to be able to put her head in her therapist's lap. She encouraged input from outside herself while, paradoxically, she was exquisitely sensitive to the threat of other people taking over and extinguishing her identity. She regularly paid the late charges on her utility bills rather than "knuckle under" to the due date specified on the bill. She regularly arrived late for sessions, blaming the alarm clock, school buses, traffic, weather and road conditions for the delays.

Indications of progress were reflected in the following exchange:

"I seem to create chaos before coming here," she said. "I don't seem to be able to help it." Later in this same session, she said, "I was thinking of euthanasia and I broke out in hives." She went on to describe a ritual in which she listened to a certain aria before she went to practice her music in a church. This description opened onto a lengthy rendition of the specifics of her own breathing exercises and the ways in which these resembled her father's method, which had enabled him to maintain a resonant voice until age 80.

Meanwhile, as he listened to this recitative, her therapist found himself at some little remove inside his mind thinking about a marina he had recently visited where many of the boats had clever, punning names. He thought of a boat named "Youth In Asia," so, following the drift of his associations, he asked her, "What about euthanasia?" The patient demurred, saying, "It's nothing." Her therapist persisted, saying that she would not be having hives for "nothing." With some irritation, she replied that the therapist always made two sides to everything. She then added, "I think of suicide." Developing the thought a bit further along, she said, "I don't understand why I experience panic whenever I think of accomplishing something. It's like murder." Her therapist commented, "When we have looked at that before, we found that, if you are competent, you will no longer be connected to the person you needed. That's a type of murder." After a pause, her therapist continued, "You have it both ways. If you do well, you anticipate being abandoned and, if you fail, you feel you will be rejected." She said, "That's right! That's right! That's right! I don't know why I can't remember about the panic when I was 3 years old. I just don't have the memory." Her therapist commented, "Maybe you are remembering it every time you have anxiety or create the chaos."

Still later in the session, the patient said to her therapist, "Your cold seems better today. You seem to get two colds a year." Her therapist returned, "And you feel threatened that I will abandon you." She said, "On the way over here when I knew I was going to be late, I pictured myself plastered up against you on the couch."

Earlier she had discussed a passage from an aria that referred to suicide. She had expressed her admiration for it and said that she wanted to buy the tape so that she could learn to sing it. Now, returning to the aria, she said, "I can hear that aria as if I had my walkman on."

Among other things, this vignette reflects the patient's growing ability to represent in fantasy the wish for actual physical contact—"I pictured myself plastered up against you on the couch"—as transitional support through her anxiety. The movement away from the concrete to the abstract also is illustrated in her use of a memory of the aria, which, she says tellingly, is as clearly audible as if she had her walkman on. Again, she does not have to have her walkman literally plastered up against her to feel the musical contact.

TANGIBLE TRANSITIONAL RESPONSES BY THE THERAPIST

Borderline patients have a tendency not only to recreate transference patterns with others but also to repeat traumatic configurations with others. They evoke a variety of intense affective countertransference responses that, in turn, result in a spiral escalation of affective overload in the situation. Under this overload, countertransference responses are generally driven to one of two extremes. Either there is overidentification with the patient or there is complete unempathic rejection. The first aggravates the fusion danger for the patient. The second accentuates the loss danger. The task, as we will elaborate in Chapter 10, is to recognize one's countertransference response and make use of it in understanding the patient.

Masterson (1989) represents the generally accepted attitude regarding countertransference. He advocates that, in response to the patient's effort to have the psychotherapist "take over," the therapist should maintain "an emotionally neutral stance" in order to "serve as guardian of the emerging real self. . . . Their hidden agenda is to get the therapist to resonate with their need to be rewarded and supported and to serve as a new caretaker for them, so that they will feel better with the fantasy of having gotten the emotional supplies they wished they had gotten earlier in life" (p. 26).

Our impression is that attitudes of nonresponsiveness are advocated precisely because of the intensity with which these patients hunger for response. The problem about such advocacy is that it threatens to locate patient and therapist in a complicated struggle that each one conceptualizes from an all-or-nothing point of view. The therapist presents the patient with a threat of loss in order to protect against what he sees as a dangerous invitation to fusion. The problem with borderline patients is to steer a middle course in the face of intensely polarizing projective pressures. Emotional experiences by the therapist are inevitable and desirable. They are the real link, as opposed to theoretical formulations that do not possess the richness and vitality of a lived relationship. The goal is to observe and utilize one's own participation.

Another treatment episode from the same patient, the 40-year-old voice student, illustrates the impact of a tangible response on the part of the therapist. We believe that it is important to provide support for the patient's developmental efforts at moving from a more concrete to a more abstract and flexible transitional process, one with more capacity to contain a wider variety of affect. Whatever responses a therapist makes will have a distinctly disillusioning impact, because the boundaries of the situation and the relationship will be highlighted by flexible responses that afford partial gratifications. These will represent very direct challenges to the patient's own all-or-nothing style of thinking.

In the middle phase of her treatment, the patient had just begun to be able to enjoy her surroundings. On the previous spring day she had enjoyed walking in the park and seeing the dogwood trees in bloom. By the following session, she wanted to throw hand grenades at the trees. They were so beautiful they would consume her interest; she would be extinguished by her ecstasy; she objected to "their ability to do what they do so effortlessly." This linked to her envy of her mother's natural abilities.

Later in the session, the patient and her therapist explored the ways in which she felt similarly about the therapist and his life, namely that everything came effortlessly to him. The all-or-nothing character of her views, with only a rudimentary sense of sequence or intermediate steps, was striking. As she reflected on her view of the therapist, she noted that she did this sort of thing with everyone, assuming that everything came easily to others. She also noted that she felt she had to do everything perfectly and resented that she and her performance should be judged by these others. She felt that she should be judged only by her own standards, serving as her own only reference point.

When her feelings of anger, envy, and resentment abated, she returned to savoring the beauties of nature. She added that the purple trees among the white dogwood enhanced the effect of both. This was an integrative paradigm in which differences were seen as acting for mutual benefit, rather than in a mutually annihilatory fashion. It stood in vivid contrast to the preceding discussion. She described the purple tree in detail, but was puzzled about its name.

As she was leaving at the end of the session, her therapist inquired if she had a moment and went with her around the corner of the office to point out a magnificently blooming red bud tree. This gesture was tremendously important to her in confirming her appreciation of the beauty of nature and her new-found capacity to sustain the enjoyment of her perceptions. However, the inevitable sense of frustration returned as she used this example over and over again to illustrate how the customary interactions between her and her therapist were relatively devoid of responsiveness. This served as a transitional device to contain her rage and make possible a more direct and explicit exploration of negative transference elements.

This concrete partial gratification enabled her to experience not only what she felt she had been missing from others, but, ultimately, a taste of the caring that she had been holding back within herself and not directing toward others. Her mixed attitudes toward the transitional dogwood trees could not allow her to sustain an appreciation of their beauty. Her intense attitudes toward others left her with more affect than she could process.

What we see is that the holding environment in the form of transitional phenomena is not functionally fully available to the borderline patient because the attachment to the transitional object threatens with reenactment of primary object fusion, while the hostility threatens with loss or destruction reminiscent of the situation with regard to the primary object. Here again we meet the fusing and losing dangers. The appreciation of the borderline patient's predicament in regard to transitional process opens up avenues for therapeutic interventions to help the patient stabilize the transitional process and move it to more abstract and flexible levels. Responsiveness can be informed and located in a process that, far from rendering it a danger to the patient's integrity, makes a significant contribution to the patient's sense of self. In our view, it can be an important aid to borderline patients in getting hold of the internal holding functions that will let them get more securely established in treatment.

4

Hazards of Change in Borderline Patients

CHANGE IN BORDERLINE PATIENTS

We will be discussing the relationships among holding environments, regressions, and negative therapeutic reactions as parts of an exploration of the borderline patient's predicament in regard to change. The notorious difficulty in helping a borderline patient achieve a stable degree of internal psychological change, so that it is no longer the case that today's realizations become tomorrow's ruins, provides the clinical impetus to this exploration.

We think of change in the patient as a process whereby concrete and not-so-concrete external holding provides the foundation for refinements in the inner faculty of illusion, including especially increased capacity to generate transitional experience that is more abstract. This increasingly supple illusion-making faculty in turn provides a solid inner foundation for new initiatives in psychological growth and development. In our view, psychological suppleness is the essential element in reliable personality functioning. It is an intrapsychic quality that is crucially dependent on interpersonal support for its development.

The paradox here is that the external holding contributes to psychological reality insofar as it contributes to an illusion-making capacity that is decisive for the patient's ability to attain, contain, and sustain emotional experience. We emphasize the importance of illusion in order to reclaim the notion of what is real from what, for lack of a less clumsy term, we may call the *thingish*, that is, something external and independent of the subject's own creative and exploratory capacity for its existence. When we speak, for example, of alienation, we are describing a lack of links, a deficiency in the operation of the mortar factor.

Our capacity to be active in making illusions in large part defines the flavor of our "realism," whether it is harsh, cold, constricted, and negativistic, or more forgiving, kinder in tone, with more complex borders and patterns, and more shadings and inflections. Borderline patients are often the ultimate "realists" when it comes to attunement to that part of experience that is harsh, painful, betraying, and without remorse. The harsh edge of pain serves them as a self-definition device, one that protects against an even more frightening inner chaos.

Our borderline patients appear unable to sustain fantasy and illusion that is more abstract and symbolic. Fantasy does not seem to be able to contain and shape the impulse. Rather, the impulse seems always to be threatening to escape, like a furious caged animal, and to produce dire consequences for the patient. So dangerous is fantasy, so near is the mental image of an action to the action, that control cannot be maintained except by extinguishing the fantasy. Again, it is all or none.

The borderline patient has no confidence in being able to maintain a controlled fantasy life. A resort to tangible transitional objects, if not to the painful use of the patient's own body as a transitional object, is required to give the patient the requisite illusion of control. There is a deficiency in sublimation, the ability to switch the aims and objects of urges. This closes off access to any variety in satisfactions. Because it is devastatingly frustrating to forego actual gratification, they cannot utilize fantasy and illusion as supports in moving on toward more complex and eventually more available and sustainable gratifications. They lack the psychological intermediaries in the way of transitional processes to bridge from the immediately expedient to what is in the long run more than expedient.

A patient began to fantasize about winning a contest. The fantasy started out as a pleasurable one. However, along the way, when she encountered the idea that she was not likely to win, the initial enjoyment turned to angry frustration. "It makes me feel worse instead of better." She said that she never liked to think about winning things because it made her so furious. It was better, she thought, just not to think about it at all. She and her therapist were able to trace out a pattern where, when she began to imagine situations, or even to plan, the fantasy brought her so much upset that she broke it off, with the result that planning and anticipating were severely compromised as internal mental functions.

Another patient was convinced that it was best not to think about sex at all, because if she thought about sex she was afraid that she would become a nymphomaniac without any controls at all. She had similar worries about drugs and alcohol, although her actual behavior had been quite responsible. Allowing herself any kind of sexual fantasy produced extreme anxiety and ill humor. She talked also about how much she hated the idea that she was supposed to control herself, feeling helpless and incompetent about doing so. For her, to control herself was to be abandoned, for it involved letting go of the fantasied negativistic relationship with an external controlling agent.

A borderline patient with an explosive temper who had been physically abused as a child decided that she wanted to make a proper Thanksgiving dinner for her family. Since she had no idea how to go about this, she used a Norman Rockwell painting of a traditional Thanksgiving as a blueprint. To her chagrin, despite her best efforts, she and her husband and son very quickly became embroiled in an argument that ended with their throwing food at each other and totally disrupting the meal. She herself was an active participant in this. Interestingly enough, this same woman had previously won the award as the most courteous employee of the year in a job where she had considerable dealings with the public. Her method for maintaining courtesy and composure involved fantasizing that there was a man with a machine gun sitting on her shoulder who would shoot her immediately if she were to utter any of the obscenities that coursed through her mind as she replied with apparently infinite patience to the requests she received. She invested this notion so intensely that it had nearly the force of a delusion. When she left work, she would cut and burn herself.

A number of questions present themselves for our attention. What can be done to help borderline patients develop more capacity to sustain fantasy and its associated affects? How are all-or-nothing positions modified? What dangers does the borderline patient meet as he tries to progress toward a more internalized, abstract, and symbolic approach to illusion formation? Why is it a clinical commonplace with borderline patients that therapeutic gains are so difficult to sustain? What kind of treatment approach and resources are required to support increased suppleness in transitional processes?

THE PROGRESSION–REGRESSION DILEMMA

Let us begin with a clinical vignette, which we will then leave aside while we present some general ideas concerning the progression–regression dilemma. Only after we have discussed these will we return to look more carefully at it.

In her eighth year of treatment, a severely ill borderline patient completed a vocational training school. This represented a great achievement for her, one that she had not believed herself to be capable of managing. She had struggled for years to find a way to move toward a more self-supporting position. Early in treatment she had stated her belief that she could not be a worthwhile person unless she was economically self-sufficent and able to take care of herself. She had identified this point of view as coming from her family and it had formed an important pole in her feeling about herself. She, in fact, came from people who were intensely invested in upward social mobility and very insecure about their capacity to maintain a position in the professional classes. She had worked at a variety of volunteer jobs and even two paying jobs for short periods of time, each of which highlighted certain aspects of her difficulties and provided important opportunities for therapeutic discussion. Frustration with a night job, which made enormous demands on her in caring for retarded men, led to her taking the initiative in going back to school. On this job she had had a great deal of trouble controlling aggressive urges toward her charges who were often obstinate.

Graduation from the vocational school coincided with her mother's remarriage, something she had long expected and long dreaded, given that she had always, with much justice, experienced her original father as an unfairly advantaged competitor for her mother's attention. Any sense of her mother as a competitor for her father's attentions was submerged in this earlier feeling. One of her deepest, darkest, and most frightening worries was that she might be just like her father.

Following graduation from vocational school and her mother's remarriage, she plunged into an affair with someone significantly more disturbed than she was. She had another outburst of drinking. Her therapist actually called the police at one point to ensure her safety after she had made a number of extremely disturbed phone calls to him at home. She postponed looking for a job and became quite discouraged, if not despondent. She had an episode of extreme confusion that was strikingly reminiscent of one that had occurred prior to the onset of this treatment. She had a very difficult time discussing any of this in therapy and could not make herself tell her mother about her fears.

The Figures 4–1 through 4–5[1] may be of help in understanding the borderline patient's predicament in regard to change. The borderline patient is often excoriated for making use of a very primitive set of defenses. In clinical parlance the emphasis is more often on the instability involved in the characteristic "stably unstable" position of the borderline patient than on the stability.

---

1. We are indebted to Cynthia Vaeth for the design of these diagrams (and Figures 4–6 through 4–10), done originally in torn paper to emphasize the importance and difficulty of borders and differentiation. The successive diagrams use the same pieces of torn paper to represent different configurations. It is worth noting that so many borderline patients feel so torn so much of the time.

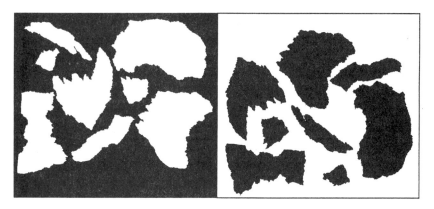

FIGURE 4–1.   Splitting, All-or-None

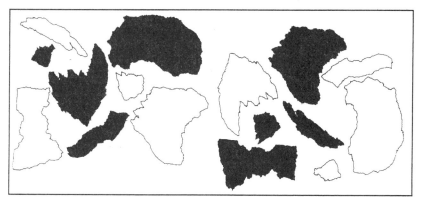

FIGURE 4–2.   Defense Disruption: Sense of Chaos, Helplessness

We have discussed the reliance of the borderline patient on an all-or-nothing approach to life that excludes ambiguity, vagueness, doubt, the middle ground, compromise, flexibility, forgiveness, and so much else. We think of this as a more general and more broadly clinically useful presentation of the splitting defense. The all-or-nothing attitude is not simply a confession of failure or a defect in the patient. It is also a significant achievement, in that it provides a form of self-organization and keeps the dangers of chaos and dissolution of the self at bay. In particular, it represents a response to what we have characterized as the fusing and losing dangers.

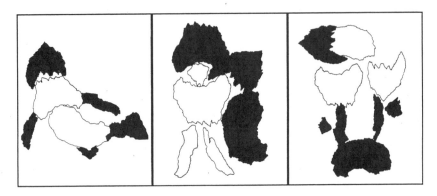

FIGURE 4–3. Insufficient Infrastructure: Competing Organizations

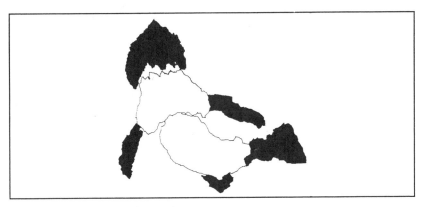

FIGURE 4–4. Early Terror Evoked: Negative Therapeutic Reaction

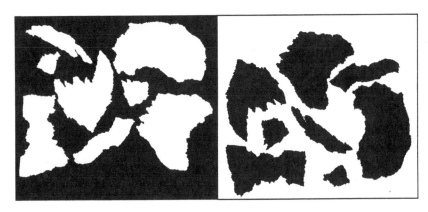

FIGURE 4–5. Back to All-or-None

This is usually where we meet the borderline patient. In the state of affairs suggested by Figure 4–1, all-or-nothing attitudes pervade. There is rigid separation of psychological elements of opposite valences. Treatment is disruptive and threatening to the patient's preexisting equilibrium. To some degree, the more skillfully the treatment is carried on, the greater the resources of understanding, compassion, and pacing that are deployed in the treatment, the more this is likely to be the case. It can be the sign of a very skillful treatment that the patient develops a sense of greater suffering, turmoil, and even despair.

The therapist's capacity to sustain interest in the patient, to attend rather than intrude, to be curious and firm as well as kind, often serves a function akin to psychological *reperfusion*. We have used the analogy of the patient who is in such severe shock that there is little bleeding, blood being such a scarce resource that it cannot be expended in this way. Improvement in circulating blood volume produces a dramatic and frightening picture in which what was wrong all along becomes much clearer. Similarly, borderline patients may be so rigid, so numbed, so distant, so closed off both interpersonally and intrapsychically that they spend large portions of their lives in a state akin to shock. With an increase in available emotional resources, the accustomed defensive arrangement may be threatened. The patient dares to take tentative steps onto a dangerous ground where the grip implied by the all-or-nothing attitudes is relaxed. This stage is suggested by the intermingling of puzzle pieces of different emotional shades in Figure 4–2. A disruption of the available defense pattern brings with it a sense of chaos and helplessness.

At this point, the patient and the therapist may both be well pleased with their work, sharing an impression that a good bit has been accomplished and that hopeful change is in the wind. What this leaves out is the insufficiency of the patient's internal psychological infrastructure. The patient is apt to experience the new state as having terrifying similarity to early states of helplessness, vulnerability, and chaos that have never been adequately mastered. Subjectively, the patient's sense, often unconsciously, may be that far from having moved forward, he has made the mistake of setting foot back into a war zone where he was severely wounded and barely survived.

Figure 4-3 aims to express this kind of predicament by highlighting the insufficient psychological infrastructure and the competing organizations that are potentially available to the patient. The shark is predatory, cold-blooded, overwhelmingly dangerous and, as the patient experiences it, unlinked to him by any relationship. The shadow expresses already a connection with parts of the self that are avowed, if also partially disowned. Here there is threat, but enough connection with the threat for at least a beginning dialogue. The tulip drawing expresses a gentler, more aesthetically pleasing, more fecund alternative in which much of the danger has been tamed.

In her second year of treatment the patient (who later completed vocational training school) disagreed with her mother for the very first time about what she should wear to a family gathering. She was very pleased with this initiative on her part and showed a bright, almost elated affect when she was telling about it in therapy. She felt that she had shown more mettle than she knew she had in her. She felt encouraged about her capacity to be an independent person and present herself as such. Two days later, hurrying across a street against the light to meet a new lover, she was struck by a car, sustaining multiple and serious injuries.

For this patient, the new initiative had been too much too quick. It had mobilized early terrors that she could not represent well enough to monitor. These represented a serious threat to her very existence. A plausible reading is that her new expression of independence evoked the losing danger to such an extent that she threw herself into a defensive affair and, so great was her urge to merge, suspended normal safety operations. The shark almost got her. She was not yet able to integrate her anger or disappointment with her mother, these shadow aspects of herself, so no gentle result was possible.

Figure 4–4 shows the dominance of the organization suggested by the image of the shark. The evocation of early oral dangers revolving around questions of trust, intactness, devouring and being devoured, ongoingness versus extinction of the self, is intended. The lack of psychological infrastructure determines the inaccessibility of more advanced organizations in face of the danger and opportunity afforded by a loosening of the defenses. The drawings are meant to suggest that different organizations are possible with the same starting materials. These psychological puzzle pieces can, with some modification, be put together in a variety of different ways.

After being hit by the car the patient had a very difficult time. With a cast on her leg, she felt very helpless, much as she had as a little girl, when she had the sense that she was always asked to wait too long. The support of a variety of therapies and a halfway house was not sufficient to prevent her from falling into a deep depression. Her psychiatrist, acting much like the often out-of-tune mother described by the patient, found the depression very hard to recognize. Ultimately, a brief hospitalization led to the initiation by another doctor of somatic therapy, which was a great help. The patient showed her resilience in attachment by making contact with her therapist to take up the work again.

Figure 4–5 shows a return to the initial defensive organization. The basic configuration of the situation remains un-

changed, although possibly a few of the pieces of the puzzle
have been modified slightly and some new potential relationships among them have been glimpsed. At the end of the
cycle both therapist and patient are apt to be disgruntled and
a bit mistrustful, not only of each other but of their own
instincts and perceptions. In many cases, it does not take
many cycles of this kind to destroy the link between the
patient and the therapist, and working with borderline
patients means sustaining many cycles of this form. Fore-
warned may be forearmed, however, so as to make it a bit
more possible for both parties to disarm before they do too
much damage to the vital link between them.

Let us pause to recapitulate where we have been in
terms that are more abstract and general. We conceptualize
three broad stages in the development of the self. The
beginning stage is an unintegrated self with an absence of
self-constancy and self-identity. Experience is intense, chaotic, and turbulent, with one part self-constellation suc-
ceeding another in sequences that can be both rapid and
unpredictable. The self is off balance and out of kilter, with
high highs, low lows, and sudden transitions.

A first step beyond this stage depends on a self that is
rigidly organized with exaggerated clarity of boundaries and
concrete thinking. Affects here are total and absolute rather
than partial. Negotiation with the avenues it opens onto
compromise, forgiveness, and collaboration is not yet possible. A subjective sense of inflexible conviction about be-
liefs and attitudes attends this stage, the one in which we
find so many borderline patients so much of the time.
Attempting to experience opposing values or feelings renders the self conflicted and torn apart: "I wouldn't know
who I was or what I stood for. It's impossible."

The advanced mode enables the self to experience
doubt, ambiguity, mixed emotions, compromise, negotiation, assurance that is only relative, and so forth. It is not
hard to appreciate that, given certain kinds of developmental experiences, the more advanced mode might seem

dangerously similar to the earliest mode: chaos, helplessness, overwhelming vulnerability, lack of any internal cohe-
siveness. Our thesis is that, for the borderline patient, going
forward seems so much like going backwards that the two
share a dangerous valence that makes the rigid, concrete,
all-or-nothing middle position overwhelmingly attractive,
not for any simply positive reason, but because of what it
excludes from awareness. For borderline patients, this can
be the *only* place to be, in that it is the only place where they
have a subjective sense of internal cohesion, however high
the price they have had to pay.

Applying this concept to the development of the transitional object and what we may call transitional object
relations, we assume that the infant experiences a relative
sense of vulnerability, helplessness, and lack of ability to
control, contain, modulate, and sustain feelings. In our
postulated middle phase, the acquisition of a transitional
object would provide the infant with a means of dealing
with the fusing and losing dangers and regulating a whole
variety of feelings, including but not limited to anger, loss,
rejection, and anxiety. We emphasize the mortar function of
the transitional object, the way in which it *simultaneously*
serves to link and wedge apart so as to make construction
possible.

Winnicott points out that the transitional object is
usually a tangible, but that, later on, the transitional zone
is occupied by art, culture, values, and religion. Our theory
is that those who have experienced the self and ego developmental difficulties of our borderline patients would find
the abstract transitional phenomena to be too close to the
original infantile state prior to the creation/discovery of
the transitional object. This leads them to cling to tangible
concrete transitional objects, such as dolls, razor blades,
parts of the body, drugs, alcohol, painful sensation, and so
forth.

We can now offer the following idea of what we like to
call the progression–regression dilemma as it presents itself

to the borderline patient.[2] The lack of psychic infrastructure renders impossible the crossing of the difficult place where the similarity of the advanced state and the early state appears. Borderline patients appear stably unstable because any venture off the ground of the very rigid defensive structures threatens them with chaos. The rigidity is confining but the avenues to more degrees of freedom are closed off by unmastered early difficulties.

These patients may have enormous trouble with "disillusionment," what we have been careful to characterize as the replacement of one form of illusion with another, because they have had inadequate help in achieving the illusive and, in their cases, elusive states in which they have an experience of control and confidence. They have been handicapped because of the relative imbalance between what they have been asked to handle and what they were able to manage at very early stages in development. Frustration has not been adequately dosed and modulated. The regression with which the ego is threatened in the middle passage is more than what these egos with limited infrastructure can manage to put in the service of development.

This progression–regression dilemma has a number of different kinds of potential uses in viewing borderline phenomena. It provides an understanding from a preoedipal point of view of the action of defenses against primordial anxieties around fusion and loss of self-boundaries. It emphasizes the importance of stable boundaries between self and object representations for affect attainment, sustaining, and ultimately affect modulation and taming. It shows how the fusing–losing paradigm we have elaborated relates to the

----

2. In part, this notion represents a generalization of ideas about female development expressed by Peter Blos (1962). We do not hold the same views Blos does on the differences in the developmental quandaries of the sexes. We believe variants of the progression–regression dilemma, leading to rigid compromise positions, can be observed in both sexes and at a variety of points in development.

difficulty in sustaining forward development. It is consistent with the observation of the use of tangible transitional objects including their own bodies by borderline patients. It also offers an understanding of the difficulty the borderline patient has in shifting to transitional phenomena, such as art, culture, values, and religion. The borderline patient is often incapable of conceiving a religion that is welcoming, tolerant, forgiving, hopeful, or compassionate. A religion of forgiveness, compassion, and hope is too unclear and threatening because it is not "definite" enough.

The progression–regression dilemma suggests an expansion of the mechanism behind the concept of negative therapeutic reaction beyond Freud's concept of unconscious guilt around achievement. It frames the matter in terms of defective preoedipal psychic infrastructure, particularly in the areas of self-representation/object-representation boundaries. A certain degree of stability of the sense of self in the face of losing and fusing dangers is required to make possible the symbolic representation, attainment, sustaining, and modulation of affects. Theories of internal object relations where part self/part object representations are bridged by affects have been proposed. Our perspective suggests a dialectic in which the affect bridges can become elaborated only to the extent that the part self and part object representation piers are firmly anchored and firmly separated.

We might part company with the death instinct theory by suggesting that the self does not seek absolute peace in freedom from stimulation, but rather a balance between what confronts it and what it can symbolize and represent to protect it from excessive strain and excessive threats of dissolution. When this balance is against it, it must take extreme measures to maintain even a semblance of cohesion. Some "self-destructive" maneuvers might actually be in the defense of a very threatened sense of self. In our view, the negative therapeutic reaction can occur when a potential step forward threatens the self with the experience of annihilation in a way that has not been appreciated and that

the self is incapable of representing symbolically. We will
return to these questions later on when we consider how we
can understand so many borderline patients' conviction that
they are empty nonentities.

WHEN REPETITION LEADS TO PARTIAL
RESOLUTION

Why should not all cycles of repetition lead to exactly
the same impasse? What factors can be called on to account
for the possibility of even partial resolution of the progression–regression dilemma? It behooves us to consider these
questions carefully and at some length so that we can form
some view of potential therapeutic strategies in dealing with
borderline patients, so many of whom have spent a lifetime
trapped in cycles of futile repetition.

Again let us turn to a series of schematic figures, Figures
4–6 through 4–10. Figures 4–6 and 4–7 are identical to the
ones presented earlier. The rigid style of organization with
all-or-nothing attitudes and disruptive unmodulated affects
is threatened by the essential features of the therapeutic
situation: constancy of concern, respect for emerging
boundaries, curiosity and efforts at understanding, support

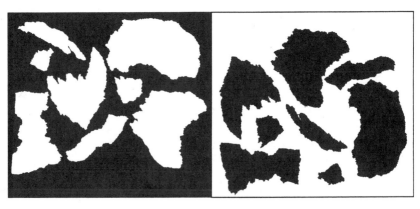

FIGURE 4–6.   Splitting, All-or-None

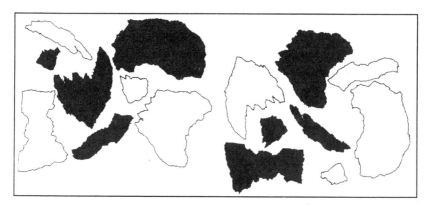

FIGURE 4-7. Defense Disruption: Sense of Chaos, Vulnerability

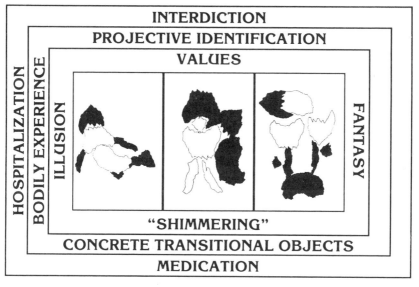

FIGURE 4-8. Insufficient Infrastructure: Supplemented by External, Intermediate, and Internal Holding

for increased symbolic expression, and a modicum of playfulness that promises a release from the realm of the shameful. Again, the patient is helped to move forward onto dangerous ground where old terrors break through alongside glimpses of new patterns of possible organization.

What is now different relates to the holding that the patient receives from the outside world and is able to

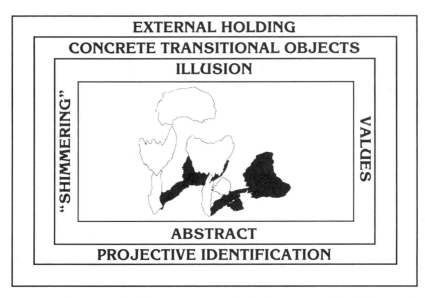

FIGURE 4-9.   Early Terror Contained: Shift to Internal Holding with
Illusion

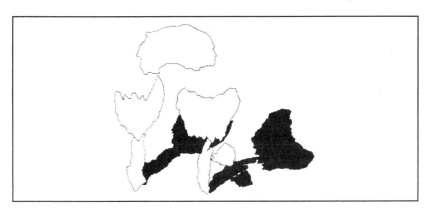

FIGURE 4-10.   Tulips with Shadows: More Flexible Inclusive Organization, Toleration of Ambiguity

provide for himself. In Figure 4-8, we distinguish three
kinds of holding, according to the degree to which the
holding comes from outside or inside the patient and according to how abstract or concrete, and how symbolic or
literal it is.

External holding efforts may include a variety of inter-dictions of particular kinds of behavior. Sometimes legal interdictions, categorical as they are, are very helpful to borderline patients. Patients can be relieved and reassured by what they see as the overwhelming power of the law. Hospitalization represents an at least relative interdiction of certain kinds of behavior, especially self-destructive acts. In Chapter 10, we will present an example in which a therapist simply declared that his back was bad and he could not physically restrain the patient. This is a different style of interdiction in which the therapist's limitations and his capacity to declare his vulnerability are highlighted. Alco-holics Anonymous provides many patients with much needed clarity and conviction through its forthright inter-diction of drinking.

Medication comes from outside and can be simply swallowed. It provides holding that is psychologically ex-ternal and relatively concrete. Medication can be very useful in reducing the affective load that the patient is struggling to contain. In certain situations, it is essential in helping the patient restore a sense of integrity and self. Facilities such as hospitals, halfway houses, and day treatment centers pro-vide a guarantee of the presence of others, reliable schedules of activities, food, transport, and interventions in daily conflicts. All this is external holding.

An intermediate level of holding, which depends on concrete interactions but is not quite so external and not quite so literal, is represented by processes involving transi-tional objects and transitional bodily experiences, not only painful ones but also regular and regulative ones, such as exercise. ''I keep moving just so that I know I exist.'' Linkages through projective identification are an important form of intermediate zone holding. In projective identifica-tion an other is used as a form of self-equivalent for the deposit and containment of unwanted aspects of the self. Processes of projective identification are extremely impor-tant in the treatment of borderline patients and intimately linked both to splitting operations and to the need for concrete transitional experience. Supportive groups, such as Alcoholics Anonymous, combine features of both external interdiction and intermediate level holding.

The most internal, abstract, and metaphorical holding involves illusions, fantasies, and the movement toward art, culture, religion, and values. A fantasy can soothe a patient at a moment of strategic exposure, or animate him at a moment when some new initiative is required. It is interesting that the soothing aspect of transitional experience is emphasized so regularly at the expense of the animating function. Fantasy is part of the creation of the future through reworking of the past. Of course, the inability to sustain fantasy without becoming too threatened by the impulse is a major handicap for the borderline patient. We are probably all always shifting back and forth through these different layers of holding all the time. The borderline patient who is struggling to manage an early danger situation as it is evoked by an effort to move toward more flexible organization usually needs help from all three layers, with an impetus from the more external toward the more internal, the more concrete to the more abstract, the more literal to the more metaphorical.

Holding represents a supplementation of the existing psychic infrastructure that both helps the patient maintain cohesion and learn new methods to maintain cohesion in the face of high stress. It assists in the constitution of a process for processing need within the boundaries of the self. It opens up internal opportunities beyond the polarities of total shamed disavowal of need and total impulsive enactment of need. With the help of holding interventions at all three different layers, the most primitive terrors may be quieted a bit, so that the patient is able to form a relation with the disavowed affects and features of himself that shadow him, leading eventually to the elaboration of a more complex structure with more flexibility. The three different layers of holding shown in Figure 4–8 represent a mixture of doing for (external holding), doing with (intermediate layer holding), and doing within (internal holding). This sequence echoes, with a modification, one proposed by Furman (1991) for toddler development in which the parents move from doing with, to doing for, to standing by and admiring while the child does for himself.

It is, of course, specially important in working with borderline patients to provide validation for what they can do for themselves within themselves. This can be one of the areas where the most sensitive judgment is required, for support that is too active at the wrong moment may be experienced as a destruction of an inner effort, while reticence in supporting may be experienced as a devastating abandonment. A therapist's spontaneous pleasure in what a patient can work out for and about himself—the unexpected thrust of the patient's feeling and understanding—may be one of his most important contributions.

The holding helps the borderline patient manage both the threat of a very primitive organization, such as the one suggested by the shark image, and a beginning accommodation of disavowed aspects of the self as suggested by the shadow image. In Figure 4–9, as a result of the support from the holding structures described by the surrounding layers, the borderline patient has been able to organize in such a way that the tulips have acquired shadows and a toothed fragment of a moderate size is still seen in the background, only now looking a bit more like a cloud than like an all-devouring mouth.

Perhaps the devouring mouth does metamorphose to become the cloud of doubt, which may change currently available forms into something else, often something richer and more intriguing, rather than simply annihilating them. This remnant also reminds us visually that the more primitive psychic modes are not vanquished or extruded. It is a matter of coming to be able to move back and forth from more primitive to less primitive layers, rather than being trapped in one mode. When we speak of "organization," we are not talking simply of making order, but of producing structures that, like organs in the body, are capable of reliably performing highly complicated functions because of the integrated and articulated relations among their parts.

In Chapter 5 we will take a much more detailed look at the concept of holding and some aspects of its practice. Examples of the need for holding in borderline patients can be easily found around experiences with vacations. If a therapist takes a vacation, the more individuated patient can grieve the loss, bound it, and even enjoy many aspects of the time without the therapist, finding reassurance and some deepening of understanding in his own capacity to accompany himself. The reunion does not threaten the patient with merger dangers that are so intense as to require extreme negativistic responses. These patients are capable not only of letting the therapist go but also of allowing the therapist to come back, because they do not lose themselves in these processes.

With the much less individuated patient, the self is lost. The relationship with the therapist constitutes the underpinnings of the holding structure for the patient. As this relationship becomes shaky with the approach of a vacation or as a result of hostile attitudes toward the therapist, often defensively related to forbidden dependent strivings, the patient is unable to utilize more internal, abstract, and symbolic aspects of the holding environment for generating stabilizing transitional phenomena. Ordinary values, cultural interests, and work and hobbies lack their usual supportive functions, and more tangible objects are employed. If these are not effective, the patient may activate self-punitive patterns reminiscent of earlier experiences with sadistic objects. Self-inflicted injury, ranging from damage to relationships to literal and severe damage to the body, may result.

In the fifth and final diagram of this series, Figure 4–10, the tulip configuration, once established, has acquired a certain dependability without the need for quite so much holding effort. It has been accepted as a functioning part of the psychological structure.

With this extended discussion in mind let us return to the clinical vignette concerning the patient who, in her eighth year of treatment, finished a vocational training program just around the time of her mother's long-awaited and dreaded remarriage.

The challenge of finishing school led to a rather dramatic regression, with a return of drinking—in identification with her father—overinvolvement in a love relationship that the patient herself knew to be doomed from the outset, and avoidance of the daunting task of job seeking. The patient's mood became more depressed. She voiced her despair openly, making subtly disguised threats of suicide.

This situation echoed the one during her second year of treatment in which, following an effort to defend her right to autonomous existence in an interaction with her mother, she had been run over by a car as she was rushing to meet a lover. During hospitalization in the first year of this treatment, she had drawn a picture expressing her wish for an entire hospital devoted only to her. This was a poignant, direct, and intense symbolic rendition of her desperate need to feel like the center of the universe—the developmentally essential illusion that had been so elusive in her experience. She could not be weaned from what she had never had. The ability to represent the urge already expressed a partial ability to let it go.

After eight years, some things were different in this patient. First of all, after some hesitation, she was able to discuss her new love relationship with her psychotherapist, her dance therapist, and her art therapist. She did not have to keep it secret to stay organized. She was able to tolerate confirmation from all three that her fears about the relationship seemed very well founded and clearly related to a pattern she had experienced in the past.

Her new lover was preoccupied with religious issues. While going to church with her, the patient was able to define differences in her own religious views. She used her new lover as a foil, setting her own newly found capacity to tolerate ambiguity and a view of religion not founded in absolute salvation and condemnation, and absolute right and absolute wrong, against her lover's more stark constructions. She also began to make use of a church that was particularly receptive to gay persons and markedly more flexible in its interpretation of scripture. She considered using a pastor associated with that church as a resource in her search for a job. She discussed religious issues at great length with her therapist as well as with her dance therapist, taking significant pleasure in her differentiation from what she characterized with wry disdain as her former "black and white borderline views."

She began to consider the life of Jesus quite seriously from a variety of perspectives, entertaining the notion that he may have been gay and that he may also have felt great resentment toward his mother for getting him into all this. The projective identification was the indication of a new degree of mental fellowship obtaining between different aspects of herself. She could feel for herself in Jesus. A shift to more abstract transitional phenomena showed in her approving reports of the atmosphere of tolerance and acceptance she met in this new church. The need for continued concrete transitional support showed clearly in her appreciation of the actual hugging and embracing that took place in this church. Also, the Easter ritual of the washing of the feet had a special significance for her, not just as the one to be washed, but as the one who washed another. The active and passive modes did not seem so exclusive one of the other as they once had.

Vocational school had represented her first willingness to function as part of a group. Now, in the aftermath of the regressive movement after graduation, she showed a new receptivity to groups in a variety of areas. Her church participation brought her into group settings, both at services and socially. She showed a new capacity to grant that alcoholism was a problem for her as well as for her father. She was even able to explore AA and an alcohol education program and to accept a vocational rehabilitation group as a support for seeking a job, even though she had previously rejected it.

A new degree of stability in the face of the losing–fusing danger made the group experiences possible. She did not need to see herself as quite so isolated and different to protect against a loss of her sense of self. As a result she did not have to bring so many losses on herself. The new stability in the face of the losing-fusing danger was supported by her capacity to represent her fears and hopes symbolically in therapy. She did not have to keep quite so much of herself secret from herself.

She was able to formulate her fear that, if she got a job, no one would ever help her. She had hoped that her mother's new husband would make possible a greater degree of financial support for her, fantasizing that her mother had forbidden him to do so because she did not wish to be a burden to him. Here the extremely difficult theme of mother as competitor for needed resources subtly presented itself, but it was not pursued either by the patient or by her therapist.

The patient went on a visit to her mother's new house and attended a family function, dressed as she thought fit. She remarked on her new degree of comfort in the family, pointing out with some humor that, while her father was still drinking, she had spent most of the time with the kids, because they were not drinking. She was able to report on bantering conversations that had involved her, her mother, her stepfather, and her father. She could even step back and reflect on the different ways all four of them stood revealed in the light of these joking exchanges.

Even in the eighth year of treatment, a long-cherished step forward that represented a real achievement posed major dangers to this borderline patient who had begun treatment on the very lip of extinction. Her new life situation challenged directly many of the all-or-nothing attitudes she had cherished. Could she be active in taking care of herself and earning a living without being totally abandoned? Could she bear a change in the relationship to her mother without the need to seek a dangerous symbiosis with someone who bore an uncanny resemblance to the most disturbed aspects of herself? Could she tolerate the feelings stirred up by these momentous changes without resort to life-threatening drinking?

Moving once more near the brink, this patient showed new strengths that had been long in developing. With holding support not just from what her therapist, dance therapist, and art therapist said now, but from memories she evoked in her mind of lengthy discussions over many previous years of similar issues, she was able to halt her regression and take steps to use new group experiences to help her with her current difficulties. She listened without rage and with some expression of appreciation as her psychiatrist told her that he thought the drinking really could kill her. Her stock reply, "With my luck, I don't believe anything can kill me," was a bit more muted and rueful than usual.

Greater stability in the face of the losing–fusing danger gave her more access to different kinds of relationships, both in dyads and in groups. She was able to conclude the love relationship that was so clearly pathological and embark on another one that grew out of new social contacts. She worried openly and steadily that here, too, she was in danger of being swallowed up.

Yet, she experienced pleasure, even as she worked hard to find a job in a variety of realistic ways. She could discuss with her therapist her quandary about how openly to express her feelings to her mother. She commented to him that the big difference this time around had been her being able to stay in contact with people and to expand her social horizon, even when she was in great distress. Yet, even so, the issues that had been joined carried great stress for her, which continued as she struggled with her expanded inner horizons.

A clinical course like this one illustrates why the notion of radical, short-term interventions with these patients can seem virtually oxymoronic. The progression–regression dilemma is a pervasive difficulty that endures and shows itself in a host of different forms at different points in treatment.

5

Holding

Running full tilt across the living room, a first-born 2-year-old tripped on the rug. She fell head first to the floor. She looked at her mother and then began to scream. Her mother, a doctor's daughter, had already thought of concussion, skull fracture, and subdural hematoma as possible serious medical consequences of the fall. She picked her daughter up, held her, kissed her forehead, and comforted her. After some little time, both mother and daughter calmed down. The child suffered no physical ill effects.

Several years later this child's sister tripped at the same age on the same rug in roughly the same way. By now mother had gotten used to these things. Thoughts of various medical catastrophes did not come surging into her mind. Upon glancing at her mother, this second child perceived a reassuring smile, accompanied by the sympathetic descriptive comment, "You went boom." The child pulled herself up, smiled, and proceeded on her way.

Winnicott (1959) was fond of emphasizing, with characteristic paradoxical flavor, the "dual unity" of mother and child, in which neither could be thought of in isolation from the other. It was the two together who made each one what she or he was. This kind of emphasis was part of a shift away from a mechanistic and deterministic way of seeing human processes toward one that was more interactionist and ecological, allowing more space for illusion. This shift calls into question nineteenth century notions of "objectivity." The following is representative of this line of Winnicott's thinking: "We are referring to the fact that there is no such thing because when we see an infant at this early stage we know that we will find infant-care with the infant as part of that infant-care" (p. 54).

Relationship is seen as a place that allows for a mutual coming to be, not entirely together and not entirely separate, but *in between*. It is probably because of his grasp of the worlds of "in between"—the never wholly definite or utterly definable—that Winnicott as a theorist is currently experienced as so congenial a companion. His thinking does not aim to convince or dominate in the style of a Freud or a Jung or even a Melanie Klein, but rather to contribute. It does not expose or shame, but, with a welcoming emphasis on play, changes the regard we have for our own work and workings.

There are no patients without a treatment environment, whether the environment is therapeutic or not. Nor should we mince words about the fact that for many patients the treatment environments in which they find themselves are not therapeutic, the fault being for the most part neither solely in the treatment environment nor in themselves, but rather, in keeping with Winnicott's emphasis on "dual unities," in the nature of the interactions that go on between them. Of course, the interactions between patient and treatment environment are strongly conditioned by the inner actions that go on within the patient and within the providers of treatment.

As we have underscored over and over again, borderline patients seek "dual unity" so often under the guise of the unity of a duel, presenting treatment environments with enormous challenges, the experience of whose intensity is hard to describe in words. This negativism is part of the psychic landscape of all-or-nothing attitudes. "If you are all *this*, then I must be all *that*, so that our only contact will be in opposition," seems to express the patient's strategy. Attachment can have an annihilatory flavor. Treatment environments can become agitated, disorganized, and fragmented in the face of a borderline patient who has an active genius for stimulating a process of shared catastrophizing imagination, which blurs the never utterly clear boundary between what in the way of disaster is possible and what is actual and imminent.

In the first head-first rug tumble described above, the mother's intense anxiety stimulated a process of catastrophizing illusion in herself. This compounded the child's difficulties, a common situation both in parenting and in psychotherapeutic treatment. In the mother's mind, the fall became worse than it was. The mother's actual physical holding of the child served to soothe and calm both the child and herself. Or should we say that a response as concrete as actual physical holding was required in order to produce such a soothing and calming effect on both parties? Certainly, with borderline patients, the concrete holding of the hospital is often required to produce even a relative soothing and calming effect. So, often, are rather authoritarian interdictions.

In the second instance the mother's reassuring composure acted from a near distance as a holding response, enabling the child to remain sufficiently stable to carry on. This holding action at a distance was mediated by a shared system of illusions. While we do not mean to ignore the role of constitutional differences between the two children, we introduce this example to highlight a difference in the degree of concreteness of the mother's holding responses and the difference that the mother's own experience and capacity for self-soothing make in her responses. An important corollary of the notion of "dual unity" is that each partner in the "dual unity" is always responding not only to the other but simultaneously to herself or himself.

A resident was listening to a senior colleague describing his course of treatment of a troubled borderline adolescent whose hobby was making bombs. The psychiatrist, who clearly identified with his patient, was appreciative in his descriptions of the patient's bomb making prowess. The resident experienced a sense of danger, to the point where he began to wonder how his more experienced colleague could sustain the treatment. He fantasized that his colleague had had his autonomic nervous system surgically removed and entertained the thought of asking him where he himself could have the procedure performed. A few years later, as he reviewed this interaction in the context of another clinical situation where he was feeling overwhelmed, it occurred to him that his senior colleague had been doing to a younger person just what the colleague's younger patient had been doing to him, namely, inspiring terror in him through a series of threats of explosions. He may even have been conveying to the resident just how hard the adolescent boy had had to work to get any response.

The resident then recalled that, as a teenager, he himself had enjoyed building backyard bombs, but never with quite the flair and proficiency of his colleague's patient. He began to experience a new surge of empathy for his parents, who had worried about him.

This is an example of a clinical interaction between two psychotherapists in which each is serving as a holding resource for the other at a variety of different levels. The older was providing an example to the younger of the capacity, however peculiar, to sustain difficult and anxious work with a difficult patient, at the same time that the younger was providing a different kind of experience with a younger person to the older. Also, the interest of the younger therapist in the line of work to which he had devoted most of his adult life surely had a tonic effect on his older colleague. Mothers and grandmothers, of course, perform similar services for each other. There is no such thing as the dual unity of mother/child or of therapist/patient except within an even wider context that holds these dual unities.

A skeptical psychiatrist said once that he did not think this whole notion of holding made any sense, because "we don't really hold our patients. After all," he said, "we don't hug them or anything like that." His approach to the question was extremely concrete. He understood holding to mean a physical action. What was "real" for him was the *thingish,* literal, external, concrete, as if the condition for being "real" was purification from any contamination by the self or subjectivity. He would have understood what the mother we have described did with her eldest child, but would not have related it to what she did with the next one.[1]

Winnicott, on the other hand, used the word holding, with its immediate evocation of the actual physical act of holding, as the metaphorical emblem for a process beginning in the external and concrete and continuing always in the direction of the more abstract, internal, and symbolical. For him, the issue was not so much the act, as the spirit of the act, which in time contributes to the spirit of the action of the internal symbolic milieu, that is, the inner world of soothing and animating illusion.

---

1. Arnold H. Modell (1976) has provided excellent discussions of the holding function. His discussions of what he calls "separation guilt" also cast important light on the nature of holding functions.

His concept has an enormous integrative thrust just because it is rooted and grounded in concrete caretaking actions that, when examined, are not so simply concrete as they may appear. Instead, they are the bearers of the spirit of an entire approach to life. We might make the analogy that concrete caretaking actions are an ink or kind of paint with which a picture is drawn or painted. They suggest a symbolic horizon beyond themselves because they are informed by values. They provide a road that can be traveled along the way to the internal use of these values and are enormously important for the organizing and reorganizing opportunities they present. They speak volumes about what is later to be symbolized and internalized, lived out in the child's approach to himself and the possibilities of experience. Their point, in addition to their concrete impact, is *that* they point. They assist in the mapping of potential space, what might with equal validity be termed space for potentials.

When we speak of holding and holding environments, it is in the broader, more abstract and symbolic sense that we intend the terms. However, what is broader, more abstract, and more symbolic, if it is to have meaning, still has to retain contact with the local, the concrete, and the literal. It has to retain contact with what is experienced now and how it is experienced. It has to be embodied. Again, it is a matter of being able to move back and forth, to integrate, to use the appropriate mode at the appropriate time. An all-or-none emphasis on the broad, the abstract, and the symbolic ends up being both empty and barren. What we use holding to describe are processes that span the concrete and the abstract, the external and the internal, and provide means for learning how to move back and forth between these poles, using each to enrich the other.

By holding we mean an action, literal or symbolic, that has the effect of supplementing the existing psychic infrastructure so as to render what might be an overwhelming situation less overwhelming, thus providing the patient a degree of increased security that allows for continued developmental effort and experimenting with new ways of experiencing that may have not only more adaptive promise but more promise in terms of self-realization. We introduce the notion of self-realization because (in contrast to Darwin) we do not believe that existence exists only for the sake of the struggle for existence. Our dissent from Darwin's ideology deserves at least a word of amplification. Psychotherapy, that quintessentially nonstatistical activity, is concerned with particular living individuals and their perils and aspirations. Such individuals are concerned with where they have come from and what they must struggle with as part of their concern with where they may be able to go and what they may be able to become. There is a deep human urge to know oneself and show oneself not just to others but also to oneself. The self must be constructed to be realized and must be realized in order to be constructed. Of course, none of this can take place without a more than minimal adaptive capacity, but, for the experiencing self, adaptation is in the service of the search for meaning, one of life's great pleasures as well as one of life's great pains.

Holding also models for patients methods of approach that may be partially imitated, used negativistically as supports in differentiation, used to initiate communication or to raise new questions. Every holding action is at once to some degree concrete and literal and to some degree abstract and symbolic, in that while it is just what it is, it also conveys a great deal about the motivations and interpersonal techniques that make it possible. In much the same way, each piece of a jigsaw puzzle occupies only its own position, but suggests a great deal about other pieces by the shape of its edges and whatever symbolic pictorial information it shows.

Holding provides support for inner psychic balance so that functioning may be maintained in the face of stress without resort to more primitive methods. Often it is an internal symbolic action undertaken by the self on behalf of the self-as-object (see Bollas, 1982). Holding is a broad concept that is useful because of its breadth. An analogy may be made to the concept of nutrition in medicine. Good nutrition helps most treatments work better. Neglect of nutrition can compromise antibiotic therapy, surgical interventions, chemotherapy for malignancy, and so forth. At one level, this is well known, yet in practice, it is a constant struggle to keep this knowledge integrated and applied. Neglect of basic nutrition crops up over and over again as a complicating clinical factor. An additional point of analogy with holding is that good nutrition consists of an appropriate supply of a wide variety of ingredients. Often it is unnecessary to identify the nutrients that are lacking because many are provided together in one package, and mild surpluses of most are no threat, but, on other occasions, it is vital to identify specific deficits in order to find a remedy.

PROJECTIVE IDENTIFICATION AND HOLDING

Ogden (1982) has offered the following useful definition of *projective identification*:

> Projective identification is a concept that addresses the way in which feeling-states corresponding to the unconscious fantasies of one person (the projector) are engendered in and processed by another person (the recipient), that is, the way in which one person makes use of another person to experience and contain an aspect of himself. The projector has the primarily unconscious fantasy of getting rid of an unwanted or endangered part of himself (including internal objects) and of depositing that part in another person in a powerfully controlling way. The projected part of the self is felt to be partially lost and to be inhabiting the other person. In association with this unconscious projective fantasy there is an interpersonal interaction by means of which the recipient is pressured to think, feel, and behave in a manner congruent with the ejected feelings and the self- and object-representations

embodied in the projective fantasies. In other words, the recipient is pressured to engage in an identification with a specific, disowned aspect of the projection. [pp. 1–2]

The virtues of this definition are many. First, the link to holding is very clear. The recipient of the projection is asked to function as a sort of safe deposit box for what does not yet have a secure place in the projector's self. Ultimately, his job is to hold on to the disavowed in such a way as to contribute to its possible return to the sender. The extent to which the recipient can perform this function depends on how safe, or at least "safely unsafe," he is able to feel with what the pressures from the projector evoke in him. What makes us so uncomfortable in the face of the patient's pressures on us is not what is in the patient but what is in ourselves that corresponds to what comes from the patient. This correspondence is an active, if mostly unconscious process. It has a back-and-forth quality, almost as if letters were travelling back and forth, but written in a language that neither party yet knows quite how to read.

In treating borderline patients and others with severe character disorders, the most dangerous character disorder is our own. In fact, a definition of working with borderline patients that stated that the central task for the therapist was getting to know aspects of himself that he did not wish to know would make good sense, provided that it emphasized that the therapist might be discomfited to find himself not only worse than he had thought himself to be but also better. Borderline patients can teach us a great deal about the silent and automatic, hitherto insufficiently conflicted workings of our own egos. Shame is a major feature for therapists as well as for borderline patients.

A therapist is most unlikely to find himself unchanged by the experience. In the treatment of the borderline patient it is therefore not only the self of the patient that is at issue or at risk, but also the selves of treating personnel. Borderline patients are extremely astute at inducing in their therapists complex "self-transferences," that is, internal transference states in which the therapists' responses are constrained by their unconscious insistence in seeing themselves in a way that does not fit the true situation. This skill on the patient's part offers to the therapist a benefit as well as posing a danger, as it can point to corresponding self-transference states in the patient that are fundamental to the patient's predicament.[2]

Projective identification is a bridging concept that does not require that we split asunder the interpersonal and the intrapsychic. Sullivan (1956) was particularly clear in making the point that we know about other people only through interpersonal processes. The rest is inference and elaboration. What we know about ourselves has a somewhat different status since we have a privileged relationship to our own experiencing selves. We use what we know of ourselves to give life and color to conjectures we make about the inner experience of others based on what is stimulated in us through the interpersonal process of interacting with them.

The projective identification concept is particularly useful in coming to grips with the effects of borderline patients on the milieu that surrounds them and in suggesting ways in which a milieu can be useful to borderline patients. In a milieu, what people around the patient feel tells a lot about what the patient may not yet be able to feel. This is as true and as important in dealing with an outpatient as in dealing with an inpatient. In both cases, the therapist's job is to help the patient profit from his interactions with the surrounding milieu and the perturbations he engenders in it and those it engenders in him to grow psychologically.

From this perspective, the principal difference between outpatient and inpatient treatment is that, when the patient is outside the hospital, the therapist's access to the milieu is likely to come mostly or exclusively through the patient's

2. For a discussion of the notion of self-transference, see Schulz (1989).

presentation of it, whereas when the patient is in the hospital the therapist can have more of his own interactions with the various figures in the milieu. This difference may be of less decisive importance than it seems at first sight, because the therapist working with an outpatient can use his vision of the reports he gets from the patient about other figures as an excellent guide to aspects of the patient that are disavowed. He can also sometimes very usefully take the parts of figures in the milieu in order to help the patient become more perplexed about aspects of himself. At first this involves taking the patient's word about these various figures, much as a therapist accepts what is projected onto him for the sake of the feeling that the projection makes accessible, both interpersonally and intrapsychically. This acceptance provides a framework for working gradually to understand what personal stake the patient has in this particular way of seeing. The projection is a contribution that the patient makes from within himself. What we put out reflects what we have taken in. As the process of living with the projections and observing what such a way of living engenders continues, things can become more complicated for the patient in ways that eventually lead to the reclaiming of important projected aspects of the self.

In discussing the long-term inpatient treatment of severely disturbed borderline patients, we distinguish a series of stages or phases in the development of the relationship between the patient and the holding environment.[3] This way of looking at the hospital courses of patients who remained in the hospital for one or more years is an effort to

---

3. The following sections are based on a paper by Christy Bergland, ATR, Maria Klement, M.D., Roger Lewin, M.D., Miles Quaytman, M.D. and Clarence Schulz, M.D., "Therapeutic Processes In The Hospital Environment," first presented at Scientific Day at Sheppard Pratt in 1984. This paper grew out of the work of a discussion group that also included Charles Peters, M.D. and James Glass, PH.D. In the extended case example presented, Dr. Quaytman was the treating psychiatrist and Ms. Bergland, the treating art therapist.

help support treatment by anticipating certain classes of conflict and confusion as regular features in the treatment of these patients. Anticipation is itself an important holding strategy because it makes preparation possible.

Preparation and reparation are intimately related. If reparation can be thought of as a variety of preparation after the fact, preparation can be seen as a kind of reparation before the fact. We have found that when treating personnel anticipate certain kinds of difficulties they are much less likely to take them personally. They can do a better job of taking care of themselves so that they are more available to take care of the patients. This discussion bears considerable relevance for the long-term treatment of borderline patients and others with serious character disorders both in and out of the hospital. In our experience, the same kinds of conflicts and the same kinds of problems in response to them have appeared whether the patient is in or out of the hospital.

A general feature of our approach is that we tend to emphasize the positive developmental potential of projective and introjective processes, even if these are operating quite primitively. We highlight the ways in which they serve patients' curiosity and their needs for contact and communication, for interactive assistance in consolidating structuralizing boundaries, and for finding out in a vital and emotionally engaged way how others have come more successfully to grips with the problems that so bedevil them. Modification of all-or-nothing features, improved toleration of limits, and increased capacity for self-soothing and self-animation all can come about if these processes are enlisted in the service of personality growth. Such personality development can be a life-saving form of biological change.

STAGES IN THE DEVELOPMENT OF THE HOLDING ENVIRONMENT

At the first stage (see Figure 5–1A), patient and staff are strangers to each other. Perhaps it is even a misnomer to describe them as if their roles were already so articulated. It

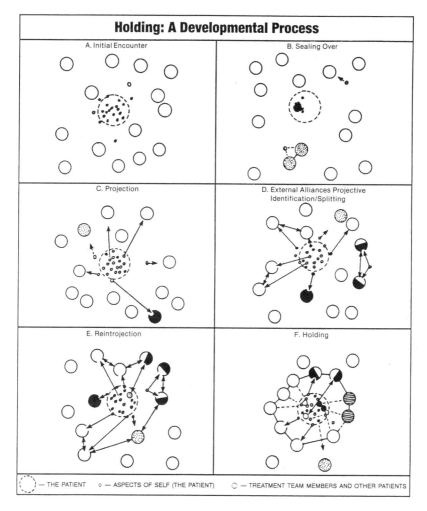

FIGURE 5-1. Holding: A Developmental Process. Diagrams designed by Christy Bergland. Reprinted from Quaytman (1987) by permission of the publisher.

might be more appropriate to say that, at the time of the *initial encounter*, a protopatient is found in the vicinity of a protostaff. The patient has incomplete ego boundaries, is fragmented, and has an amorphous undifferentiated inner self with incomplete and inconsistent self and object representations. The fusing–losing dangers are largely unmastered. Hence, the defensive structure must be rigid.

It is hard to overstate the initial bafflement and anxiety on both sides. While the patient confronts an awesomely complicated new environment, most commonly not because he wishes to, but because, as he usually sees it, circumstances beyond his control have left him no viable option, the staff is virtually as awed by the complexity and seeming incoherence of the patient's symptomatology.

A second phase of treatment (Figure 5–1B) commonly involves a deceptive *sealing over* of the patient's symptomatology. As one watches how the patient goes about his daily business on the ward, it can be very difficult to understand what the patient is doing in the hospital, so assured, confident, and competent is the appearance. At this stage, some borderline patients may actually be mistaken for staff members. The patient says he feels better. Indeed, he looks better. The routines of hospital life, the set schedules for sleeping and eating, the round-the-clock availability of responsible others, the rather clear behavioral expectations, all help the patient to seem more integrated and better functioning. A certain aloofness and paucity of real emotional content are often the only clues to how thin the veneer is. What is essential to grasp is the dependence of the apparent improvement on conditions external to the patient. Holding is of a very concrete and external nature at this point.

Looking better without being better, in other words without any internal change, can actually be a life-threatening problem for certain patients. In our experience, the so-called "high functioning borderline" can prove to be a patient at specially great risk because it is so difficult for treating persons to avoid entering into some collusion with the patient's defenses and actually becoming convinced that the patient is better. Many treatments end prematurely during this sealing over phase. A better measure of the depth of the patient's difficulty might be the difference between the apparently "high-functioning" part and the more reclusive "low-functioning" part. The inability to bridge the two testifies to the lack of integrative resources and the deficits in transitional process.

A merely cross-sectional view of these patients does not provide an adequate basis for treatment planning. The indication that the treatment ought not to end here so often comes from history, which proves to be a form of prophecy. We have seen patients of this kind who have had as many as fifteen or twenty rather stereotyped short-term hospital courses before entering treatment that aims at more fundamental change. Of course, the costs of this revolving door situation, not only in monetary terms, but also in terms of the patient's despair over communicating the serious nature of his trouble, are enormous. A similar revolving door syndrome may occur in outpatient treatments. Often, at the first sign of negative attitudes or the first separation stress, treatments are broken off, only to be started up again to pursue an identical futile course a few months or years later.

During a third phase (Figure 5–1C), mostly utilizing various forms of *projection*, the patient begins to establish tentative, partial contact with other people in the immediate environment, staff and patients both. Using a venerable psychoanalytic metaphor, we can say that the patient sends out *pseudopodia*. It is often striking how much can be learned about a patient simply by watching where his affinities lead him in seeking relationships in the milieu. Early attachments in the milieu can foreshadow material that will emerge with clarity only many months later in treatment. An affinity for a certain patient very often expresses an underlying similarity that determines the liking. Or an antipathy may reflect a deeper recognition.

Because of the poorly differentiated self and object representations, which do not allow the patient to use relatedness in a healthy way, primitive defensive operations begin to break down the preexisting inadequately integrated internal structure. The patient is specially vulnerable to fusing and losing dangers. Internal conflicts that cannot yet be tolerated as such are projected into the surrounding world. Incipient splitting operations are a feature of this stage, as some staff are regularly seen as supportive and sympathetic, while others are seen as frustrating and even malevolent. What the patient sees may bear only the most tenuous relationship to the actualities of the individual characters or intents of the others involved. Even so, there is a certain relative truth to how borderline patients see those around them.

The challenge for the treating personnel during this phase is to receive what is projected onto or into them, to accept it as an initial gambit in a deepening relationship, rather than righteously refusing it as wholly alien. It should be admitted with an interest in finding out more about it, not only in terms of its present function, but also of its meanings from the past and promise for the future. If it is refused, the patient, given his propensity for part object relationships, will experience the refusal of the part as a global rejection of all of him. Such righteous rejections impoverish not only the patient's developmental efforts but the staff's, and lead to treatment stalemate, with both staff and patient frozen into painful defensive positions. Neither side has much awareness of its own contribution to the emergence of this unfortunate state of affairs for the treatment.

At the next stage, characterized by the formation of *external alliances* and the full-scale influence of *projective identification* and *splitting* in the milieu (Figure 5–1D), the patient's engagement with treatment becomes much more compelling. The patient has consolidated relationships with many different staff members. Fragments of the patient evoke part object representations within the staff members involved with the patient. It is around these part object representations that external alliances coalesce, organizing the milieu into clusters of people who share similar views about certain aspects of the patient and engage in characteristic dialogue with the patient and with each other on the basis of such views. Of course, these different clusters may be very much at odds with each other.

At this stage, the patient's pathology is at work and at play within the treatment setting. It is easy to see how this stage can be very intense and conflicted. The patient has gotten under the skin of many different treating persons, and, as a result, these people may find that they begin to get on each other's nerves. The dissension among staff may go beyond the professional level to serious personal disputes. A borderline patient engaged in this stage may seem to dominate the whole workings of a milieu, with concerns about his treatment remaining on the minds of staff members throughout the work day and beyond. Staff meetings may come to be taken up with details of the treatment of just one patient to the exclusion of much important material having to do with other patients. An analogous situation can occur in outpatient treatment when one aspect of a borderline patient's life dominates sessions so entirely that it is impossible to develop a broader picture.

Conflicts around the patient may often threaten to divide a well-functioning milieu intensely along regressively personalized lines. This is the stage at which one borderline patient can seem one too many, too much of a burden for everyone. It is also the stage where, after much strife and striving, a certain therapeutic despair may be experienced. Particularly when it can be openly acknowledged and discussed, rather than simply acted on, this often heralds the beginning of the movement into the next phase, with both staff and patient starting to recognize realistic limitations in their respective points of view and realistic virtues in opposing ones. The acknowledgement of the difficulty and even the despair (see Farber 1966) is essential, because it presents the patient with a view of the vulnerability of the treating personnel. This can be an enormous aid to the patient in beginning to integrate his own vulnerability.

A crucial notion in managing this stage is that splitting and projective identification are not best seen as negative influences to be eliminated by strenuous efforts to present an artificially unified front to the patient. (A therapist, discussing a borderline patient's need to be over definite, slipped when he meant to say "party line." What came out instead was "potty line," placing the issues in relationship to

a developmental period when crucial issues in self-definition, separating self and object representations, dealing
with shame conflicts, and managing the losing–fusing dilemma are at center stage.) Rather, if the projective identifications are seen as attempts by the patient to deal with the
otherwise overwhelmingly conflicted complexities of his
encounter with his internal affective chaos, they can be
moderated and placed in a wider perspective through cultivation of open and impassioned, but tolerant discussion of
incompatible points of view. In this way, they can provide a
royal, if rocky, road to a dynamic understanding of the
patient.

An observation we have made is that in this fourth
stage, because of the pervasive influence of projective identification, it is common to see conflicts arising in the treatment system that are not seen as related to the patient's
pathology or predicament but will later come into focus as
introducing a neglected problem in treating the patient. The
virtue of being aware that such split-off conflicts can exist is
twofold. It can provide access to hidden or incompletely
appreciated clinical material. Also, it provides a modulating
tool for staff, as the clinical habit is fostered of trying to
understand whether observed conflicts in the treatment
system actually have their basis in patients' pathology and
what the pathology evokes in staff. During this entire period, cultivation of lines of communication among staff
members, particularly those with opposing views, is a task
that calls for heightened attention. In outpatient treatments,
it is essential that the therapist be able to hear the voice of his
own doubts.

In the fifth stage, *reintrojection* (Figure 5–1E), the
patient begins to be able to take back into himself, in
modified form, some of what he has put into play around
him. This can be a very difficult time for the patients, who
often report that their views of themselves and of the world
around them are changing in ways that are extremely baffling. Also, staff alliances tend to change at this phase. A

common experience is that staff members feel they have learned something in the course of the treatment and have become aware of perspectives they had not seen before (Lewin, 1985). Staff members who have been through this phase together have developed a shared understanding and appreciation of differences as well as agreement that strengthens their capacity to work together, not just with this patient but with those that are to come. The recognition by staff members that they have learned something may be a clue to the productivity of the treatment for the patient as well.

The patient can begin to recognize that conflicts he has staunchly maintained were external to himself actually have myriad relations to the chaos within. While there is often at least the hint of a tone of hopefulness at this stage, it is also a time when the old adaptations, however unsatisfactory, need to be grieved. Learning to grieve is, in fact, a major task that can begin to be undertaken at this stage. Patients will express a wistfulness for what they have lost, the symptoms they have given up, the defensive certainties they have renounced. At the same time, they feel great sorrow that they were not able to navigate these developmental passages earlier on in their lives, without becoming so sick. As they strive to integrate what they have taken back in, patients may show significant neediness and dependency that recall early troubled points in treatment. There may be a shared sense of the fragility of what has been accomplished.

Reliable Holding, as we conceive it (Figure 5–1F), occurs when the patient and the surrounding treatment milieu have negotiated a sufficient degree of mutual trust, a sufficient repertoire of meaningful communicative behaviors, to enter into a partnership that can endure in the face of considerable stress and agitation. The patient is not in any way free of conflict, but rather can begin to notice and manage the conflict as something that occurs within himself. Far from being free of conflict, he is enriched by this new awareness.

After many months of treatment—or even years in some

cases—the struggles that have been played out, observed, and, to some degree, modified in the milieu begin to pay off in greater internal containment. The patient begins to find validity and use in connecting conflicts experienced in the hospital milieu with similar conflicts experienced during developmental years. Memories may well come back to the patient's awareness.

At this point, staff communication about the patient tends to flow more freely, with more mutual recognition of differentiated contributions to the patient's care from different quarters. There is more shared sense of who the patient is and what the problems and appropriate emphases in the treatment are. Argument is often replaced by mutual recognition of dilemmas that pervade the patient's functioning. Because the patient's own activity is now something for which he begins to take more responsibility, the work of integrating the treatment is less arduous. Much of what previously had to be transacted among staff members while conflicts were externalized is now managed more efficiently, internally, with the patient being aware of his role, his doubts and ambivalences, and his choices. What has been built by this point in treatment is reliable mutuality in relating, sufficient so that difficulties that arise can be handled as difficulties *within* the treatment relationships at whose center the patient finds himself, rather than appearing as insurmountable difficulties *with* the treatment relationship itself.

It must be understood that these stages in development of the holding environment are intended as suggestive conceptualizations, navigational aides in the arduous task of clinical decision making with severely ill borderline patients. They do not occur once and for all in a straight line. Much back and forth movement is possible. Different conflictual affects and the units of self and object representations associated with them may move through this process at different rates of progression, with some lagging far, far behind others.

The complex metamorphosis of a chaotic, undifferentiated core with rigid defensive operations to a more harmoniously integrated person is a process requiring considerable time—both for the patient in the hospital and for the staff, who will need hours each week to work together to metabolize what comes from the patient. This requirement for time, in both senses, applies equally well to outpatient work, which is a much more lonely effort for the therapist. While a few therapists may be able to manage the complex internal dialogue required among differently stimulated parts of themselves, in our experience work with borderline patients goes much better on an outpatient basis if the therapist is more generous with himself in terms of holding resources.

CASE EXAMPLE

Mrs. D., 36 years old, was transferred to Sheppard Pratt from another hospital. She had had numerous short-term hospitalizations, which, on review, conformed to a basic pattern. After being admitted in an acutely distressed and disorganized state following some self-destructive action, Mrs. D. seemed to improve rapidly. Following resolution of surface symptomatology, she would be discharged. Long-term treatment was recommended when a treating physician made the clinical judgment that this repetitive cycle was futile.

Although they were in college at the time, Mrs. D.'s parents married when her mother unexpectedly became pregnant with her. Finances were always a problem for this very young couple. Mrs. D.'s father struggled to support a family while continuing his education. During Mrs. D.'s early years the family moved often, as work and educational opportunities for her father became available in different places.

When the patient was 5 years old, a pediatrician discovered through testing that she had quite superior intelligence. She herself interpreted this as meaning that other people expected great things of her. Because she was convinced that she would be unable to deliver, such a notion filled her with dread. Although she became an excellent student and participated in a range of extracurricular activities, she derived little internal reward and somehow always felt badly about herself. She shied away from involvement in close personal relationships, as if these too might reveal her deficiencies.

The first time she left home was at age 14, when she was accepted into a National Science Foundation summer program, which proved disastrous for her. Instead of making new relationships, she became withdrawn, retreating to her bed, where she spent much of each day. Nonetheless, upon returning home, she was able to complete high school.

Despite her superior intellect, it took her eight years to complete college. While she did very well in some courses, she did equally poorly in others, presenting in the academic sphere a characteristic picture of bafflingly mixed functioning, as if both success and failure contained unacceptable dangers. At one point when her turmoil was heightened, she decided to take some time off to visit a paternal aunt who happened to be living in Africa. During her stay, this aunt confided to her the fact that it was because Mrs. D.'s mother became pregnant with her that her parents had married. Upon hearing this important piece of history, she became extremely despondent. As she later recalled it, something came over her, impelling her to burn herself with a cigarette.

When Mrs. D. returned to college her struggle continued unabated. She was unable to take hold and organize her life in a way that suited her. While in times of relative calm, she was able to make some progress in school and maintain a social life, she frequently resorted to self-destructive behavior, including suicide attempts. When her parents separated, she relocated to live with her father.

As the patient perceived it, there was little rhyme or reason to the onset of her periods of intense distress. She could identify no clear precipitants. Similarly, it was a puzzle to her why she felt better after short stays in the hospital. While she received considerable treatment, continuity was lacking. Very little, if any, inner gain was carried over from episode to episode. She was repetitively successful in hiding the severe stormy fragmentation of her inner world behind a veneer of shortlived good functioning.

It was during one of these short hospitalizations that the news came to her that her mother had been killed, suddenly and tragically, in an auto accident in which she had been struck head on by a drunk driver. Her sister was injured in the accident. Mrs. D.'s reaction was to decide to pull herself together because she felt that her sister and her brother and her father needed her help in getting through this very troubled time.

Not long after her mother's death, Mrs. D. herself married and started a family of her own. She devoted herself to becoming, in her phrase, a "supermom." While there were serious difficulties in her marriage, she experienced relief from the self-destructive impulses. This respite proved to be only temporary. Once she stopped nursing her youngest child, she found herself becoming restless. The problems in her marriage now loomed even larger. It was in this context that she conceived the project of returning to school to get an advanced degree. To her surprise, her self-destructive impulses returned. She was again caught up in turmoil very like what she had suffered in college. Four short-term hospitalizations during this phase brought the long series to a close.

When the treating psychiatrist first saw her at Sheppard, large parts of her were in bandages. Prior to her last short-term hospitalization, she had had bilateral subscutaneous mastectomies performed to repair damage from previous silicone implants that had not been done properly. In addition, she came with a huge self-inflicted burn. She was subdued and tearful about entering the hospital for long-term treatment.

After one week in the hospital, Mrs. D. seemed in better spirits and stated that she was ready to leave. She did not see the relevance of trying to come to grips with what had transpired just in the last few weeks, let alone in more remote portions of the past. The global nature of her denial and avoidance was startling. She was adamant about wanting to leave and submitted the legally required notice stating that, after seventy-two hours had elapsed, she intended to depart. It took much work on the part of the nursing staff to make it possible for her to withdraw this notice, which she did reluctantly. The transitional function of the three-day notice, providing a negativistic support for the patient's sense of autonomy, is apparent.

The subsequent reemergence of her symptoms was as abrupt as the "improvement" had been. She was found, just a few days after having retracted her notice, huddled in the corner of her room, having once more burned herself. The next day, Mrs. D. appeared much better. All she could say about the events of just a few hours before was that some unspecified kind of a malevolent force had taken over. Whenever this force took over, she did "weird" things. As she saw it, the whole episode was past. It had nothing to do with her in the present. She still held to the view that she was ready to leave the hospital, and it was difficult for her to understand how anyone could see the matter differently.

Similar incidents of burning ensued. The patient now began to attribute her difficulties to the outside world. She was adamant in maintaining to her therapist that, if she were only at home with her children, none of this would be happening. It was because she was in the hospital and separated from them that she was experiencing such turmoil—a malevolent environment caused the malevolent force to make her do "weird" things, like burning herself.

So far, our description of Mrs. D.'s hospital course has taken us through the phases of initial encounter and sealing over, on into the period where projective mechanisms are used to achieve more, if still quite tentative engagement, with important figures beginning to acquire definition in the milieu. As a series of burning incidents occurred, tension around the patient increased in the hall. Her actions eventually succeeded in raising the staff's anxiety level so high that they felt it necessary to place her in locked-door seclusion. As with so many other patients of this type, seclusion had, with Mrs. D., an effect opposite to the one intended. She felt more frightened, farther out of contact and out of control. The locked-door seclusion accentuated the "losing" danger.

In an atmosphere of concern and even consternation, the decision was reached to prescribe daily cold wet sheet packs.[4] The clinical thinking was that these would provide Mrs. D. with a reliable period each day of a soothing and stimulating bodily experience in a safe context where, unlike in seclusion, human contact was continually available. Observation verified that the treatment—two hours each day spent swaddled in wet sheets—helped reduce Mrs. D.'s anxiety and agitation, diminishing her tendency to hurt herself.

It was the staff, initially, who had to decide when in the day to give the packs. The patient, despite her intellectual gifts, could not identify either internal or external cues leading into her dangerous agitated states. Connections that seemed clear on close observation to staff escaped her notice. For example, Mrs. D. would receive a telephone call from her husband. After speaking with him, she would not look obviously upset, but, after a short delay, would begin to look frightened and withdrawn. Knowing where this sort of sequence was likely to lead, the staff would initiate the cold wet sheet pack before she could act self-

---

4. A patient described the impact of cold wet sheet packs as follows in a poem: Oh those cold wet sheet packs/take me away/to a far off place/that is really so close/to that body that lays/all wrapped and secure/in that cold wet sheet pack that brings out/the little girl in me—/who hurts so bad and is enraged beyond words. For discussion of cold wet sheet packs, see Kilgallen (1972) and Ross et al. (1988). The poem is quoted from this second article.

destructively. Available as an intervention they could use before a crisis ensued, the packs served a soothing function for the staff as well as for the patient.

In addition to their soothing and sedating effects, both psychologically and somatically mediated, the cold wet sheet packs—these times of respite with another person in attendance and available for discussion—provided a useful support for the patient's emerging capacity for self-observation. Given this degree of security or, to phrase it slightly differently, enforced abstinence from previous self-destructive tension releases, she could begin to attend to what was happening within her. The notes documenting Mrs. D.'s response to packs during this period described over and over again her shifting from what seemed dissociated panic states into reflective discussions with the person in attendance about what she was feeling and fearing.

Such capacity to shift, testifying to ego strengths crucial to the unfolding of a treatment based in large part on symbolic means, represented an encouraging sign. At this point in her treatment, with the support and underpinning she received from a ward staff capable of responding in a helpful way to her extremities of distress, Mrs. D. was able to begin art therapy. A few of her drawings are reproduced (Figures 5–2 through 5–6) to convey visually, in her own idiom, a sense of the dynamics we have been discussing.

The nurturing of these symbolic representational resources was itself an important treatment achievement. Arduous struggle with concrete caretaking responses to behavior whose significance was very puzzling was required to help the patient begin to communicate not only with others but with herself on more economical and less dangerous symbolizing channels. Showing and knowing by drawing, as by talking, helped her spare her body the ravages of doing, that is, burning. This was a step forward in transitional object relations.

Figure 5–2 is the first picture the patient made in art therapy. Its disorganization is evident. Mrs. D. was not able

FIGURE 5-2.

FIGURE 5-3.

FIGURE 5–4.

FIGURE 5–5.

FIGURE 5–6.

to talk about this drawing; she simply made it and left it. As time went on, she developed a name for the malevolent force that made her do "weird" things. She called it the shadow. Figure 5–3, which shows a huge shadow, perfectly in step, pursuing an obviously frightened Mrs. D., was made at a juncture when Mrs. D. was struggling with impulses to run away from treatment and all that it involved. She said that her feelings were all hidden from her, that she had no idea how to come to grips with them. She told the art therapist that she made this picture instead of running away from the hospital.

Figure 5–4 shows Mrs. D. and the shadow positioned differently with respect to each other. In commenting about this drawing, she talked about having felt as a child isolated and utterly alone in the face of her feelings. She also talked about her mother's death and the impression it had made on her. She said that she had felt at that time that she had no choice but to maintain total control over her feelings. Vividly, she went back over what she had felt when she had gone to see her sister in the hospital after her mother died. However, she was not able to cry.

Mrs. D. told the art therapist that the wall (done in red) in the fourth picture, Figure 5–5, represented the hospital. This drawing was made as Thanksgiving approached and Mrs. D. was feeling considerable pressure from within herself to go home to be with her children to live up to her image of the ideal mother. The organization and coherence of what lies within the wall as opposed to the graphic disorder of what the patient puts outside makes a forceful visual impression. The patient's hands convey feelings of longing and loss. While we did not come upon this picture until we had completed our own graphic efforts to illustrate our notions of phases in treatment, a kinship of idiom, suggesting the relevance of issues relating to internal organization, projective processes, and need for containment, seems apparent.

In the final picture of this sequence, Figure 5–6, the

shadow is no longer wholly out of scale and alien to the figure of Mrs. D. In fact, one way of looking at this drawing is that the shadow has become two shadows, one of which seems much like the patient, not yet attached to her, but reaching out. Mrs. D. was now able to talk, after a long negativistic phase, about positive transference feelings toward her therapist. She also described sensing herself more in touch with feelings of doubt and fear. She said that, although she felt slightly more able to tolerate angry feelings, she was convinced that there was a much larger monster waiting for her in the background. Although these pictures are reproduced in black and white, the brightening of mood is reflected in the colors of the originals. The background in the first picture is blue; here it is a robust yellow. Bergland and Gonzalez (in press) have recently made an effort to develop a reliable instrument for characterizing the degree of disturbance in patients' art works. Their instrument successfully discriminated the works of six patients with borderline personality disorder who ultimately suicided from a larger cohort of hospitalized borderline patients.

On the hall, a significant new line of development was Mrs. D.'s beginning ability to ask for cold wet sheet packs when she felt she needed them. This change reflected her increased trust in several staff members, as well as more stable self-observational capacity. However, an intense controversy around the use of the packs in treating Mrs. D. surfaced. We want to detail this controversy and its therapeutic management as an example of the dynamics characteristic of the stage in the hospital course of a patient dominated by external alliances, splitting, and projective identification. At this stage, the location of the relevant pathology is perhaps best specified as in the field shared by patient and staff, in the "interperson."

Two parties emerged. The staff divided into opposed groups. One felt that the packs had been very effectively utilized by the patient, which represented a high return on the effort invested. They pointed out that the patient was progressing rather well, developing means to identify and control her own self-destructive impulses. This group favored continuing to use the packs very much as they were being used. The other group felt the packs were too burdensome. They felt other patients on the hall were being deprived of needed attention from nursing staff and Mrs. D. was being encouraged to be too dependent. They worried that the packs were actually more disabling than helpful and insisted Mrs. D. could and should do more for herself.

As is so often the case, this controversy gathered energy and intensity as time passed. Different staff members argued their positions with the fervor of cherished ideological stances. Clinical discussion moved toward the border that demarcates argument about treatment strategy from *argumentum ad hominem.* Staff members found that it was hard to keep from being extremely irritated with their colleagues' obtusity and inability to see what seemed so plain to them.

During this time in individual therapy, the patient was working at delineating two different views she held of her therapist, the one in force depending on her own internal affective situation. When she was able successfully to deny her illness and maintain a surface calm, her therapist seemed harsh and cruel, wanting to impose pain on her by insisting that she see herself as ill and perhaps even enjoying it. During her periods of pain and panic, when she felt out of control, her experience of the therapist was the opposite. She was impressed with his compassion and patience, in short, with his good qualities.

While the patient struggled with this aspect of her splitting operations, the controversy in the staff raged on and found subtle expression beyond the immediate ward milieu. For example, a nursing supervisor introduced for discussion in a ward nursing meeting a paper describing another hospital's approach to borderline patients with self-destructive tendencies. This approach was simple and

direct: if the patient cut or burned, the patient was sum-
marily discharged. When Mrs. D.'s therapist, who was himself an advocate of continuing cold wet sheet packs for her,
happened to find this paper in a prominent position in the
nursing station, he assumed that the staff was addressing this
issue in direct relationship to his patient. A nurse standing
there assured him it had nothing at all to do with his patient;
it was merely, she said, a topic being discussed as part of a
staff development effort. This had an effect on him opposite
from the reassurance consciously intended. He worried that
the urges to get rid of his patient were so split-off that they
were more likely to get acted out, much in the way the
patient's own urges to hurt and get rid of herself had been
split off and then enacted.

In individual therapy the therapist tried to let Mrs. D.
know the nature of the controversy about the cold wet sheet
packs. While at first she had trouble connecting this controversy with herself in any meaningful way, after a time she
did begin to see that it might have something to do with her
own intense conflicts over being dependent. She began to be
aware of the fact that she had quite a split view of her
mother, who had been a successful and respected school
teacher. Mrs. D. described saving a clipping from the school
paper in which her mother was praised for her special
qualities of patience and forbearance. In contrast to this
rather idealized image of her mother, Mrs. D. became aware
of the fact that, in important regards, she herself had experienced her mother as perfectionistic and harshly demanding. In particular, Mrs. D. had found her mother to be nearly
totally intolerant of any expressions of painful or angry
feelings emanating from her child.

Mrs. D.'s developmental quandary revolved around
what to do with her own painful or angry feelings. She
resorted to putting them out of awareness, which had much
to do with the creation of what she represented as the
shadow that made her do weird things. The staff's quandary

revolved around how to deal with Mrs. D.'s behavior when she was driven by painful and angry feelings she had trouble avowing as her own.

The staff split, recapitulating the split in the patient's view of her mother, found one party seeking, probably unrealistically, to meet the patient's needs with a patience and forbearance that went well beyond what might be regarded as "good enough mothering." The other party, again taking up a projected aspect of an object representation from the patient's early experience, sought, also probably unrealistically, to shift most of the burden for managing painful and angry feelings quite swiftly and abruptly back to the patient herself. The extent to which happenings on the ward during Mrs. D.'s treatment were tied to significant events from her past was brought home forcefully when she remembered that her mother's response to her getting angry and upset had often been to put her into a closet. Only when she appeared calmer was she allowed to come back out. This was reproduced in the early use of seclusion with the patient. For years, Mrs. D. had had what she regarded as the "weird" habit of sequestering herself in a telephone booth when she was upset. This, too, began to make sense to her in light of her early closetings.

The controversy within the staff over the use of cold wet sheet packs lost its intensity only as Mrs. D., beginning to move toward integrating her fractured inner self and object representations, was able to join with the staff in working out plans for employing them. As she could see more clearly both the realistic strengths and the realistic limitations of the care available, she could start not only to depend more comfortably, but also to be more dependable herself. The waning of her need for the packs correlated with a much greater sense of reliable connection with a variety of other people. These included the nursing staff and other patients on the hall, as well as staff and patients she encountered in activities off the hall.

Needless to say, there were significant changes in the character of her transference to and communication with her therapist. As increasing personality integration made possible increased differentiation, articulation, and richness of self and object representations, "the shadow," resolved into elements, lost its hold on her. With her reintrojection of projected part representations, which had been modified during the milieu's intense efforts to understand them and withstand their effects, Mrs. D.'s treatment moved toward completion of the development of an assured holding function.

A second series of Mrs. D.'s drawings, Figures 5–7 through 5–12, illustrates the scope of the changes we have been describing. Mrs. D. produced these drawings after the Christmas holidays, which had been very stormy for her. While her therapist was away on vacation, she had experienced a serious regression, during which she again burnt

FIGURE 5–7.

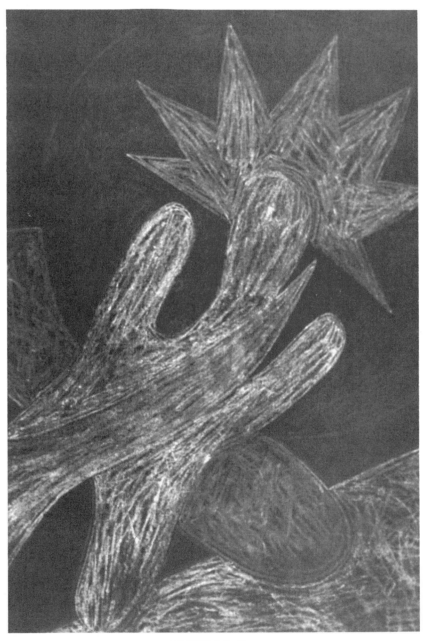

FIGURE 5–8.

FIGURE 5-9.

herself. This cycle, however, was different in that she was able to discuss what she had felt. She reported that she had made one particularly terrifying discovery, which was that she needed people—if you needed people, she said, then you were awesomely vulnerable.

Figure 5-7, shadowless, represents painful feelings as being contained within. The geometrical elements echo what was beyond the restraining wall of the hospital earlier in Figure 5-5. Mrs. D.'s cutting was a way to bring herself out from trance-like numbness. She told the art therapist that this drawing had to do with an incident on the ward where she had, instead of cutting, been able to scream, thus bringing her distress to the attention of others more safely and directly. The scream shown here is in her head. More self-containment and more object relatedness go together.

In the next drawing, Figure 5-8, one shape, yellow in

FIGURE 5–10.

FIGURE 5-11.

the original, is a child, the other, orange in the original, a knife. Mrs. D. associated to a memory of having cut herself when she was three or four. She remembered being wrapped up in a white sheet and rushed to the hospital. In Figure 5-9, Mrs. D. represents herself and her mother. Mrs. D. told the art therapist that she felt shaky because everything was changing around her and in her as well—she could now see her mother as more of a real person with real problems of her own. She expressed anger at her mother for compelling her to try to be all good. In this connection, the tooth-like edge surrounding the figure of the mother catches the eye.

Figure 5-10, drastically different from any of the others, dates from a session in which the patient was enormously upset. She produced this image of a black child screaming, then said she had to go immediately back to the hall because she was having violent thoughts. She saw the hall as a container for her fearful feelings. A day later, in the trance-like state that usually preceded cutting or burning,

FIGURE 5-12.

she went into the bathroom. She had an experience of herself as two people, an adult and a child. The adult allowed the child to cry, providing a release that Mrs. D. had keenly missed as a child.

Figure 5–11 dates from the one-year anniversary of hospitalization. The whole landscape has changed. Mrs. D., far from fleeing, gazes at a reflection that has defined features. Colors are mixed, on land, sea, and in the air. A path connects her to the wizard-like figure she uses to represent her therapist. There is containment without confinement. Fiture 5–12 dates from the eve of the patient's discharge. It is fascinating to notice that, at the very bottom of this drawing, a portion of shadow has attached itself to the figure of the patient.

TEN YEARS LATER

When, through the art therapist who had kept in touch with Mrs. D. after her discharge from Sheppard, we contacted Mrs. D. to make certain that the reproduction of her art work met with her approval, she expressed the desire to come to talk with us. She said she thought that, if we were writing about the kinds of troubles and treatment she had had, we also would want to know about her struggles after she left the hospital. In particular, she felt that it was important for us to hear about her struggles with drinking. She had had, she said, some very bitter feelings toward Sheppard at one point because she felt that she had not gotten sufficient help with the drinking problem she had while at Sheppard.

Her account of treatment at Sheppard focused on the affective dimension: "I felt like I was born here at Sheppard in a lot of ways and that, well, this was the first time I'd ever really gotten in touch with my emotional self." When asked if she could single out anything in particular in her treatment, she replied:

I remember that there was an incident that happened that I felt was very moving, and it feels like that was where it got started. . . . Something had happened and I was struggling to keep, to stay in control, which is kind of the way I usually felt, like I kind of couldn't let any feelings through, but I went off the hall into the bathroom and I just . . . the way I felt was I sort of squatted down on the floor and huddled myself together and it was like I was hugging myself and telling myself it was okay to feel the way I was feeling and it was almost like communicating with somebody, with my child. I felt like a child and I felt like an adult at the same time . . . and I was crying. I was sitting there crying and I was like rocking myself and it was sort of like I was trying to tell myself it was okay to be a kid and, you know, it was okay to cry . . . I just felt like it was okay where I was.

Mrs. D talked about her art work meaning much more to her now than it had when she was in the hospital. She described herself then as simply making pictures in order "to entertain" the art therapist. Only years later did she realize that her drawings were drenched in feeling. When she talked about her drinking, she made it quite clear that she used it to cover up intolerable feelings. She would get drunk after discharge in order to be able to talk when she went to therapy, to the point where her therapist, who had caught on to the importance of her alcoholism, would wonder whether it was she talking or whether it was the booze. While she felt some bitterness that the drinking had not been recognized sufficiently as a problem in the hospital, she could recall an occasion on which a social worker in the hospital had pointed out to her very directly what a difficulty it was. "I was like, I couldn't hear that that was a problem, which was exactly the way I was with the therapist I had after I left Sheppard. She tried for two or three years to suggest that maybe the drinking was a problem."

It took an encounter with the police in which she actually ended up in the police station in leg irons and handcuffs before she was ready to see that her drinking mattered. "The way I felt about booze was that, if it wasn't for booze, I would really be crazy . . . I felt that, if I didn't have the booze, it would be all over. I would really, really be crazy and I don't even know what I thought really crazy would be, but to me the booze was the solution to the feelings that I was having."

The role of negation in introducing a thought was evident in her remark, "I remember thinking 'Thank God I am not an alcoholic because I could never do AA and AA is the only thing that works for alcoholics.' " She felt that what was so forbidding about AA was the religious part:

> I just thought it was a religious organization and I couldn't possibly get into all that stuff. I was reared to live in a very universalist and a very, very rational kind of thing . . . You know, it was just like everything had to be very neat and scientific and I wasn't at all in touch . . . I really felt that it would have been nice if I could believe in God because it could be a comfort, but I felt like it was a very childish, uneducated, unintelligent thing to do.

For her, science meant certainty and religion was threatening because of its fuzziness: "It didn't make sense, you couldn't prove it."

Alcoholics Anonymous proved to be very useful to her, providing a coterie of friends and a sustaining organization for her living and her efforts to come to better terms with her feelings. In her account of her participation in AA, the hands on, contact-oriented approach of her fellow AA members seemed to be especially helpful in ways that echoed helpful interventions by the nursing staff in the hospital. Her neighbor's husband poured her liquor down the drain, because she could not trust herself to do it. People came and asked her to go to meetings. People called to see how she was doing. She went to ninety meetings in sixty days, each day marking on a calendar that she had gone, which offered her tangible proof that she was doing something. She remarked that what she got from her first AA meeting was "hope."

Interestingly enough, during the early very stormy period of sobriety, she kept with her and took sustenance from a remark that had been by made by her therapist at Sheppard:

> When I was here, Dr. Q. used to say that it's okay to have murderous thoughts as long as you don't act on them and, I mean, that was something that he told me. I was kind of at the time shrugging and saying, "Well, what do you mean, murderous thoughts? I don't have murderous thoughts." There were times in early sobriety when I would just get very upset and think it was all too much. Suicide occurred to me. The thought occurred to me, and it was almost as if the thought came in when I was feeling upset and depressed and hopeless. I have had some physical problems that have made me realize I would be better off dead, but the thing is I never really thought seriously about killing myself. It was like the thought would come in as an option. You know, there would be five possible options to this scenario, and suicide would be one of them, but then I would say, "Okay, that is an option, but it's one I reject."

Mrs. D. emphasized that she had had and still had quite a struggle with her feelings. However, she made it clear that she was pleased to be alive and had found great satisfaction in many relationships, expressing pride in her children and also talking with some warmth and forgiveness about her former husband and their very confused and tumultuous time together. She said explicitly that one of her main motivations in coming to talk with us was to see if she could help us in any way with others struggling with similar problems. As she left she reflected on the conundrum that she, on the one hand, wished that she could have been helped with her alcoholism earlier; on the other hand, she wondered if she could have availed herself of the help earlier, when she was so utterly disconnected from her emotional self.

6

More
on Holding

OUTPATIENT APPLICATIONS

Whether to confide or not was a major issue throughout the treatment of a young woman who had had the terribly unfortunate experience of having her previous therapist suicide early in their work together. In the aftermath of the suicide she received virtually no help with her reactions either from the local psychiatric community or from her family, both of whom responded in a denying style. She was left with an accentuation of her feelings of despair and of her own sense that life was not worth living, as well as her fear of her own hostility.

This denying defense was prominent throughout her growing up, particularly where losses were concerned. As she put it, "The important thing was to look good, no matter what the cost." The suicide of her previous therapist was particularly unfortunate because it reinforced her belief that confiding in others was extremely dangerous. Her conflict over confiding in herself presented itself for quite a long time in terms of confiding in others. She was also quite unaware of how angry she had been at her therapist *before* the suicide and how much she internally accused herself of having been responsible for the therapist's suicide, through omission, if not through commission.

One of her major activities in therapy was to discuss her discussions with others of highly charged material that she had not discussed directly in therapy. She would disclose something about which she had terribly conflicted feelings to a member of her family or someone at work. Then she would report on the reactions of the person to whom she had made the disclosure. Often, she was extremely indignant about the reception she had received, and it particularly bothered her that her disclosures received wider distribution than she had consciously intended. She would end up castigating herself for having been foolish enough to disclose anything in the first place. It was as if all the containers had holes in them.

What she was reporting, as her therapist saw it, were interactions with her holding environment. These interactions were important in providing a view of the world of not only her internal object relations but her relations with herself, that is to say, her habitual ways of seeing herself, what might be called her internal "self-relations." By reporting on such interactions, the patient was able to bring material into therapy and to keep it from being more intensely affect laden than she could manage at her current stage of development. She was communicating on long circuits, but, from her therapist's point of view, the important matter was that she was communicating and confiding, if in a displaced manner.

She would, for example, describe some of her recent dating experiences to a friend who was not dating. Then she would report on the friend's reactions, which she perceived as withdrawal, icy condemnation, and envy. Or she would take up some of her views about the dynamics of her family with a sister and then report the way in which the sister had spread her views through the family without her consent, causing her both embarrassment and pleasure, which was harder to acknowledge. The processes she described resembled very much what her therapist was used to working with when projective identifications were influencing the hospital holding environment.

Thinking of the treatment along lines analogous to those sometimes used in play therapy with children, where it is understood that much of what the child plays out describes what is at work within—and that much work on what is at work within can be done by participating in the play that is presented so vividly—the therapist was very willing to participate in discussions of how and why the various people the patient confided in reacted as they did, what purposes of their own might have been served, what feelings they had particular difficulty coming to grips with, and so forth.[1] As in a dream where everything is about the dreamer, so in this sort of narration of social drama everything ultimately refers to an aspect of the dramatist.

As time went on, the patient began to see that the telling she did was useful in a variety of ways. She noticed that, even when she vowed not to say anything, she ended up telling just what she had promised herself she would not tell. She was appalled at the trouble others had in keeping confidences and worked hard at being able to keep the

---

1. Ablon (1990), in reporting the analysis of a boy whose mother died when he was very young, remarks, "The use of play and displacement in the analysis facilitated structuralization as fantasies and feelings were elaborated and integrated" (p. 350). In our terms, it is worth noting that both play and displacement can help with shame by keeping what is difficult from coming into view too quickly and too overwhelmingly while still allowing it to come into view. Play and displacement both can help in countering the massive inhibitions of shame. Shame is a major issue for most patients with serious character disorders.

confidences of others, achieving considerable success in this area even in environments where keeping confidences was not the norm. She was able to see that, in her telling, there was a considerable degree of curiosity at work. She wanted to know how someone else would react, so that she could have more information about the other, also so that she could have a basis for comparing and contrasting herself to the other. The transitional function of the other in both bringing her closer to her therapist and keeping her separate was apparent.

She noticed how much she liked feeling superior, although she regularly presented herself as someone who felt inferior. She was also able to begin to see not only that there was malice at work in many of her revelations but something much harder for her, which was that her malice was not simply sinful and unacceptable and worthy of the harshest condemnation. In more human terms, it was often a reasonable response to some of the malice that had been directed her own way. She liked to ignore the hurtful things others did, because she was so fearful of her own rage and because she depended on her idealizations of others to protect her against a sense of inner chaos and loneliness.

Another way of viewing this entire piece of work was that it involved confiding in her therapist at a variety of levels her *difficulties with confiding*, not just in him but in herself. The projective technique reflected the pain of containing what nonetheless had to be contained if it was to enrich her personality. The therapist demonstrated his capacity to identify not just with what was being projected but also with the need to project it so as to be able to identify with it, rather than being simply overwhelmed by it. What the patient could not help revealing had, ultimately, to do with what she did not dare either to reveal or to remember. Her inability to keep from confiding was the inverse image of her inability to let herself confide. Of course, this related to her trouble both in depending and being dependable.

As in the example of Mrs. D., the processes of projection

and identification were significantly modified when the patient was able to bear recovering extremely painful early memories, of which she said, tellingly, "The trouble is the rage. That's what scares me so much. That's what I can't stand." As with Mrs. D., a place had to be made for the rage before memory could provide the links between the current situation and the past. Some new ways to manage and accommodate rage, resulting from what could also be seen as advances in transitional processes attained through work on fantasy material presented in terms of problems around charged confidences, made it possible to move beyond the old pattern of blaming and denying toward a more realistic approach to hurt and grief.

For a variety of reasons, including the importance of keeping the patient's confidences, this account leaves much out. It is meant to illustrate the application of the concepts about holding and projective identification that were developed in response to the tumult of inpatient treatment in an outpatient setting in which the therapist meets the figures in the patient's holding environment only as the patient describes them, that is, only as they figure in the patient's narrative. In managing outpatient treatments that involve halfway houses, day treatment centers, family therapy, Alcoholics Anonymous, dance therapy, and art therapy, these concepts have an even more direct application.

Also, when patients present their previous therapists and previous treatments in a negative light—not to mention picturing their parents in such a light—it is well to remember that here again the processes of projective identification are at work and that this very presentation has a holding function for the patient. Eventually, with a further development in holding functions, the same negative valences that are now contained in this way will be liberated and able to find other objects. As this process takes place, the patient will have a more free and more flexible access to different aspects of his own experience of himself.

When we see that holding depends not just on concrete

actions but on the creative uses of illusion, then we can begin to understand the factors that make for the holding environment becoming more portable, an essential requirement for carrying on an outpatient treatment where the patient has to make the voyage from session to session largely under his own power. The borderline patient's need for concrete holding makes outpatient treatments very difficult if they are conducted without regard to what is available to the patient outside of therapy. There may be many borderline patients for whom a residential setting is required in order to provide the concrete holding that is needed to facilitate a maturation of transitional functioning.

ON VARIETIES OF HOLDING

Even after her discharge, Mrs. D. would drive past the hospital when she was upset because the sight of the hospital provided her with a soothing and comforting experience. Another patient, who had a stormy course in the hospital, developed a pattern in her outpatient therapy where, from time to time, she would become agitated and seem near collapse, with all manner of threats of harm to herself and other dire actions. Her threats were given special force by what she had actually done in the past. On a number of occasions, she was in such dire straits that her therapist offered her hospitalization and she accepted. She would drive to the Sheppard parking lot, stare at the building for a while, then drive home, leaving both the admissions office and her therapist in uncomfortable suspense.

At her next session, she always reported the same sequence, namely that she had stared at the building for a long time, thinking to herself something like, "I'd rather be dead than go back into that place where I was so miserable." She would find herself enraged at her therapist for even suggesting such a thing. After a suitable interval, she would resolve to go home. It was as if these visits to the hospital parking lot, with their highly negativistic tinge, served to make the hospital and her therapist sufficiently present to her internally so that she could use them for transitional soothing. After this pattern was repeated a few times, the therapist had to deal with some irritation on the part of the admissions office, complicating his dealings with it about other patients. The patient's hostility was at work in the broader treatment milieu.

Many patients will call their therapists' answering machines, simply to hear the recorded message. They know full well that they will not get their live therapists. For some, this is actually a comfort. Knowing that they will not have to deal with the therapist as an actual, unpredictable person makes the experience more rewarding: it prevents the therapist from spoiling it. Others become regularly enraged when they cannot get the therapist in person, but call anyway. This would represent an example of actively seeking a negativistic interaction. Some patients even go so far as to record this recorded message, so that they have a sample of their therapist's voice available. A recently discharged patient called her hospital therapist from another state. After hearing the sound of his voice, she said that she now remembered being at the hospital and what had been accomplished. She said that before hearing his voice she had thought it had all been a dream.

A borderline patient had a work therapy job in the residency training department as her discharge from the hospital approached. She was terrified about this, because she said she was not even able to imagine life outside of the hospital. Many months after discharge she told her therapist that she was feeling very guilty because she had stolen a picture of him from the residency training department. She wanted to know if he wanted the picture back. In her mind, she had stolen the picture from him. Mindful of the boundary confusions that were so much a difficulty for this patient, her therapist pointed out that she had not taken it from him and that he thought that she should take the matter up with the administrative secretary in the department of residency training. He inquired about why she felt she had needed the picture. She replied, "I just had to have it. I felt like I was losing you and I needed to have it. It isn't even so much that I look at it. It's just knowing that I have it." Here, the concrete representation, the actual picture had intense importance for the patient as a guarantor of magical control. The picture functioned as a fetish, an overvalued object endowed with magical properties used to ward off an immense danger, in this case, one composed both of the patient's worry about her hostile feelings and her worry about her affectionate feelings.

This recalls the idea that to possess a man's image is to possess his soul. The secrecy surrounding the deed gave it a negativistic charge. She, the powerless one, had managed a feat about which the powerful ones did not even know. The stealing of the picture stood at once for an intense cherishing of her therapist and for his annihilation. It was a response to the losing–fusing dilemma. It was this mix of feelings at high intensity that made her so uncomfortable. When her therapist asked her why she had not felt that she could ask for a picture if she needed one, she was utterly shocked. The idea had never occurred to her.

As she thought about it, the patient realized that she had assumed that her therapist would disapprove severely of her even wanting a picture of him, feeling that she always wanted too much and was too needy to be acceptable. This was a lifelong conviction about herself that she cherished, as it guaranteed her sense of having a separate self. She had previously forged checks from her parents for reasons that were not dissimilar. The patient wrote a letter to the administrative secretary describing what she had done, why she felt she had done it, and expressing her mortification over the action. The administrative secretary, a very sensitive woman, was touched by the letter. The patient returned the picture. After some discussion, her therapist offered to provide her with a copy of the picture if she felt that would help. She remarked that it was a totally different experience to have a picture in this way. It was both a more fulfilling and a less fulfilling experience.

Another borderline patient actually broke into her outpatient therapist's house while the therapist was on vacation, removed pictures, had them copied and returned them, all without the therapist's knowledge.[2] This kind of problem and process is not uncommon. The example of the woman who stole the picture of her therapist from residency training illustrates a change from a very negativistic and concrete transitional process to one that is less negativistic and a bit less concrete. The therapist offered to provide a copy of the picture because he saw this as a support for the patient's move to a more collaborative and abstract position. In fact, collaboration always calls for more abstract thinking because it involves a more complex vision of the possible relationships between oneself and an other.

This example is not so different than the one discussed in Chapter 3, in which the therapist invited his patient to stop for a moment after her session to see the redbud tree in full bloom. It involves a receptivity on the therapist's part to meeting the patient at a transitional point in the development of her transitional process. The therapist provides a

2. For a rich and full discussion of this patient's course from a variety of perspectives, see "Treatment Of The Hospitalized Borderline Patient," edited by Donald R. Ross, M.D., *Psychoanalytic Inquiry*, Volume IX, Number 4, 1989, The Analytic Press, Hillsdale, New Jersey.

form of holding that supports the movement from more primitive forms of holding to more abstract and symbolic and collaborative forms. He values the transitional process and takes a part not simply in confirming steps forward but also in showing the forms such steps might take.

These partial gratfications of wishes ask of the patient a capacity for renouncing more global and literal aims. In obtaining the picture, this patient had to move from extreme notions of powerlessness and omnipotence toward a middle ground in which the price of getting something more or less like what she wished was giving up on the literal enforcement of her wishes as a tyrant who needs to consult no one.

Probably the most crucial forms of holding are the ones provided internally by the self for itself, or, to put it another way, by the self for the self-as-object.

A patient who had been wrongly thought to have organic brain damage eventually managed to learn his way around the hospital. Of special use to him was a work therapy job that involved delivering things to various locations throughout the large hospital campus. One day on his rounds he chanced to encounter a patient from his own ward who announced to him that she was going to leave the hospital in the near future. This news completely disorganized him, presumably because of the losing danger, which may have heightened his urge to fuse, thus precipitating a loss of the sense of self. He had no idea where he was or how to proceed. He was back to the state in which he had been mistaken for a case of organic brain damage. After a frightening interval of confusion, really a panic state, he was able to call up in his mind a memory of a very pleasant occasion on the ward with this fellow patient, whom he liked. As soon as he could do this, he knew once more where he was and was able to proceed with his rounds.

This example makes explicit and visible what we believe is ordinarily implicit and invisible. It serves much the same function in highlighting psychological processes as a defect in metabolism does in highlighting ordinary physical metabolic processes. When something does not work or works only marginally, it provides an excellent model for scrutinizing the ordinary everyday workings of similar systems that are not so stressed. This patient, faced with a sudden loss danger, experienced a loss of self organization consequent upon the psychological loss of the stabilizing object. In the face of this danger, he provided a holding experience for himself by evoking the memory of a pleasant occasion on the ward with that person. This remembered presence counterbalanced the present loss. He went "boom"—in a way that bears a significant relationship to the two little girls with whom we began our discussion of holding (Chapter 5)—then reached out to himself from within himself through the holding power of illusion.

In our view of normal mental functioning these kind of processes are occurring subconsciously all the time. They enter into awareness only at times of special stress. Shortly after admission a schizophrenic patient told his therapist most emphatically that his mother was on the ward. When the therapist inquired how this was so, the patient proceeded to describe how her various features resided in different patients and different staff members. This one had her nose, that one her ears, another her lips, and so forth. It was as if the unfamiliar people on the ward represented a drawer of type, which he could use to compose a familiar person. This is, of course, what we all do with children, using names and resemblances, often quite illusory, to establish the linkages we require.

A therapist who had recently and suddenly lost his wife, and was aware of having a very hard time working, found himself immensely comforted one day in the midst of a session with a young patient whose hands suddenly seemed large, quiet, and gentle in a way that suddenly and forcefully evoked for him very pleasant memories of his wife. A sensitive woman patient in her 40s remarked that, although she had not been aware of it at the time, she had used gifts of her mother's clothing at the time of her death to turn various of her woman friends and relatives into pieces of her mother. In this way she both managed to continue her extremely difficult relationship with her mother and to make efforts at modifying it even when her mother was dead. She had spats with many of the recipients that were just like those that had gone on between her and her mother.

If we were to push this line of thinking to a logical conclusion, we might want to define one central function of memory as to provide a link to the past and the familiar, that which already has for us the protective illusion of a form. In this way, we might see memory as a device to protect us against the baffling openness and intriguing lack of definition of the present. Instead of responding creatively to a current feeling that presents us with new opportunities, we experience a threat of dissolution from which we retreat into memory and the familiar habits of the self. We retreat from opportunity, again because it takes us into the dangerous territory of lack of definition.

Painful memory has the virtue of maintaining an inner organization from which we are as yet unable to distinguish or detach ourselves. A cue in the present may present us with the chance of a dangerous freedom from which we escape by repeating especially what is most painful. We dare not respond innovatively and creatively to the cue, often for fear of losing ourselves as we have become accustomed to knowing ourselves. We are habituated to ourselves and, in the face of potential change, confront something like a withdrawal syndrome.

In therapy, present cues lead to the recall of past experiences, past ways of relating. We use this recall as a container, one that channels the unfamiliar in the direction of the familiar, more abstractly than the schizophrenic patient who created his mother from pieces of people on the ward, perhaps, but certainly in a kindred manner. The threat of the newness of the therapeutic situation is at least as great as the threat of the repetition, which bars the way to anything satisfyingly new. Here "we" refers both to the patient and to the therapist, each of whom is at work in the face of tensions over how to use the old to make possible an encounter with the new, rather than as a fortress against what life offers in the vast and undefined present.

But this recall also presents in the present the opportunity for changes and repairs. We talk about a product being "recalled" to the factory, a place that has the tools and designs that make possible some change. We may think of therapy as a kind of recall, a half-way station along the way to a form of integration where what is being "recalled" no longer is so problematic as to need to stay "fixed" in exactly this form. That which is deeply integrated can be both remembered and forgotten. It is available without being terribly demanding.

When we can learn to use memory as a reassurance that does not take us captive, we are in the position of being able to visit an accustomed state of the self without becoming trapped there. We can travel old roads to look for new branching points. We can begin to have the experience of finding ourselves in what we remember so that we can go on, rather than of being imprisoned in ways of being whose obsolescence we dare not admit. We can use memory then to inform new essays into feeling, variations that are neither utterly alien nor utterly familiar. Here again, at a more abstract, internal, symbolic, and feelingfully nuanced level we have suggested a geography of experience that situates itself between the twin poles of the losing and fusing dangers.

ON IMITATION AND HOLDING

Imitation is at the core of virtually all learning processes. The capacity for plastic imitation of a vast repertoire

of forms of behavior is one of the great evolutionary tri-
umphs of the line leading to man, where it is extended to the
capacity for imitation of symbolic behavior and symbolic
imitation.

The saying, "monkey see, monkey do," encapsulates an
important observation regarding primate behavior. We may
easily become a bit too habituated to what is a wondrous
ability. If we stop and think for a moment about what is
required to turn a set of pictures into a copy of an action, the
wonder should return. Consider for example something like
watching championship divers at play, imitating each
other's dives impromptu. How did they turn what they saw
into a program for a complex acrobatic movement in just a
few seconds? Watching young children take on the postures,
gaits, facial expressions, characteristic rhythms, and variations in intensities of their parents' repertoires will also
reawaken this kind of awe concerning imitation. Clearly,
there are a set of neurological apparati dedicated to imitation, that is, to taking in through sensory modalities external
impressions and then modeling inner neurological sets on
the basis of data extracted from these sensory impressions.

These apparati are especially active and influential in
basic patterning of other parts of the nervous system during
certain privileged periods early in childhood. No doubt
there are specific neurochemistries and neuroanatomical
dynamisms related to these periods. If the history of the
development of the individual brain is the history of the
development of inhibition, then it makes sense to think of
these apparati becoming progressively inhibited in their
operation as development progresses. As attachment and
self-object boundaries are consolidated, the capacity for
totalistic imitation wanes. In a sense, imitation becomes less
overwhelmingly intimate and physiological as symbolic
modes become available. Here, too, transitional object relations play their part.

The genius of Woody Allen's movie *Zelig*, about a man

who is an obligate chameleon, lacking the ability to resist imitating whatever model is presented to him and therefore losing all sense of personal cohesion and autonomy, is that, by no great leap, it suggests the hypothesis that the predisposition to imitate is still highly active in adults. Under normal circumstances, however, it is adaptively held in check in the name of organizational stability and the preservation of previously learned behavioral sets and inward dispositions, which are too valuable to risk disturbing. Learning always carries a risk, because it puts what was previously known in question. Learning is at once the basis of the possibility of social and personal order and a threat to it.

What role does imitation play in psychotherapy? Or perhaps it is more accurate to ask what the possible roles of a variety of forms of imitation may be in psychotherapy. Let us start with the idea sketched above that apparati to support imitation that are both very complex and very diverse are not only built in, but functioning under varying degrees of inhibition throughout life. We have been impressed over and over again in work with patients by the phenomenon of observing that the patient and therapist have assumed the same posture, have fallen into breathing in the same rhythm, sigh at exactly the same moment, and so forth. One therapist noted that he became aware of pain in his stomach just a second before his borderline patient began talking about how much her stomach hurt. Videotapes show therapist and patient beginning nervously to bob their feet at exactly the same frequency.

These chance observations are only a very small part of the set of observations of this kind that could be made. (How does the vulnerable infant catch his mother's anxiety so that he is not able to eat when she tries to feed him, but settles down as soon as she leaves the room?) It was a common observation at Chestnut Lodge in Rockville, Maryland, a site of pioneering hospital work with severely disturbed patients, that patients, after long association with their therapists, began to look and move like the therapist. We have seen the same phenomenon at Sheppard Pratt.

What is the experience of being with an other person? How do we go about knowing the other? Along what channels, within and out of awareness, do we communicate? How do we identify threat, enticement, allure, offers of cooperation, competition, good faith, bad faith, and so forth? Being with another person is just that: an experience. It is richer than any set of logical and theoretical propositions about it. Our attunement to the other—what we receive and what we send, our accommodation—occurs along multiple channels, physiological and symbolic, probably even at different levels of neurological organization.

When we talk about getting a "feel" for another person, about the "vibes" we get, the vagueness of the terminology actually expresses the complexity of the integration being attempted when we try to describe our position vis-à-vis another person. We take in and put out so much of which we are not consciously aware. We probably do a lot of matching of the other's physiological state in order to be able to model it internally and respond to it with a state of our own. We undoubtedly do this with a variety of separate apparati that interact with each other as well as with stored experiences. We also assess symbolic communication in terms of the physiologic status of the other and we do this both in and out of awareness.

Being with a patient is not so simple as "listening" to the patient. Or to put it another way, this "third ear" with which we are enjoined to listen is actually a compound organ of enormous complexity and diversity. It reaches deep into us, certainly travelling a visceral circuit. From time to time the question comes up regarding supervision of psychotherapy, "How do you really know what is going on between the doctor and the patient?" Some have advocated the use of tapes to know what is "really" happening. Others have suggested videotapes. The *reductio ad absurdum* of this relatively concrete notion of what is "real" would involve suggesting—facetiously—that we use intrathecal electrodes, noting then that issues of where to place them and how many to use would become vexed. What goes on between people is not of finite complexity. Each technique for reporting may add something, but it certainly does not exhaust the field.

Suppose we take seriously these ideas of communication through imitation, matching, and internal modeling along many channels, many out of one's awareness. One immediate result is a heightened awareness on our part not only of how much of the patient is available to us to be known, but also of how much we are available to the patient to be known. This leads to a different way of looking at the whole question of self-disclosure, one that we will explore at length in a later chapter, for the real issue may be not how much we dislose to patients but how willing we are to avow our disclosures. When we are with another person, the openness constituted may be of a staggering complexity and profundity. When we bracket only parts, we also run a reductionist risk.

Everyone who has worked with more disturbed patients is aware of the often uncanny accuracy of patients' ability to discern sensitive and intimate aspects of the doctor's character, disposition toward them, current states of feeling, and life circumstances. This may seem uncanny only because we so wish to deny how actually and actively present we are, wherever we are. Our denial may be in the service of protecting ourselves as therapists against the fusing danger more than we care to admit. Patients are often in the position of the child in the story of the emperor's new clothes. They are, like children, unable to buffer themselves against reality by buffering themselves against what they take in.

In his very stimulating book, *The Primitive Edge Of Experience* (1989), Ogden quotes the following passage from one of Winnicott's letters (in Rodman 1987):

I know an autistic child who is treated by very clever interpretation and who has done moderately well. What started off the treatment was, however, something which the first analyst did, and it is strange that I have never been able to get the second analyst to acknowledge the importance of what I will describe. The first analyst, Dr. Milda Hall, died. Dr. Hall found this boy who had gone autistic after being normal and sat in the room with him and established a communication by doing everything that this boy did. He would sit still for a quarter of an hour and then move his foot a little, she would move her foot. His finger would move and she would imitate, and this went on for a long time. Out of these beginnings everything showed signs of developing until she died. If I could have gotten the clever analyst to join on to all this I think we might by now have had something like a cure, instead of having to put up with one of those maddening cases where a lot of good work has been done and everybody is very pleased but the child is not satisfactory. [p. 76]

Ogden refers to Winnicott's discussion as addressing "the role of imitation in a primitive form of object relatedness" (p. 76). Perhaps it is a useful extension to talk of imitation's *fundamental* role in all object relatedness and in all communication. A theory of the growth of human intelligence out of the need and adaptive advantage and pleasure of imitating not only the behavior of other animals but of other members of the protohuman group possesses great appeal. It would give a different slant on our view of intelligence.

When we talk about "liking" another person or about "being liked," the language itself seems to be pushing us in the direction of a recognition of the fundamental importance of imitation, so close are the senses of "like" as liking and "like" as likeness. Likeness is the link that makes liking possible. A borderline patient described how she acquired an eating disorder during a hospitalization. She pointed out that she had lived in isolation most of her life and found a way toward contact with two peers through her eating disorder. She acknowledged that it was a problem, but felt that no one had appreciated its positive side, and worried that to give it up meant to lose touch with these two friends and the feelings she had about them. When one friend suicided, this highlighted the problem. This line of thinking casts a different light on the commonplace that criminals learn new ways to commit crimes in jail.

In subtle ways, the kind of relatedness and reassurance, the kind of imitation that is described by Winnicott, is a central feature of all human contact. There is a negotiation going on that probably has an ethologically determined basic vocabulary, but yet admits of infinite variation. Even effective negativistic response, developmentally at its height during the periods when imitation is the strongest, presupposes the imitative capacity, because without the capacity to imitate and the allure of imitation, there would be no possibility or need for the dissent of negativism. To put it another way, imitation is the foundation of differentiation, because without it there would be nothing *from which* or *with which* to differentiate. What we mean by differentiation is not the achievement of a state of utter alienation, but a state that reconciles similarity and the capacity for autonomous reordering of many shared elements.

The example of imitation provided by Winnicott is probably atypical in that it rests heavily on the conscious volition of the therapist. She knows that she is doing what she is doing and she organizes it deliberately and sequentially. It is likely that most imitation, and probably the most important imitation capacities, depend on pattern recognition paradigms that work more like face recognition (e.g., "That's him.") than by more stepwise reasoning (e.g., "Let's see. That nose resembles his. Those eyes are like his eyes. Therefore, it's probable that it's he.").

Sometimes it is very hard to say something very simple. If the capacities for imitation are as central both in evolution and in development as we think they are, the means at their

disposal are likely to be highly sophisticated, highly integrated, and largely beyond awareness. Such capacities and
how they work would have to be inferred from their
achievements.

    We have had the sense that what can be called *imitative
convergence* occurs most frequently in therapy at times of
heightened interpersonal strain (or at least is noticed most
frequently then, perhaps because therapists require reassurance most at such points and therefore tune to a channel that
is always operating). We also believe that such convergence
often occurs just before a departure into some line of
discussion or relating that carries the strain of newness and
increased differentiation. As the internal repertoire for imag-
ining and simulating sequences is enriched, so behavioral
capacities are enriched. Psychotherapy's setting replicates
conditions of opportunity for the kind of attachment and
intimacy that are developmentally associated with particularly vigorous learning through imitation. (Marriage is another relationship that sets up these conditions.)

    While we do not believe that psychotherapy operates
through consciously intended corrective emotional experience, we do believe that, especially through ongoing opportunities for imitation, often of complicated sequences of
response, often beyond awareness and equally often nonverbal, an enriched repertoire of inward pieces of potential
responses becomes available to the patient. At certain points,
a critical amount of enrichment may make possible an
experience of a qualitative change in behavioral capacities
and internal experience of affective states. This may happen
without being reported in words. That is, a new conception,
conscious or not, of the range of possibilities enables new
patterns of behavior, symbolic or actual. A borderline patient reported with some amazement: "My butterfly stroke
just changed. I don't know how to describe it. It just flowed
inside my body."

    Consider a typical sequence in the treatment of a patient
prone to affect storms. The patient becomes enraged after a

response that she says she perceives as cold, rejecting, and withholding. She launches a long exhausting attack on her therapist. The therapist sits in a certain way, looks at her in a certain way, breathes in a certain way, moves or does not move, assumes different hand postures, and so forth. All this is generated from within the therapist in a complicated way that depends on how the cues from outside interact with previous experiences and the available repertoire of expressive responses, kinesthetic and autonomic as well as symbolic. Particularly in the context of a long-term relationship in which both parties have access to a great deal of information about each other, an enormous amount can be communicated in this way. This is often described as "surviving" the patient's anger, but we should remember that surviving means living through, and that "living" is always of a particular sort, rich in form and rich in information.

Quite often, particularly in discussion of borderline patients, the idea is advanced that patients learn from their therapists by inducing in the therapists states that are akin to the most difficult aspects of the patients' experience. The therapist deals with this state in himself, making himself available to be watched while he does this, so that the patient can see a new possibility. This commonly goes by the name of projective identification and metabolism of projected contents, followed by their return to the patient in a less threatening form, because of the modifications that have been made. Most often the process is described as a matter of verbal transactions, or at least as culminating in verbal transactions. This misses the much more complicated matter of the ongoing back-and-forth flow of communication through mutual imitation. The words may be signposts along the road, but they are not the road and would mean nothing without it, that is, the shared presence and all that goes on within it.

As the patient watches the therapist and monitors the therapist's responses along many different channels all at once, an extremely complicated dialogue goes on. The patient whose mother would become enraged and end up in physical fights with her sees and feels in the most important physiological ways that the therapist is different. Even when the transference is near psychotic this difference registers. Many doctors neglect work with psychotic patients, those whose transferences reach psychotic proportions, or those prone to affect storms because of their discomfort with these nonverbal channels and their lack of faith in their own capacity to respond along these channels.

We should stop and notice that just as imitation is the core of the process that leads to enrichment of the personality, it can, if it is too global and overwhelming, become a toxic roadblock to enrichment: for example, the infant who catches its mother's anxiety and is rendered literally unable to eat because of it. One sees many examples of children who have caught their parents' anxieties and conflicts in ways that are equally debilitating at later steps in development.

Imitation always brings along with it a merger danger. It can have very hostile motivations, as, for example, the patient who becomes so much like his therapist that the therapist starts to feel that there is no space left for him. It is, in these situations, as if the patient said, "I will become so much like you that there will be no you." It takes a very secure therapist, with considerable flexibility, to stand his ground in the face of this without being driven to active and extreme distancing measures that ignore the amalgam of love mixed in with the hatred. Here again, the capacity to relate and to tolerate being related to in a negativistic manner is essential.

So much of play involves imitation. Transitional processes like play provide for imitation with variation, the variation being essential to dealing with the merger danger. As the transitional object helps the child play through various troubling aspects of experience, repeating and reworking, modifying what is stressful in a relationship with a real other and thus stabilizing his own inner organization and predilections, so imitative play allows the adjustment of what is being imitated and taken in so that it does not represent a series of monkey wrenches thrown into the existing intrapsychic structures. Play is the handmaiden of structure building.

When we see borderline patients who seem internally to be battlegrounds for conflicted massive introjects, leaving little room for the emergence of anything distinctively individual, we can surmise that there has been a terrible defect in the capacity for play and transitional relatedness. Imitation has not been nutritive because of what we might call the failure of digestion and metabolism. Therapy will have to provide opportunities for imitation and also for the secure metabolism of what is imitated through play and playfulness in therapy. Sometimes even the most agitated acting out can best be seen as an effort at play under the most extreme anxiety conditions. Play represents the effort to utilize what has been taken in by imitation in the personal developmental project of the person playing.

SUMMARY

In the past two chapters, we have advanced a concept of "holding" that takes early concrete caretaking actions as the emblems of processes that span from the concrete to the abstract, the literal to the symbolic, the external to the internal. "Holding" provides for a reduction in tension that makes for a more open range of internal adaptive possibilities by protecting psychic balance. At the same time, it provides many clues to possible modes of adaptation and integration.

We have used a conceptualization of stages in "holding" derived from long term inpatient work to illustrate the complexities of holding and how these bring up questions of the linkage between intrapsychic processes and interpersonal processes. An extended clinical example showed how a patient developed an increased internal capacity for more abstract transitional process. We then proceeded to apply the ideas illustrated through inpatient examples to one aspect of an extended outpatient treatment.

Finally, we focused on imitative processes obtaining between individuals at a variety of levels, conscious and unconscious, symbolic and physiological, to suggest the richness and complexity of the dynamics of "holding" as they take place between individuals who meet under conditions that foster intimacy. Our goal has been to give experiential content to the idea of "holding" in ways that are suggestive and challenging. Our hope is that these ideas will provide some "holding" for clinicians engaged in treating borderline patients, suggesting new horizons of practical clinical action, inquiry, and abiding, rather than rigid theoretical concepts that move the clinician away from the flux of clinical experience.

7

Emptiness, Self-Participation, and Self-Observation

It's a waste of your time and it's a waste of my time. You talk about how therapy is about getting to know yourself. That's all very fine for you to say. In my case, there really isn't anyone to get to know.

My basic worry is that when you get to know me, you'll find just emptiness, nothing there. So naturally I'm afraid.

Me? Forget it. There's nothing to me.

One of the most perplexing problems encountered in relating to borderline patients is their bedrock conviction that they are nonentities. Whatever their faculties, abilities or achievements in the world, however great their impact on the lives of others, including their therapists', however massive, intricate, intriguing, and appalling the chaos they can generate around themselves—none of it seems to make any impression on their inner worlds. It is as if all the

179

telephone lines have gone dead so that no news can reach the area of the personality where these individuals really live, if there is any liveliness to their living at all.

Even their own protestations of suffering do not move them. It is as if they turn two deaf ears on themselves, often grinning sadistically as they do so. This inner deafness is at least as profound as any receptive block they interpose between themselves and outside interlocutors, such as psychotherapists. In what follows, we will explore the idea that this inner conviction of emptiness reflects linked dynamic defects in self-participation and self-observation. That is, it is a process that has its benefits for the patients as well as enormous costs.

The treatment of borderline patients may be thought of as an effort to resolve a constricting form of self-transference in which the self is seen as not having the rights to experience, autonomous will, meaning, or significance. By self-transference we indicate a focus on the way in which the self is caught up in seeing itself as it once was but need no longer be. The concept is analogous to object transference, but with the focus back on the self.

SELF-EXPERIENCE AS FLUX

Heraclitus long ago observed that it is impossible to put one's foot in the same river twice: "You could not step twice into the same river, for other waters are ever flowing on to you." The constancy of the river—the commonplace that the Mississippi is the Mississippi is the Mississippi, yesterday, today, and tomorrow, so that it makes sense to characterize it as an old man who just goes rolling along—is an illusion, a magisterial feat of abstraction and linking. Illusion lets us let go of particulars in order to get hold of larger patterns. We abstract to pull ourselves out of chaotic flux. The constancy of what *seems* constant to us is *constructed* by the marvellous selectivity of our attentional capacities. We are as active as the most gifted writers of music in *composing* the appearances that move and soothe us.

Heraclitus focuses on the river and its vicissitudes, leaving unchallenged the foot that seeks to dip into it. Yet, does it not make as much sense to say that it is impossible to put the same foot in the river twice, because, even as in the flow of time the river changes, so does the foot? Where Heraclitus focuses on the object of experience, the river, we can turn our attention back on the experiencing subject, whose relative constancy, continuity, and coherence are as much constructed and composed through dynamic—that is, vulnerable and variable—internal processes as the corresponding features of the experienced objects.

When we talk of *self-constancy* or *self-continuity*, or *self-cohesion* or *identity*, we are discussing not things but processes, not once-and-for-all achievements, but dynamics in which there is relative stability, which is but another way to say that there is relative instability as well. To the extent that we experience ourselves as *constant, continuous, cohesive,* or having an *identity,* it is because we are adept at establishing links that bridge what might well become chasms between states if we did not have this ability. Nor are these transitions without peril. Experience, after all, means "that which comes out of peril." Each new state questions the one that went before it. The quandary is that, if we keep the states separate, working to isolate and insulate different pieces of ourselves from each other, then we produce a style of experiencing that is at once rigid and brittle.

In this style, difficult experiences are encapsulated in brittle shells, as if they were so many dragons' eggs waiting to hatch. Anything that resembles the encapsulated, isolated experience has to be avoided, lest the shell crack and the dragon come rushing forth. A patient said, "I can't even let myself lie down and try to rest, because if I do, I'm afraid I'll be just like my mother who spent weeks and weeks being sick in bed when I was a little girl." While we are accustomed to worrying a great deal about the drama of the opening of Pandora's box, for fear that all sorts of dread and fell creatures will come rushing out, we pay less attention to the more subtle and complicated question of how the box got built in the first place. Another patient remarked with some heat, "You want to connect everything. I want to keep everything apart."

On a number of occasions we have seen borderline patients who had seemed incredibly young, not just in their behavior and thinking but in their physical appearance, age rapidly before our eyes as they began to take into themselves as genuine experience what had happened to them in their lives. In this transformation, which had its sorrowful side, "incredible" youthfulness was replaced by a more mature and credible aspect, as a policy like the one expressed in the fighter squadron's motto, "Stay Pretty, Die Young," was replaced by one that admitted more vulnerability and ambivalences, more blending of loss and gain, permitting an aging and curing whose spirit went deep into the flesh. Our cultural obsession with youth may express a greater despair about the possibilities of experiencing than we normally care to admit.

A style of self that allows for connection instead of disconnection, integration instead of isolation and insulation, aims for the kind of strength that is flexible and resilient instead of rigid and brittle. The price to be paid is numerous repetitions in quest of something like mastery of difficult aspects of experience. Where the isolating and insulating style aims to "feel better," to avoid emotional pain by avoiding in general, the connecting style aims to get better at feeling, which is a very different matter. Getting better at feeling means feeling what hurts, what disappoints, what threatens as well as what heartens and gladdens. It means tasting the bitter in life as well as the better. It means doing this over and over, and having the experience of doubt, disillusion, and change over and over again. In this style of self, there is no fixed star by which to navigate. If there is a capacity to create a constancy in change, there is also an awareness, however implicit, of the fragility of the senses of constancy and continuity. There is also a fundamental sense of humility, as the individual comes to appreciate his own place.

Integration is not proven by the capacity to be adamant and unyielding alone, but by the more complex capacity to mix yielding and firmness to change, rearrange, give ground in order to make new grounds on which to sight new figures. When Goethe remarked that he had been an adolescent numerous times in the course of his long life, he was admitting that his remarkable gift for inclusion and self-renewal had its very stormy side. He could even, near the end of his life, pay a balanced tribute to the different states of self he had known, without trying to judge among them. "People always fancy," said Goethe, laughing, "that we must become old to become wise, but, in truth, as years advance, it is hard to keep ourselves as wise as we were."

> Man becomes, indeed, in the different stages of his life, a different being; but he cannot say that he is a better one, and in certain matters he is as likely to be right in his twentieth as in his sixtieth year.
>
> We see the world one way from a plain, another way from the height of a promontory, another from the glacier fields of the primary mountains. We see, from one of these points, a larger piece of the world than from the other, but that is all, and we can not say that we see more truly from any one than from the rest. When a writer leaves monuments on the different steps of his life, it is chiefly important that he should have an innate foundation and good will; that he should, at each step, have seen and felt clearly, and that, without any secondary aims, he should have said distinctly and truly what passed in his mind. Then will his writings, if they were right at the step where they originated, remain always right, however the writer may develop or alter himself in after times. [1984, p. 310]

The hallmark of the connecting, weaving, and reweaving style of self is the capacity to use regressive experience in the service of constructive extension and revision of the domain of the self. Old pains and old problems, even old catastrophes become the touchstones of new initiatives.

There is a sense, different than the enormously painful one intended by the borderline patients, in which we are all as nothing. Cultivated, this sense, far from detracting from us, can enhance our vitality as well as our capacity for compassion and ethical behavior. We need not take ourselves quite so literally and concretely as we so often do.

VARIABILITY AND VARIETY IN SELF-PARTICIPATION

The appeal of the concept of variability and variety in self-participation is that it introduces the notion of the vastness of the self, not just as a set of potential experiences but as a set of potential ways of experiencing. Vastness, which can under unfortunate conditions be experienced as waste, implies space for exploration, openness to curiosity, room for disparate elements to coexist, and the opportunity for a whole series of comparisons, contrasts, blendings, refinings, findings, and refindings. Vastness implies the kinds of processes that are combinatorially so rich that they go beyond procedures and predictability. Actually, the idea of the vastness of the self, which entrains the idea of a similar vastness of the other empathically construed, is a very simple idea with profound consequences.

We have a whole host of ways of referring to variability in self-participation: "I see myself as a little girl. I don't want to grow up. Whenever I get a hint that I'm behaving even a little bit like a grown woman, I just want to run and hide." "I had a dream in which I was boxing Mike Tyson. He was huge and I was terrified. I kept hitting him and knocking him down. It wasn't that I was so strong, but I knew just where and when to hit him. I used my skill in boxing." "I don't feel

right when anyone around me isn't getting what they need."
"I can't feel and function at the same time. I have to
choose." "There's a part of me that wants to be a girl. I want
that kind of attention. I know a man isn't supposed to feel
that way, but sometimes I do." "Some days I go through the
day like I was sleepwalking. I can't seem to get hold of
myself. I wonder where I am." "I don't want to have
children. If I had children, I'd be just as bad as my mother
was. It would be the same old story all over again." "When
the music starts, my body just wants to move. I love it, but it
scares me." "My children laugh at me. They're almost
grown now. They can't understand why I let my father talk
to me like that. They scold me, but it's no use. He's my father
and when I talk with him I'm a little boy again." "I'm never
glad. I don't think that's what life is about." "I have to keep
beating myself up about losing him. If I don't, then it might
seem to me like it all never happened at all, like I never had
him at all and I just made it all up."

We could go on and on compiling such a list of references. Our goal is not to exhaust or categorize them, but
simply to convey a bit of the richness and flavor. We are our
own partners in experience, and our exquisite disjunction
from ourselves opens up a potential space that can be filled
with a richness in texture, flavor, phrasing, and dynamics,
perhaps better suggested by music than by any metaphor.
Listening to patients on any day of clinical work reveals a
tapestry of references to change in the fervors and flavors of
their participation in themselves. Many of our heuristic
terms achieve generality and reach by overlooking—or
should we say "looking over"—what is particular, individual and, quite possibly, crucial: local color. This con-
duces to much of therapy taking place in locales that are
more emotionally, relationally, and cognitively colorless
than need be.

An example might be the notion of "conflict." Conflicts
are not struggles of energy. Nor are they simply working out
puzzles encoded in arbitrary and bizarre ways; nor are they

clashes of stereotyped internal agencies. Conflicts pit bits of particular people against other bits of those same individuals in ways that are as peculiar to the individual as the bits are. "I get mixed up in more things at once than most people do. I think I get so confused because I just don't know how to pull myself out." "I can't even ask myself what I think or want. Things happen so fast. They're already over before I can do that." "The thing about me is that, if I were going to put the apple back, it wouldn't be enough to get it back in the bin. I'd have to put it back just on the right tree in the right branch in exactly the place it was picked from. Otherwise, it wouldn't be worth bothering." Conflicts are meetings, encounters that put our capacity to invent an existentially fit vocabulary to a test that is at once exacting and a searching critique of exactitude.

What we say about conflict can also be said about devices to avoid or mitigate affect. No two people split, project, introject, and displace in quite the same way. Psychotherapeutic work that attends carefully to the scent and style of the individual has as its goal opening up horizons for the self that may change the self's range of reference.

Affective states reflect differences in self-participation. We are with ourselves differently when we are sad, happy, shamed, scared, angry, lonely, exultant, guilty, and so forth. We are with*in* ourselves differently in these different affective domains. Nor should we assume that one person's sadness or joy is like another's. To overemphasize likeness, to assume we know someone else's affective states and their characters, is like dismissing painting by saying, "A painting is a painting is a painting," or dismissing wine by saying, "Wine is just grape juice that is a little bit over the hill." To appreciate another's feeling is to enter into a neighborhood.

We are accustomed to talking of *selves having feelings*. In a partial way, we might also want to think of *feelings having something like selves*. What do we mean by this turn of phrase? Feelings are internal experiential domains that bring together quite a bit in the way of internal mental phenomenology. Feeling always has conceptual and memory contexts, and autonomic, muscular, and perceptual contexts. We should attend carefully to the links that exist in our language, that great conceptual and experiential reef laid down over the ages by countless incessantly tinkering tiny individual creatures linked to us. For example, the complex of motion, emotion, and motive is highly suggestive. It recapitulates linkages in the brain that join old motor patterning centers, newer limbic centers, and very new frontal planning centers in larger communicating exchanges.[1]

We do not want to try to specify how conceptual context, memory context, autonomic, muscular, and perceptual set constellate together in feeling. This is beyond our current scope or capabilities. They do so differently in different feeling states. We do want to point out the high order of integration intended when we discuss the experience of "feeling." When we talk about feelings we are not discussing anything elementary. Feeling domains may be more like continents on plates in tectonic theory, that is to say, huge arrays with dynamic and local environments all their own. Feeling states are so highly organized that we may also usefully think of them as organs that function. When we say that we might want to think of feelings in a partial way, as having something like selves, we mean that particular feelings—sadness, joy, rage, for example—may be associated in individual people with particular styles of thinking, ranges and arrays of remembering, dispositions, and body skills. What is available of the self to use, to remember, to plan may be very different in different feeling states. This is quite clear in young children and can be observed at many

---

1. McHugh (1989) offers an interpretation of the syndromes of dyskinesia, dementia, and depression in Huntington's Chorea, Sydenham's Chorea, and Parkinson's Disease that emphasizes the integration of the brain and the complexity of function of such old structures as the basal ganglia.

different levels. For example, learning proceeds quite differently under the influence of angry and loving feelings. Nor is it certain that what has been learned in one state will be available in the other.

When we meet patients who experience themselves as fragmented selves with a high degree of autonomy associated with the fragments, and no clear sense of conscious self-continuity, we need some ideas such as the ones sketched above to relate their experience to the broader continuum of our knowledge of the less fractured personality. In complex multiple personality patients who develop hundreds and hundreds of "alters," we need a notion, such as the creation of different carriers for ongoing streams of feeling, to help us with the enormous task of integration in the clinical work. Otherwise we are apt to lose our heads in the fading in and the fading out, unable to focus on the feeling that is unbearable and the current situation that is bringing it up again. Once we have such an idea, much of what we know about the role of transitional processes in mitigating losing–fusing dangers and in affect attainment and containment becomes relevant.

It could be argued that we invent, to a certain degree, a different form or style of self for each relationship, each inflection in social role. Certainly, internal object relations denominate domains of the self. Among a host of others, mentors and tormentors each stake out their territories within us. We participate differently with and within ourselves according to who our relational partners are, not just in reality, but also in fantasy: "Sometimes when I'm not here, I try to get hold of you and I can't do it in my head. Then I'm really confused and lost. If I can think of you, it changes how I feel and what I can do to take care of myself." This kind of statement from patients, not at all rare, describes the use of a relationship as a device to change and integrate feelings and fantasies. It illustrates the notion that, like feelings, relationships are integrative domains, quite large and quite abstract by the time we get around to using them as terms.

It could be argued that feelings are important ways of linking experiences across a broad range of relationships, and that relationships are important ways of linking experiences together across a broad range of feelings. Here, of course, relationships is meant to refer to relationships with other people. It could also refer to conceptual relationships, such as sequence, likeness, reference, and causality. The capacity to tell a story depends crucially on these, and the formulation of identity is in many ways an act of story-telling. It is tempting to urge that concepts, feelings, and relationships are all large integrative operators that play a part in constituting that union we call the self. Now a union, if it is a unity at all, is an achieved unity. Just as concepts, feelings, and relationships can all serve as large integrative operators, so each one can take a particular part and, in so doing, play as important a part in taking apart as in putting together. The same tools that can be so vital in construction can be central in destruction.

In every self, as in every political confederation, there are forces pushing in the direction of breakdown and disunity as well as in the direction of integration. These forces can make an enormous positive contribution by breaking the hold of constricting established sets. A virtue of Jungian thought, too little celebrated in Freudian circles, is its emphasis on maturational reconstitutions in the self as it moves from a narrowly personal sphere of concerns toward links with a self denominated on deeper grounds. The richness and reliability of the self depends on the disposition and interplay of these different tendencies toward union and disunion. In every self, there are places that it is nice to visit, even fascinating and invigorating to visit, but you would truly hate to be trapped and forced to live there all the time.

This observation brings us quite naturally to the question of how we make the transitions. How do we move from place to place, from position to position, from disposition to disposition within ourselves? If we get stuck in a certain narrow domain of ourselves, what processes can help us restore our freedom of movement? How do these processes develop? If they are compromised, what can be done to help restore them?

ON SELF-OBSERVATION

Self-observation is at once a commonplace of psychotherapeutic discourse and, perhaps, an oxymoron, with a U-turn built right into the term. Self-observation requires that the self, subject, take itself as the object of its own curiosity and vigilance. An internal split into subject and object is required.

The self-observing function is not a simple one. It is not the same in different people, nor is it the same in the same person from epoch to epoch in that person's life. "I don't know why this is, but I think I have a glass-bottomed boat. I can see what is going on inside me. I don't always understand it, but at least I can see it. I think most other people's boats don't have glass bottoms." This young man who had been suicidal and severely compromised in his functioning over a long period of time also remarked, "I was always able to keep my observer going. He watched what was happening, even when it was terrible. He was watching and he put a lot together, even though I didn't have any idea what I could do with it."

What he was describing was a very rich self-observing internal relationship. He was able to note differences between himself and others, positive features in his capacity to observe himself and even the limitations of what his observing function could do for him. A few years later in therapy he said, "My father's voice is distinct enough inside me now so that I can argue with it. My mother isn't even a voice. She's just actions that happen to me. Or maybe her voice just sounds so much like mine that I can't tell what's happening to me." His self-observing function helped him to note the effects of others on and in himself as well as his effects on others and even his effects on himself: "I think I overwhelm others when I feel overwhelmed. I'm good at it. I think I overwhelm them when I'm reminded of how I've been overwhelmed. What I don't understand is why I go on overwhelming myself. It doesn't help me."

In contrast to this patient's robust and resourceful self-observing relationship with himself, there are patients whose capacities for self-observation are terribly blocked and impaired, as if any self-observation carried with it dangers of such enormity that even to move back far enough from them to notice them could be obliterating. One such borderline patient subjected her therapist to hour after hour of grueling silence, sitting in a posture at once withdrawn, defeated, and terribly hostile. Finally, one day, she announced, "Either you have a white cat, a white dog or both." When pressed to elucidate, she said that she had been staring at her therapist's knee for a long time and had noticed on his pants white hairs of two different lengths, from which data she had reached her conclusions.

This woman rarely, if ever, made statements about herself. She had no lack of observational powers, no lack of curiosity. Mostly what she did was to scrutinize others and find fault or blame. She did not have at her disposal the kind of regard that could turn inwards and guide her in the search for connective threads within herself. This problem was quite consistent with the history of extreme abuse and neglect. It was an enormous job to help this woman find even brief instants when it was safe to look at herself and to see a little bit. Often, these moments were followed by new outbursts of chaotic behavior, as if, slight as they were, they had been too much, perhaps because of the new internal contexts and experiences of self they made available.

That self-observation is a very peculiar activity becomes apparent if we step back just a bit to observe what is involved in observing ourselves. Self-observation involves taking a distance from ourselves, but not so great a distance as to break the link with ourselves. Insufficient distance makes for blindness: we are too close to see. Too great a distance leads to the predicament of depersonalization: what we see lacks living meaning for us. Another way of stating this point is to say that self-observation, like a sense of humor, requires the capacity for a modulated, non all-or-nothing investment in the self. We can only change the frame if we are not totally invested in this particular one. We must have the flexibility to contain variability, to dip back into earlier ways of experiencing things that are less tightly organized without wholly losing organization.

To say that self-observation involves taking a distance from ourselves is to say that we must be able to situate ourselves in an inner representational space that we share not only with others, but also with remembered, envisioned, and expected versions of ourselves. We must be able to see ourselves, at least temporarily, as if we were an other. The creation of the requisite internal representational space is no simple achievement, requiring a great deal of capacity for symbolization, a skill that starts in symbiotic attachment to another in very early childhood and is crucially involved in catalyzing the emergence from such enmeshment, even as the emergence from such enmeshment is crucial to its development. The capacity for self-observation may be one of the most important legacies of the individuation process.

To observe ourselves, we have to be able to separate ourselves sufficiently, not only from ourselves but from others, to use the others as reference points of comparison and contrast. Such a task of sufficient separation from past hoped-for, idealized, or devalued versions of ourselves calls for considerable resources in separating past, present, and future, passive and active, possible and impossible, as well as harsh and indulgent.

The fact that what we learn in the process of observing others is essential in observing ourselves, just as what we learn in observing ourselves is indispensable in observing others, has significant psychotherapeutic implications. As a matter of technique, we are at work in supporting the faculty of self-observation when we help our patients enlarge and refine their observations of others. It is not that they are avoiding the task of learning to see themselves, but that they are gaining essential skills through practice in a zone that is perhaps less threatening.

Of course, patients' observations of their therapists deserve support and validation for just this reason. Such observations have a special value. There is a regular progression, where an issue is discussed at safe remove in terms of the extratherapeutic world, then as a transference issue, and, finally, as an issue within the patient between different aspects and tendencies. It is really an internal design problem. The transference relationship thus serves as a privileged port of entry for material that needs to be accommodated within the self. Another way to say this is that the transference relationship is the gateway to consideration of self-transference.

To observe ourselves we have to take up a distance. Yet, for the observation to have an animated and animating quality, the distance cannot be too great. There are patients who speak a great deal of themselves but seem to have no idea either of whom they are talking or even that they are talking. Some patients talk of themselves as if they were mere things, without even noticing that they grant themselves no more vividity or initiative than is allowed an inanimate object. They have a form of what might be termed symbolic catatonia. Any inner mental movement beyond a very constricted range threatens disaster. Some patients are so enclosed in an attitude of contempt, embarrassment, or shame, which covers up a primitive and stilted grandiosity, that they cannot connect (or disconnect) enough from themselves to have a vital observing link. The development of a genuine self-observing function would require noting this and allowing for it, that is, not trying to eradicate it, but understanding how it works.

When we speak of self-observation, we are talking about more than watchfulness. We are talking about an observer who is not only *detached* but *attached* to the one who is being "watched." When young children talk of being "watched," of being "seen," of being "looked at," they often mean something that would more aptly be described as being "invested," regarded as having value and being worth being noticed and cared for.

This stops far short of ownership or control, but represents a real response, one that contributes to inner responsiveness, whether directed to the self as an object or to other objects. This sense that someone is watching, that someone is there in a living sense, that someone is, as the telling phrase goes, "looking out" for one is an important component of the internal sense of safety that lets us feel that we can trust ourselves enough to explore ourselves. When we talk about self-observation we mean that the self both serves and conserves itself as an object.

SELF-OBSERVATION AS A TRANSITIONAL FUNCTION

Winnicott (1953) spoke of the transitional object—the blanket or the teddy bear—as the first "not me" possession. He emphasized a process that is simultaneously linking and separating, one that produces a "middle space" or "third space" where certain paradoxes—as, for example, whether something is created or discovered, found or given—need not be resolved. When we note that a central requirement of self-observation is the capacity to place the self in a mental representational space shared with others and subject to a set of common rules and organizing concepts, we are noticing that self-observation relativizes the self. It enriches it in relations and connections, which increases both its definition and its distinctiveness, while at the same time opening up a new horizon for further such gains in form.

It looks at the self as if it were "me" and yet simultaneously "not quite me" or "not entirely me" or "not yet me" or "no longer me." It brings the self into question. Another way of putting it is that it introduces the leaven of uncertainty (or should we say "choice") into the self, so as to make of the self more a set of questions and less a set of answers.

"You know, my father doesn't approve of therapy. He never has. He keeps asking me what therapy does for me. It's not the right question, but it's very hard to answer. I've thought about it a lot. I think that I use therapy to try to find the thread of myself. Once I find the thread, then I can follow it where it leads. My father wouldn't ever understand this."

For this young man, therapy has represented a way to find a thread ("thread" used here as the insignia or emblem for a very complicated dynamic process) that will lead him through a variety of different spaces, places, experiences, hopes, and disillusionments. He sees himself as looking *at* himself and *for* himself so as to be able to make transitions *in* himself and *as* himself. Whenever we describe something about ourselves, we introduce a potential space between it and ourselves. We objectify a part to stretch the whole. This may be frightening because what will later become part of the whole may be experienced at first as just a hole. To put a quality into words, to describe how we do something or feel something, is already to enter a neighborhood where other qualities, other ways of doing or feeling live. It is to introduce a new dimension of at least potential sociability, by which we mean the chance to interact, both internally and externally to the self, allowing for new learning of the kind that changes the patterning of the self.

Winnicott's concern with early transitional process can be described as a concern with how very young children use illusions to move simultaneously away from the previous form of relationship with their mothers and toward future forms of relationship not just with their mothers, but with themselves. The change in the form of the relating is every bit as important as the change in the object. A young child has a very rich and changing relationship with his transitional object, especially if the transitional object and process are invested and respected but not appropriated from the side of the mother. The favored object does what the child wants to do and fears to do. It feels what the child feels, what the child can not avow feeling, what the child wishes and fears to feel. It helps the child complement and extend the scope not just of his relationship with others, but with his own self.

"I hate Seal," said a 2-year-old angrily. When asked why she hated Seal, she replied, smiling and hugging Seal, "Because I love him," as if this were the most obvious thing in the whole world. Like self-observation, this early relationship with the transitional object is a dynamic process that not only goes back and forth but changes the nature of the back and forth as it does so. The use of the transitional process to master splitting can be seen in the quick flicker between attitudes that may eventually lead to blending, much as a swift enough succession of images produces the illusion of continuous motion.

What we call self-observation may be thought of as a developmental continuation of transitional processes in which what has been added on includes more capacity for complex symbolization and greater cognitive reach and clarifying power. All of this serves the capacity to move back and forth from the concrete to the abstract and from the literal to the symbolic.

We are now in a position to pause and look back at the question we asked earlier: "How do we move from place to place, from position to position, from disposition to disposition within ourselves?" A part of the answer lies in the faculty of self-observation, what we might perhaps better term the *transitional* faculty of self-observation. To see where one is, one cannot be 100 percent there. At least a tiny part of oneself must be far enough away to see, to name, to begin to wonder, to make at least a portion of a map. To put this in terms of a different arithmetical metaphor, a process of benign doubling that enables one to keep oneself company, converse with oneself, and, eventually, convert oneself has already to have been set in motion. We might even go so far as to describe self-observation as a form of self-participation from an inner distance that increases the capacity for abstraction and metaphor. We should note here that movement and physical action and sensation can be abstract and metaphorical as well as concrete and literal.

When a patient says something like, "I can see what I'm like. I can see how I go about things. I can see the part I play in making all this happen, but there is no hope of it ever changing," a hope of change, however thinly disguised behind the veil of fervent negation, is already there. Even when a patient says, "I have no idea who I am," the self-observation has a defining and constituting function. This does not mean that the change or the self-definition will be radical or swift. But it does mean that the patient has invested a part of himself in a project of change, which is already a major modification in internal process.

"I hate to see how mean I can be," said a young borderline patient, quite oblivious to how mean she was being to herself with the flavor of her self-observation. "I don't like to see myself that way or anyone else that way. It's too scary. Besides, I like the pleasure of being so righteous, even though I hate it when other people are self-righteous." A statement like this one shows a patient who, after many years of therapy, has achieved the capacity for significant intrapsychic contained and sustained conflict about a variety of her fundamental dispositions. In many borderline patients, the capacity to experience internal conflicts, as opposed to conflicts with the environment on the basis of splitting, externalization, and projective identification, is a major and hopeful developmental achievement. Also, as the patients point out over and over, it is a very painful one.

Conflict and conflict resolution depend crucially on self-observation, which may be phrased in words or in graphic, musical, or kinetic form as in dance. Self-observation abstracts from and organizes the flux of experience, showing the patient that he is more complicated than he thought, but that the complexity can be articulated. It shows him that there is more clamoring to be contained inside and that, through a project of remodeling and reorganizing, he may discover further aspects of self-experience that he may not previously have conceived as possible.

In some patients it is possible to see the relationship between transitional process, self-observation, and opportunities for transitions to new states of self quite clearly.

A young borderline woman, burdened also with a serious neurological illness and substance abuse problems, had made numerous suicide attempts in the context of deteriorating relationships with others who were at least as disturbed as herself. She had had periods both in and out of the hospital of being totally out of control. Her alcoholic and musical father had been the source of severe disturbance in the family and, on at least one occasion, had assaulted her murderously.

As an inpatient, she had a very hard time talking in therapy. She seemed miserable in her silence, yet unable to break it, as if it were a prison from which she could imagine no escape. The silence was part of a negativistic presentation that clued her therapist in not only to the fervor and furor of her dependency needs, but also to her terror of losing herself through merger. The negativism held at bay a repeat of a predicament she had found herself in over and over again with her lovers: violent attachment gave way to violent disengagement, bringing intense and life-threatening suicidal action in its wake.

The silence went on for a long time. Her therapist made a number of experimental efforts to open a channel of communication and was rebuffed over and over again. After some weeks, he had become more or less resigned to this agitated and provocative withholding silence. One day he said, ''I just wonder what goes through your mind while you're sitting there.'' She said that nothing went through her mind. Her therapist responded skeptically. When she said that she wasn't thinking about anything, he replied, a bit caustically, that it would be quite an achievement to have nothing going through one's mind. The patient replied that she didn't have any words and said that she had heard that psychotherapy was talking therapy. As she didn't have words in her mind and couldn't talk, she had been sitting there feeling terrible, a failure at therapy from the outset.

Her therapist persisted in inquiring what went on in her mind, feeling a bit sadistic as he did so. She said that she didn't hear words. She heard tunes, but was certain that her therapist wouldn't have any interest in these, because therapy was about talking, not about tunes. The therapist replied that, even though he couldn't carry a tune, he was indeed very interested in the tunes that went through her head. Much later on, he realized that his remark about not being able to carry a tune served the useful purpose of distinguishing him not just from her but from her father. It represented unconscious cooperation on his part with her negativisitic defensive style.

The patient had had a promising career as a singer in clubs before the fateful intervention of her neurological disease. Going back as far as she could remember, music had been the only part of her life that had brought her satisfation. It seemed to soothe and protect her in times of despair and terror and was performing this function once again as she confronted a new male therapist who showed signs of wanting to get to know her. She was genuinely surprised that her therapist was interested in knowing about the tunes in her mind and wondered why none of her previous therapists had been similarly interested. Tellingly, she later described one therapist as being much too forward and scaring her by being too interested in her. Her worry was that his interest was sexualized. In conjunction with the discussion of the tunes she heard in her mind, she was even able to provide a few associations radiating from the music and from the lyrics.

Shortly after this recognition and acceptance of the place of her transitional process in therapy, she was able to contribute an observation of herself. "I had a light bulb," she said. What she meant, borrowing the visual idiom of the cartoons, was that she had had an idea. *Eidos* in Greek means vision, a picture, an illumination. Her pleasure in noticing was striking. Something of value had taken place within her, surprising her. Her light bulb was that she reacted on the ward just as she had at home.

The ward atmosphere reminded her of home, with one particularly loud and bullying patient playing the role of her father. The nursing staff played the role of her mother, always having too many to take care of and waiting to intervene until things were already out of control. As she had at home, the patient withdrew and, when her resentment at having to wait got too great, turned to hurting herself, both as accusation and as appeal. This "light bulb" was the beginning of her capacity to start to interact on the ward as if it were something other than home. In her case, feeling that she was, literally, at home made her feel anything but "at home" in the metaphorical sense of being comfortable. The "light bulb" opened the door to the idea that the ward did *not* have to be just like home and she did not have to be restricted to the experiences she had had at home. It shed a new light that let her see a choice in how to experience herself, which we can describe in terms of the resolution of a self-transference.

For the most part, borderline patients seem to take to psychotherapy as fish do to air, gasping, flopping, and thrashing about, seemingly at death's door. The element is new and they do not feel they have the necessary equipment to adapt. Therapy often feels life threatening to them because it takes them back over territory that has felt life threatening. Often it has been literally life threatening in a variety of ways.

An important part of the work in dealing with the protean and prolonged problems of the borderline patient is to help the patient find his way to observing something about himself that makes a difference to him. This can take years and require the surmounting of formidable obstacles, because such figuring out requires a well-developed capacity to use symbols to organize inner experience and some movement away from seeing the self concretely and literally. It requires a change in the tool kit that is available for shaping experience. This is a technological revolution that ranks in profundity with any in the history of the human race.

The patient who is able to make this sort of self-observation and to allow it to make a difference in a *feelingful* way has taken a significant step not just in getting the hang of psychotherapy. He has taken a step toward a new way of getting the hang of getting the hang of himself. The emergence of this kind of self-observational resource from the dynamic matrix of the transitional process signals a new form of relationship to the self. As the transitional process simultaneously links together and wedges apart self and object, so self-observation simultaneously links together and wedges apart self as subject and self as object.

ON PSYCHOSIS AND SUBLIMATION

Freud (1924) described psychosis as akin to a patch on "a rent in the ego" (p. 151). By this he meant that the psychosis was a kind of prosthetic device or process pressed into service to manage what the ego was not up to managing in a way that respected the demands of reality. In psychosis, the ego with its at least relatively more reality oriented policies, gives up hard won territory to the rule of more magical and idiosyncratic policies that are not so respectful of reality and the potential dangers of conflict with it.

By sublimation, Freud connoted processes that make possible the resolution of conflict without either a breach in the practical respect for reality or the burden and pain of the renunciation of cherished wishes. Sublimation has to do with the plasticity of desire. Under certain conditions we can change not just what we want, but who we want it from. An analogy could be made to a form of psychic punning: we take *this* for *that*, experiencing the same intensity from our satisfaction with *that* as if it were *this*, even though at another level, to which we also have access, we are quite well aware that *this* is not *that*. There is a disjunction of frames at one level and a conjunction at another.

Freud describes switches in the aim and object of a sexual urge and also describes such switches in regard to destructive urges. A crucial feature of most sublimatory processes is the replacement of a concrete literal satisfaction with a more abstract symbolic satisfaction. In sublimation, an instinct changes its aim and its object, allowing gratification without the burden of conflict recognition. Both what we want to do and who we want to do it with are changed.

The transformation is analogous to that by which some materials go from solid to gas without passing through the liquid state. A creative burst, which links and separates the new aim and object and the old aim and object, extends the territory of the ego. New territory is often claimed for the culture in intellectual and artistic pursuits as well. A more sublime and socially valued and approved aim and object replaces the old aim and object.[2]

This involves the use of illusions in a transitional process. What psychosis and sublimation have in common is the intense investment of illusions. For example, what Heidegger (1971) said of the work of art, that it possesses the capacity to world forth a world, can be said as well of psychosis. We might be tempted to say that sublimation is psychosis in the service of the ego.

The capacity for sublimation may be a measure of the general combinatorial richness and flexibility of the ego, depending on the orchestration of many defenses, including passive into active, reaction formation, aim inhibition, idealisation, splitting, and repression. Coordinated operations in an internal symbolic space allow the ego to realize symbolic satisfactions that have undiminished intensity and flavor. Just as thought comes to be able to stand convincingly as experimental action, internal modelings of satisfactions, both erotic and destructive, develop the capacity to satisfy, even if they are symbolically displaced and disguised. The self develops a capacity to believe in itself without being deluded by itself. Play becomes the means by which desire is consummated without destructive disruption of reality.

In borderline patients, as in very young children, action commonly has to be viewed as experimental thought. Very literal and concrete simulations are required as platforms to explore possibilities. An analogy might be to the differences

---

2. For a helpful summary and outline of the complex place of the term "sublimation" in psychoanalytical discourse, see Laplanche and Pontalis (1973), pages 431–433.

between throwing oneself off a cliff, a test flight in an actual airplane, and hours in a flight simulator as ways to learn about flying. With borderline patients, much of the challenge is to take what is intended concretely and enacted literally by them not so literally and not so concretely. Potential delusions must be nudged repetitively in the direction of potential sublimations. The rehabilitation of play depends on a movement toward the more abstract, metaphorical, and mobile use of illusion.

A seriously ill borderline patient who was only tenuously maintaining herself as an outpatient came to therapy one day in an unusually agitated and shaken state. She could hardly sit still. She reported that her father had had a stroke and was seriously, possibly mortally ill. At her next session, she was in worse shape. She said that her father had died. She went into mourning and took time off from work. She expressed not just sadness and shock, but also anger along the lines of, "How could he do this to me without any warning?" Her therapist found himself feeling quite sympathetic toward her and worrying how she was going to maintain her tenuous functioning without slipping into the agitated suicidal states that had been such a trouble in the past.

In the course of almost a month, it came out that things were not quite what they seemed. One day, the patient said she was feeling terribly alone and hopeless, because it was not only her father who had died but her entire family. When her therapist wondered about this, she was adamant and indignant. Not only was she an orphan, but she hadn't a relation in the world. Her therapist was by now well aware that he had very little idea what was going on as opposed to what was reported, which was usual with this patient. He told her he was convinced that there was more to it than what she had said—or possibly less.

Over the next two weeks, corresponding to an improvement in the patient's mood and a return to work with slightly better functioning, a more sensible version emerged. The father had had a transient ischemic attack and been hospitalized. She had called to express her concern and he told her, brusquely as she experienced it, that he could not talk with her because the doctor was there. He asked her to call back, but she felt so rebuffed and hurt that she became enraged at him to the point where she regarded him as dead. When she stated her grievance against her father to her mother and siblings, they expressed little sympathy for her position, so the patient declared her whole family dead and deepened her mourning. Needless to say, as she broke all external contact with her father and her family, they were even more central in her thoughts and feelings than usual, illustrating a simultaneous linking and separating process.

Here we have the anatomy of one of those "minipsychotic" episodes that are said to characterize borderline patients. In response to intolerable hurt, rage, and longing, the patient invested an illusion so intensely that it became real for her. She conducted herself on the basis of this conviction so convincingly that it was difficult for outside observers to avoid being at least temporarily infected by her conviction. Since the patient was not able to accommodate any view of herself that included both her own murderousness and her longing to be close simultaneously, she had to see actual deaths where she had only wished for deaths. She was the kind of person who drove others away because she could not tell herself or them how much she missed them.

Of course, she was responding to a real predicament. Her father had been violent with her, beating her throughout her childhood. Her perception of him as extremely self-centered and unable to accommodate the needs of others or to respect their feelings was firmly grounded in reality. Nor had she received any more support or validation from the other members of the family as a child than she received in the current instance. The flight into temporary psychosis also probably protected her against the suicidal impulsivity that she had shown on previous occasions. In this regard, her therapist's temporary sharing of her delusion, an instance of his mistaking a metaphor for a literal statement, was probably a help. She put him in a position where he did offer her some of the validation and concern for her feelings that she so desperately missed in her development and that she could not supply from within.

If there was a transference event, a small slight or neglect on his part that felt abusive to her, that set this off, he was not able to find it with her. Perhaps it was in a certain ongoing guardedness on his part in crediting what she said literally that evoked for her the atmosphere of her childhood where her perceptions were disregarded. Certainly, though, with her psychotic episode, she brought both her rage and her need for closeness into therapy at one time, but split apart, the appeal for closeness directed to the therapist and the rage at her father. What is often missed about the borderline patient's minipsychotic episodes is that they are associated with efforts to move forward. The patient makes a forward moving assay and is then thrown back into a chaotic state when unable to deal with the progression–regression dilemma.

In contrast to this patient, Goethe was able, as a young man, to use his capacity to coin and invest coherent and harmonious illusions to good effect in resolving an internal impasse. When he found himself hopelessly in love with a married woman who was unavailable, he turned his attentions to the composition of *The Sorrows of Young Werther*, whose protagonist, Werther, was a young, lovesick, despairing fellow who found himself in a predicament that bore marked resemblances to Goethe's own in real life. Refusing to accept a compromise on his emotions, Werther commits suicide. Through *fantasy and illusion* Goethe was able to give free rein to his rage. In the fundamental hopeful irony of sublimation, Werther's suicide, founded in his refusal to compromise the intensity of his passion, actually represented the means for Goethe's effecting a real-life compromise. Werther's inability to tolerate rebuff and hurt showed Goethe's ability to tolerate, contain, and symbolize his own hurt and disillusionment. Goethe could have his curse and survive it, too. In fact, *The Sorrows of Young Werther* made Goethe's artistic reputation. We might say that destroying Werther in fantasy created Goethe in reality.

A number of young people, finding their own images reflected in *The Sorrows of Young Werther*, but unable to avoid the trap of taking reflection literally, actually committed suicide shortly after the book's publication (Hatfield 1963).[3] This illustrates how perilously thin the line between illusion and delusion can be.

Unlike the patient, Werther, or the suicides in the wake of the book, Goethe could include his own murderousness in himself, while simultaneously taking a step back and away from the inclusion. His ego could invent a symbolic alter on which he could vent his enraged hurt, making a virtue of his capacity to use *virtual* action in the service of *actual* emotional experience.

We enter here the vexed territory whose underside Shakepeare takes up in Hamlet's famous, "What's Hecuba to him or he to Hecuba . . ." soliloquy. What is fake and what is real? What is genuine expression and what is sham? How do we establish criteria of authenticity within ourselves? How should conscience and consciousness be related? As Goethe and Shakespeare both knew, art carries jest to the pinnacle of the serious.

Whereas psychosis represents the extreme investment of illusion to the detriment of the ego, sublimation represents an equally fervent investment of illusion for the benefit

---

3. For a novelist's treatment, see Thomas Mann's *Lotte In Weimar*, recently back in print, University of California Press, 1990.

of the ego. Whereas the first, psychosis, *deranges*, sublimation *rearranges*. What makes the difference in the capacity to put illusion to one or another of these uses? Certainly transitional process, the ability to use symbols in the service of self-organization and reorganization, are crucial. Well before Winnicott, Freud reported watching his grandson, then 18 months old, play with his toys and, particularly, a wooden reel and piece of string in the absence of his mother, whose leaving he habitually did not protest (1920). The little boy threw the object and then reeled it back in, showing intense, apparently pleasurable interest in both aspects of the game. He was working on the problem that confronted him in real life in what has to be regarded as, if not a symbolic dimension, at least a protosymbolic dimension. Rather than being passive and helpless, he was active and in control. He sent the object away in what can be interpreted in our terms not just as a vengeful getting rid of, but a defense against an internal merger danger. He brought it back in what can be interpreted as a defense against loss. Freud remarked on his grandson's pleasure in both aspects of the game.

Freud's grandson used play and illusion to orchestrate a considerable number of internal maneuvers, not just as a comfort in a threatening situation but in the service of increased mastery and internal differentiation. Anyone who has watched a child of this age or just a bit older fall apart and lose functional capacity—including, literally, balance on occasion, if mother is absent just a bit too long—not to mention anyone who has watched a borderline patient in the face of a separation, will appreciate the crucial importance of this kind of inner resourcefulness.

Transitional process, play, the use of illusion to extend the scope of the capacity to understand and cope, the development of the capacity to invest symbols without breaking links with essential realities, the achievement of the capacity for self-observation from a position at once attached and detached—all these go towards the ability to use sublimation instead of being used by psychosis. It is possible that sublimation changes the nature of the self of the sublimator, so that what lies beyond the pleasure principle is not a state of extinction of stimulation, but a state in which the literal makes less difference and the symbolic more, so that the threat of stimulation is decreased in proportion as the promise of simulation is increased. To put it another way, the faculty of simulation confers a certain sovereignty over stimulation.

A delusion, after all, is an illusion that has us rather than we it. The sublimatory use of illusion is not a matter only or even principally of the creation of works of art. To overvalue works of art is to fall into a form of idolatry that devalues what is probably much more important, the ongoing, everyday uses of sublimatory illusion to make possible amalgams of comfort and vitality, being linked and differentiated that lead to some sense of being "at home" in the world in a different way than that experienced by the patients discussed here.

ON EMPTINESS, MONOTONY, AND
SOLITARY CONFINEMENT

After this long excursus, we can return to our starting point. Why do borderline patients protest that they are empty nobodies? What do their claims mean? How can we go about conceiving a strategy for therapeutically useful responses?

We have discussed the crucial role of self-observation in making possible transitions from one sector of the self to another. From our point of view, self-observation, an outgrowth of transitional processes, represents a living internal relationship within the self in which the self takes itself as an object. It is both linked and separated from itself, both attached and detached. An internal potential space makes an enriching dialogue possible.

It is not simply a question of "I" statements. The patient who says repetitively, "I am the worst patient," shows a constricted capacity for self-observation. It is an advance beyond saying nothing, but still most eloquent of what cannot be said, noted, or admitted into the self. It reflects how much difficulty he has in self-observation and probably his limited capacity for play. It is terribly all-or-nothing in form.

A living, vital, self-observing relationship with themselves is precisely what is missing in borderline patients. They are blind to themselves, or deaf, or perhaps internally mute. Or perhaps it is a matter of all this together. If every communication has two loops, one toward an object and one back to the self, it is this recursive self-challenging and self-enriching loop that borderline patients are missing. This was well illustrated by the patient Mrs. D., who noted that she had thought of her drawings in art therapy principally as a means to "entertain" the art therapist, as if the only possibility of a response could be one from outside herself.

It is common for therapists to have the sense that there is so much substance to borderline patients and that the patients are deliberately and viciously frustrating them by refusing to recognize and utilize this. We can experience them as actively nihilistic, stuck in very narrow, monotonous and, above all, bleak internal solitary confinements. We feel like missing links to realms of experience that are at once so near and so far. We may also feel, complementarily, that we are unable to help the patient extricate himself from realms of experience that are also so near and yet out of reach of observation by the patient.

This perception that what is missing is so near and so far is substantially correct.

Another patient noted after four years of therapy, during which she was also very active in Alcoholics

Anonymous, that her craving for alcohol, while still present, did not bother her as intensely and actively as it had through years and years of chaotically monotonous turmoil. She said that, instead, she felt sad all the time, especially when she thought about or had actual contact with her extremely disturbed mother. She said that she understood why she had spent so many years avoiding this kind of experience and she had a keen sense that, if the cure was better than the disease, it was a very close horse race indeed.

When we admit a new feeling, in this case sadness, we are facing the task of accommodating within ourselves some aspect of ourselves that we had previously been able to store at least partially outside. What is so painful about letting go is that it requires that we take hold of ourselves in a new way. It may sound paradoxical, but one of the major difficulties of any separation is that it involves a new reunion with ourselves, one that calls us into question and requires of us significant internal reorganization. We have to find ourselves anew, and this discovery is, inevitably, of a self that is at least partially new and unfamiliar. Similarly, any reunion, any new investment requires a new separation from an aspect of ourselves.

Because the borderline patient is so concrete, letting go and taking hold are both enormous problems. The borderline belief is that we have only what we can possess by clinging and controlling. Letting go relativizes, makes more abstract, and allows new things in. Borderline patients are glued so tightly to themselves that they cannot get the distance they need to appreciate themselves. They are not aware that what we truly have is not what we can possess by clinging and controlling, but that which we can let go so as to make possible refinding and refining both in the outside world and in the internal world of representation and illusion.

Clinging and controlling close off the potential space of

experience. They prevent the experience of response that borderline patients hunger for, not just from outside, but even more importantly from the inside. They hunger for response precisely *because* they deny it to themselves. Whatever the historical antecedents of this denial, we encounter it as a living force in therapeutic interaction with these patients.

Borderline patients, with much justice, are terrified of what will come rushing in if they let go of the terribly constricted and confining views of themselves that they hold. They *are* the Pandora's boxes they fear to open. What comes upon them as they take the risk of relaxing their strangleholds on themselves is at once old and new. It is old in the sense of having its roots in often traumatic pasts. It is new in the sense of never having been mastered, assimilated, understood, integrated. It has not become experience that is available to the self to be put to work to further self-chosen ends. It is unforgettable because unrememberable: "When I talk about it, it happens again, so I don't talk about it."

Treating borderline patients is not about rescuing them and having the vastly increased sense of effectiveness and self-esteem that comes from a rescue. Those who need this kind of thrill to protect against out-of-awareness despair in themselves find working with borderline patients an appalling experience. Treating borderline patients is more like sitting in a lifeboat afloat on freezing waters watching them tread water. Waves toss them about and pull them under, sometimes for so long it seems they will never come up again. The watching and the waiting and the attendant feelings of being ineffectual, cruel, and useless, feelings that reflect so much in the patients, go on a long time, while the patients' entire lives pass before their eyes and ours, not only in review but often in such a new view that it is shocking. Finally, it is the patient who must discover the combination of strokes that brings him to the lifeboat.

We can encourage, admonish, advise, nourish, model, disagree, dispute, discuss each scene as it comes up, help the patient make links, but the patient's autonomy remains fundamental. The patient has to be the one who takes the decisive steps of rearranging the internal relationship with himself so that it is not too close/too far but allows for a nearness with enough separateness to allow for caring inner communication, inner modulation and inner remodeling. The patient must learn to dwell in himself.

Because of their incapacity in bounding, modulating, naming, symbolizing, and playing with inner experiences, borderline patients *are nonentities for themselves*. Before their distinct sense of a relationship to a nobody, someone who is fundamentally *not there to himself* can change borderline patients' need to discover/create an internal process of discovering/creating themselves. One borderline patient who had had twenty-six years of treatment said she knew there were no shortcuts, because there was nothing wonderful waiting to be discovered in her. Every little bit had to be built bit by bit. This was a severely ill patient, but one who is by no means unique. For others the road is a bit easier, the discovering/creating a bit richer. But it is important to respect the difficulty and devastation of the borderline patient's internal relationship to himself. Some simply do not make it.

A psychotherapeutic strategy for caring for borderline patients must take as its object the highly abstract goal of providing the resources that will facilitate broad, subtle, and profound changes in the patient's inner processes. It is not simply a matter of providing the patient an opportunity to "express" himself. The patient's "receptivity" toward himself is every bit as important. The patient needs to learn to "receive" himself as much as to "express." What therapy turns on is a set of cycles of putting out and taking in that involve both the therapist and the patient. The challenge is to create a holding environment that helps the patient get hold of himself in a new way, more symbolically, more abstractly, more receptively.

The borderline's complaint of emptiness does not mean

that there is an existing container that has nothing in it, but that the lack of containing processes makes it impossible to experience the self as having valid contents. Only the capacity for internal playfulness can lead beyond emptiness. By playfulness, we do not mean anything frivolous. Greek tragedy and Greek comedy both figure in a certain manner of play, a very serious playing indeed.

The long run chance of even a measure of contentment depends on creating/discovering internal holding processes. Change in the experience of the self depends on changes in the relationship between the self as subject and the self as object to allow both for greater linkage and greater separation.

8

Loneliness

TOWARD A DEFINITION OF LONELINESS

Loneliness is such a private privation that to try to discuss it is to feel a certain measure of diffidence. Loneliness is different at different times of life. A 2-year-old, a 5-year-old, an adolescent, someone in young adulthood, someone in middle age, and someone in old age experience different kinds of loneliness. Each type deserves study in its own terms with careful attention to developmental and historical contexts. The loneliness that comes as a person confronts the possibility that a cherished wish will never come to pass is different than the loneliness that comes as someone confronts the certainty that a particularly cherished love will never come again. A discussion of loneliness must be tentative to respect the complexity and diversity of the family of affective experiences collected under the rubric "loneliness."

That loneliness is little discussed although much felt already testifies to the difficulty of the discussion. To try to discuss it is already to *feel* a little lonely. It is to bring to mind our own feelings of loneliness, past and present, and also our feelings in regard to those whom we have known and for whom we have cared who have suffered with loneliness. When we start to think and feel about loneliness, overtones of mistrust and lack of self-confidence enter the discussion. An intuition of a fundamental vulnerability at the very core of being human attends any discussion of loneliness. The experience of loneliness and the shaming question, "What is wrong with me that makes me unloveable?" are closely linked.

All individual thinking and feeling may invoke some loneliness in that to think and feel as individuals we have to withdraw just a little bit from others, both actually and in the internal world. When we think and feel for ourselves and as ourselves we encounter a losing danger. Insofar as our thinking and feeling for ourselves and as ourselves changes us, it brings change into our relationships with others, both as we enact them in the external world and as we imagine them in the internal world.

Loneliness is one of the central concerns of many borderline patients. It is not uncommon for a borderline patient to feel so threatened by even the inward experience of a feeling that belongs authentically to him that he avoids any awareness of such experience for fear that it will entrain terrible loss. This can make treatment very difficult, especially when this dynamic operates stealthily, so that so much is left out. In a sense a patient like this has a difficulty even achieving loneliness. He is in a state where even the capacity to miss is missing.

Loneliness may be thought of as a name for a family of related affective states that emerge in response to the risks involved when a person has to change his method for relating to objects, including himself as an object. As one prototype of this kind of risk situation, we can take the predicament that confronts an adolescent when he has to move from relying so heavily on his parents to being more sufficient within himself. This developmental task brings the teenager onto ground where the losing and the fusing dangers are both heightened. As the teenager pulls away from his parents, the loss accentuates urges for closeness of kinds that threaten the very work that he is undertaking. Adolescents commonly have the experience of careening from states in which they feel much too far from their parents to ones in which they feel much too close. Of course, an adolescent's experience draws on all his developmental achievements and all his previous developmental vulnerabilities. It is at once new and not new.

A tentative definition of loneliness might be that loneliness is a state of object relatedness in which the lack of the object is experienced as a threat to the self. Loneliness is an affective state that involves relatedness. It represents a developmental achievement in that feeling has been attained, but the feeling is painful. It is a state with a certain stability, and as such, it may protect against much deeper pain and disorganization. Becoming less lonely often involves a progression–regression dilemma, in that the first steps forward may seem indistinguishable from a plunge into past terrors.

It is often striking how intensely related to objects within himself the lonely person is. In loneliness the problem of relating to objects is one that can be so consuming that it leaves very little room for anything else. The lonely person may be figuratively glued to internal objects from which he cannot achieve enough separation to allow any satisfaction. When we describe loneliness as an affective state of object relatedness in which the lack of the object is experienced as a threat to the self, the phrase "lack of the object" is ambiguous. When a lonely person talks, he tends to talk about lacking the object, rather than about a lack that he is experiencing in the object in the sense of a deficiency in the object that causes him pain.

Often the lonely person is defending an idealized internal object by withdrawing from all that brings to mind the object's lacks and so brings on the terrible fervor of his blaming and resentment. The idealization is necessary precisely because of the opposing devaluing trends, which often have a firm basis in reality. A familiar depressive introjective dynamic is at work, founded in the lack of consolidation of boundaries between self and object representations. Of course, the availability of objects with some empathic capacity in reality is an important part of providing the chance to consolidate boundaries between self and object representations. Attempting to quote the young boy who said, "Mother, I hate you: everything I do, you blame on me," a patient came up with the marvelous slip, "Mother, I hate you: everything you do, I blame on me."

In loneliness the self is threatened and painfully aware of the threat. Lonely people are commonly worried about very serious disorganization within themselves. A complaint of loneliness is no small complaint and it should, as a matter of course, alert us to a very high level of internal danger. Selves need others in virtually all they can do or become. The lonely person complains of something that is, at least metaphorically, akin to a lack of oxygen. What is missing produces serious developmental impasses.

CLINICAL ISSUES

In an earlier chapter, we discussed a borderline patient who, after an effort to assert her own autonomy vis-à-vis her mother, suffered serious injuries when she was struck by a car while she was crossing the street on foot. After he heard about the accident, her therapist went down to the emergency room to see her. She had been given no pain medication because of the worry that she might have sustained a concussion in the accident. She had fractures both of the collar bone and of the leg.

Much to her therapist's astonishment, she told him very calmly that the physical pain was not a problem. It hurt, and that was all there was to it. However, as she told him that she could not stand how lonely she felt when they left her all by herself in the treatment room, she burst into shaking sobs. Her therapist had the sense that the physical pain, like the cutting that she did, actually helped her to organize psychologically. It seemed to reassure her of her ongoing existence and her capacity to feel. Being left alone, on the other hand, brought with it a terror she could not withstand. It threatened the ongoingness of her self.

A compound fracture of the leg required that she stay in the hospital for an operation to insert a pin. She had a paranoid reaction to the nurses, and especially at night, felt that they made her wait too long for everything because they wanted to torture her. This read back to childhood feelings that her indomitably martyred mother, preoccupied with sick and difficult boys, including her alcoholic abusive father, always made her wait too long.

The mother had seen her as an extension of herself and expected a forbearance and patience from her only daughter that she sought nowhere else. She later confirmed this to the patient, who was shocked because she was unused to any kind of validation of her own feelings. She found the confirmation a mixture of relief and disillusionment, because she had long hoped against hope that what she asserted would somehow turn out not to have been so. In a sense many of her angriest assertions were in the service of a deeper denial.

Irritated with what they saw as her highly critical and unfairly demanding posture, the nurses moved her into a room by herself that was farther away from the nursing station. This intensified her loneliness to the point where she was cursing and threatening in the style of her father, as if she could find no other comfort. Her therapist, who was making virtually daily visits to the ward to talk both with her and with the nurses, helped her to ask for a roommate. She was moved in with a debilitated elderly woman who had a hip fracture and was more helpless than she. Adopting a protective attitude toward this elderly woman, she did much better with the nurses. By projecting her own helplessness and terror onto this elderly woman, then adopting the attitude toward it that she wished others would take toward her own helpless feelings, she found a much less frightening position. The nurses appreciated her helpfulness and spoke of how much better she was doing. It was as if she were once more joined to her mother as an adjunct in a caretaking task.

After a week in the hospital, she told her therapist that she had not yet looked in the mirror. Her therapist asked why, and she replied that she was not able to face it. She knew she looked hideous and could not bear the thought of what she would feel when she saw herself. Her therapist helped her to find a mirror and to look in it. The patient was surprised that she did not look as bad as she had expected. She had had the idea that no one could possibly bear to be with her because of how awful she looked. Once she had looked in the mirror and saw that her ugliness was in her fantasy, it was as if she had reestablished a connection with herself that had been shattered in the accident and its aftermath. She was on a bit better terms with herself and so able to allow others a nearer access to her.

How do patients like this one come to be so vulnerable to loneliness? What strategies offer some promise of helping such patients assuage their loneliness? Loneliness is not a matter of the behavioral state of being alone. Rather, it depends on the entire drama of experience with others that is performed within a person, whether or not the person is physically alone. Representations of others pervade the fantasy lives in which we are continuously immersed. As borderline patients regularly report, the most excruciating loneliness can occur in the midst of others, along the lines of, "Water, water, everywhere and not a drop to drink."

One important practical test of whether mothering has been good enough for a particular child is whether the child has been able to learn to soothe and stimulate himself appropriately with illusions that take off from, extend, and transform the character of experience with the literally present, active, and receptive mother. In other words, a test of good enough mothering is whether the mother has been able to support the development of robust transitional object relations and transitional processes in the child. The child has to be both met and left alone in a rhythm of graded intensities, so that he learns to be with himself when he is alone.

Another one of Winnicott's paradoxical formulations (1958) has to do with the developmental sequence leading to the capacity to be alone, or, to put it another way, the capacity to experience solitude rather than loneliness. Solitude is really a very pleasurable state, representing not just a freedom from external impingements but a sense of inner sufficiency. Of course, it is also true, as we shall discuss later, that pleasure confers an element of being on one's own that, while it is essential to solitude, may also carry with it a risk of feeling so lonely and deprived that this risk may provide the grounds for avoiding pleasure.

Winnicott says that the capacity to be alone, to enjoy one's own company in solitude, must rest on a primordial experience of being alone in the presence of another person. What does this mean? We think that Winnicott means to suggest that it is a mother's job to tend the emerging border between herself and her child with a tact and moderation that includes a measure of error that allows her baby or toddler to become centered in himself as she, the mother, remains centered in herself, even though she is available to the child and committed to the child. But the commitment is to a relationship with the child as a separating human being. As a patient put it, "A mother's job is to love herself enough so that she can take care of her baby. It's a free deal."

In our terms, being alone in the presence of another person is a way of describing being able to cope simultaneously with the losing and the fusing danger. The mother's presence provides safety against the losing danger. Her capacity to leave the child alone in her presence provides safety from the fusing danger.

Borderline patients are so often castigated for being dependent, whining, clinging, demanding, entitled, and so forth. In fact, there is a whole host of adjectives of a pejorative nature that are regularly applied to borderlines. Many psychiatrists now believe and assert with great fervor and righteousness that borderline patients are not simply beyond treatment but beyond redemption. We do not mean to imply that borderline patients are not whining, clinging, and demanding. The pejorative litany is founded in clinical experience. Nor do we mean to suggest that clinicians stop complaining. The complaining serves a holding function for those who are trying to sustain difficult work. It is important to stay in touch with the feelings inside ourselves that correspond to what the patients struggle with. However, when these feelings provide the underpinnings for attitudes that seek to deny treatment to patients because of qualities that are in the patient, we must wonder whether we are not in the presence of a countertransference containment failure that recapitulates the patients' earlier experiences only too well.

What so easily gets lost is the actual experience these patients have had of being continually pushed away, rejected, and ignored, or, at the other extreme, intensely and intrusively dictated to, rushed, overwhelmed, used, and abused. So many of our patients have had little experience of being valued for themselves as separate and separating individuals who have something to offer. Their needs have so often been subsumed under the needs of others. The danger of neglect is that it leaves the child so alone in the face of urges that are heightened by enormous levels of frustration. With many borderline patients, as we know them over years, we become more and more impressed by the fact that they have survived at all.

A patient who had had an extremely anxious, intrusive, and demanding mother who had regarded his developmental milestones as her achievements said, "I can't stand to be around other people. I can't stand to be around any other people, because when I'm around other people I just don't know what is going on. I can't do things that I can do when I'm alone. I can't even tell you what's wrong with me. That's how confused I am. I'm afraid to be around anyone and I'm very lonely, because I like people."

Young children who are subject to a projective barrage that tells them what they must be if they are to have a claim on any care or attention have an experience of loneliness that is so profound as often to be unrepresentable. Often, parents of borderline patients have used their children in a way that suggests that the patients were enlisted into service as concrete transitional objects for their parents, who were stuck at this level of development in regard to many significant affects. Physical battering of children can often represent an effort on the parent's part to manage affects that the parent has experienced as unbearable. Certainly sexual abuse can have a similar dynamic, namely, to make the child the receptacle for unbearable shame.

Physical and sexual abuse are common themes in the treatment of borderline patients. So are separations that are so long, so unprepared for, and so without succor that they qualify as abandonments. Experiences of physical and sexual abuse have the special quality that they are concrete and overwhelming bodily experiences. They often have a near

annihilatory quality that produces an experience of loneliness under the most extreme circumstances. These experiences can have the continuing force of malevolent revelation
as their objects, so often in isolation and secrecy, struggle
with the fact that they have had their own vulnerability
underscored in an unmistakable fashion and their own
helplessness made so clear.

They feel they know two things. First, they know that
they cannot count on others, professions of helpfulness
being grounds for terrible mistrust. Second, they know thay
cannot count on themselves, because they have known
themselves powerless to prevent the near annihilation they
have already experienced and powerless to manage the urges
that come in the wake of this experience. A great deal of
self-reproach about traumatic experiences is elaborated to
protect against the feelings of helplessness and vulnerability,
the abject condition of not being heard. Better to feel guilty
than to face how little power you had. These abusive
experiences have a terrible impact on the narcissistic balance
of the patient.

This dark and shaming knowing based on actual misfortune heightens the inner sense of vulnerability and the need
to defend against it with a variety of strategems, including
hurting before being hurt, leaving before being left, and so
forth. It is as if the part that knows whispers always to the
other parts inside, frustrating involvement with others because others cannot be trusted, preventing even the utilization of what resources the patient does have to connect and
construct because these have already been shown to be so
shamefully and woefully inadequate.

The lonely borderline patients have not had the experience of a tactful tending of their emerging boundaries with
others. That is why contact is so hard for them. Availability
without intrusion is not familiar to them. If they are dependent, it is in large part because they have experienced so
little that is dependable. If they whine, it is because need
brings fear in its wake. If they cling it is because they have

had to hold on so hard to an evasive object. If they demand, it is because they have had so little experience of the mutuality of asking and receiving.

The borderline patient who had the accident and then was terrified of being left alone in the emergency room was a marginally invested child. She arrived at the baptismal font without a name. Her mother was stunned to hear one issue forth from the father's mouth in response to the priest's question. Yet not only had the mother allowed the situation to get to that point, she did not raise a protest about it until many years later. This story is important not so much in itself but because it can serve as an emblem of so much of her childhood experience. When the patient reacted in a paranoid way to the nurses in the hospital, this represented a familiar way of trying to remain involved with others.

When this patient worked as a volunteer in a day care center she reported regularly on the children who were not being noticed by the regular staff. Her envy of the more aggressive ones, the ones who were "the squeaky wheels who got the grease," was passionate. She pointed out to her therapist that for her to be bothered by loneliness and to have trouble with what she felt when she was alone was already a major improvement, for it showed that she was not so withdrawn into her shell. She contrasted this with her use of alcohol and drugs during high school in order to numb herself and withdraw from a reality she found too painful.

She drew a vivid portrait of herself as an elementary school student in Catholic school. Learning, she said, was so difficult for her because all she thought about was going to hell if she committed the least transgression. She was so frightened by this that she often had no idea what was going on in the classroom around her. Certainly, she did not dare ask a question. This was the best that she could do in keeping herself company. "I got," she said, "that S+ in deportment each time but not much else." After a few years out of the hospital, when she had begun to interact a bit more, she bought an "I Survived Catholic School" sticker, which she displayed proudly on her guitar case. Still, she projected so much of her rage onto others that she kept herself largely sealed off from others.

Four years after a suicide attempt that brought him to treatment, first briefly as an inpatient and then as an outpatient, a late adolescent patient was much concerned with getting some internal space from his insecure, critical, bullying father and his insecure, conscience-ridden, seductive mother. "I've got so much junk inside me that there really isn't any room for me at all. I'm lonely all the time because I miss myself," he observed.

This patient was terrified of his own rage, displacing it onto a host of phobic objects. He had previously formulated and brought to therapy the palindrome, "Ma is as selfless as I am," which he then simplified a few sessions later to "Ma is as I am." These palindromes showed his intuition that his problems with feeling secure in himself were related to his mother's similar problems, as well as an awareness of how much difficulty he had distinguishing himself from his mother.

The junk he referred to was various notions and convictions he had gotten about himself in interactions with his parents. He had already been able to test some of these and call others into question. What he was able to put into words so strikingly is that the lonely person is most often a very crowded person, who has very little room to maneuver within. This particular patient was even able to recognize that what was so hard about getting rid of the junk to make more room for himself was that there was much that was of value and much that was very dear to him mixed in with all the junk. Mere "getting rid of" was not going to suffice.

So many lonely patients are so harsh with themselves that they are truly monstrous to themselves. One can compare this harsh inner presence to a teddy bear, which is desperately needed despite its capacity to maul because of the internal threats of deeper states of exclusion or abandonment or abolition through merger. The internal struggle that is so painful represents a negativistic way of relating in the world of internal objects, bringing loneliness in its wake because it is such a consuming struggle that it leaves little margin for progression beyond it.

Loneliness at least represents the urge to move to another way of relating to objects, both intrapsychically and interpersonally. Often borderline patients begin to complain more and more of loneliness as their attachment to treatment deepens. This apparently paradoxical result makes sense once we realize that often the provision of something makes clear a previous lack and so deepens the pain of it. The man emerging from a desert where he has been wandering parched and near despair may suffer a moment's intense confusion when offered a drink of water. He struggles to master the urge to assault the one who offers the water because this succor has been so long in coming.

If, then, the lonely person is inaccessible from within, sealed off by illusory fears or fearful illusions that in turn protect against still deeper and darker fears and disillusionments, how can we go about being of use? First of all, it helps to recognize that the kinds of loneliness we have been discussing are profound problems not amenable to prescription and intrusion. The lonely person has come to the point where his dilemma is that he is painfully aware of his discontent with what we can term his own way of keeping himself company, yet also painfully aware of his difficulty in finding another way.

It is only too common for interested others to offer behavioral prescriptions along the lines of, "You should make friends," "You should go to the movies," "You should become involved in community activities," "You should give people more of a chance than you do," "You should have more self-confidence." These apparently well-intentioned prescriptions have an undermining quality. The "shoulds" highlight the patient's sense of a lack. If it were that easy, the patients would already have done it. Usually it is not that the lonely person has not thought about all this and more. What prescriptions, especially those of a concrete and behavioral cast, leave out is the essential problem of intrapsychic blockade. Other forms of access to others are blocked off by the consuming inner preoccupation with warding off the losing and fusing dangers.

One of the keys to being of use to the lonely patient is to leave the patient alone. This returns us to the terrain of Winnicott's paradox (1958), because the other key is to be present with the patient while we are in the process of leaving the patient alone. The person who attempts to be of use to a lonely patient may reliably expect to experience two intense and contrasting pressures. One is to be remote and poorly attuned to the point of near total deafness. The other is to be intrusive and to rush in with all manner of misconceived and ill-timed comfort, advice, admonitions and censure.

Nor is it clear that either of these two classes of dangers can be avoided. To avoid them is to avoid bringing the inadequacies of the objects that the patient has known into the treatment as current transferential reality. Many therapists are much more willing to assume the mantle of the good object than the cloak of the bad or threatening object. Perhaps this is why so many of us are shocked when we realize the degree of anger and abuse we have to absorb from patients in the course of a career.

While the paired and opposed dangers of the therapist's being too aloof and too intrusive cannot be avoided, they can, however, be monitored, discussed, and understood in the context of repetitions of patterns from earlier in the patient's life. This kind of monitoring, discussion, and search for understanding introduces a new element. It represents a different kind of relationship with a potential for helping the patient to develop a capacity to use symbolic expression to make more tactful and reliable contact, not just with others but also with himself.

Symbolic processes are very disturbed in many patients who are lonely. Many borderline patients are able to use symbols extremely adeptly to refer to elements outside themselves, and, when we compare their performance in using symbols with the performance of others, they often seem outstanding. They can put together extremely complex and nuanced strings of symbols with marvelous technical skill. We might even notice that they use symbols to refer to what we would think of as elements within themselves, as if these elements were outside themselves. Symbol using has an evacuative function, a "getting rid of" job to perform. Very impressive intellectual achievements of real and undeniable worth can be the result of these processes. Nor do these observations apply only to the use of words or scientific and mathematical symbols. Visual art, music, dance, and other pursuits like athletics, gardening, and building can all be used in this way.

When we look, however, not at the performance aspect of the borderline patient's symbol use, but at the way in which the symbols can be used to help the patient come to grip with inner problems, the way in which the symbols are available to pattern the patient and give him reliable inner shape and form, the picture that emerges is very different. The loop in symbol using that carries a feelingful message back to the user is undeveloped. It is as if the one who played the piano were unable to hear the music at all, certainly unable to respond to the feeling that he put into it. It is the in-forming feature of symbol use that is underdeveloped.

Particularly in the so-called higher functioning borderline patient, this gap is of signal importance. These patients can show the dilemma of being sometimes too aloof from their symbolic productions to understand their feelingful relevance to themselves and, on other occasions, especially when angry or frightened, so concrete that for them symbols do not stand for anything but are used to enact the drama of their feelings on someone else. Biting words are so common in dealing with these patients.

One way in which expressive therapies like art and dance therapy are of special use with these patients is in helping them question and revalue their use of symbols, taking the emphasis off performance and putting it on questions like, "How do you feel when you look at what you have drawn?," "How do you move when you feel this way?," "What does the way you move now suggest to you about how you might be feeling?" These questions need not be asked explicitly at every juncture. They can be implicit in the kind of attention paid by the art or dance therapist. Again, the issues of tact and contact come to the fore.

Both the late adolescent patient who constructed the palindromes, "Ma is as selfless as I am," and "Ma is as I am," and his therapist regarded their construction as an important event in the therapy and brought them up for discussion at later junctures. As time went on, the patient's sense of a need to perform for the therapist came into much sharper focus, as did the fact that these palindromes represented the application of the patient's enormous technical skill with symbols to problems that were very near to him and intensely invested with feeling. This was for him an important revaluing of the use of symbols, one that opened the way toward moving much closer to what he felt and being able to contain it much more reliably.

Helping a lonely patient with his loneliness is a process whose elements can be specified only in terms that retain a certain generality. It is necessary to meet the patient in a space to which both patient and therapist have access but that belongs exclusively to neither one. The construction of this space for collaboration is itself a collaborative task. It must be at once familiar and unfamiliar, not simply to the patient but also to the therapist. If the therapist does not have a sense of the unfamiliarity of the venture, this is a sign that he is out of touch with a significant aspect of the patient's feeling, possibly because the patient has had such extensive experience of being forbidden the expression of his own discomforts and fearfulness. The task in helping a patient with the loneliness problem is nothing less than the negotiation of a process that leads to a change for the patient both in the meaning of what it is to be with someone and in the meaning of what it is to be without someone.

An experienced dance therapist made the observation that in her work at Sheppard, she had been able to classify therapists along a spectrum according to the ease with which they admitted others into their work with patients.[1] At one pole were those who had a generous countertransference, and at the other were those who had a stingy countertransference. She remarked that it was very hard to find a place to work with a patient when the patient's treatment had gone in such a way that the psychotherapist had been drawn into a stingy countertransference. One impetus to the stingy countertransference is a repeat of a pattern in which the mother has had such an overweening need for what the child has given her that she has held onto the child as if he were a possession that existed for her own sake. This denied the child a way out from the dyadic pressure into the transitional zone.

The borderline patient who found the hurt of being left alone so much greater than the pain of her physical injuries

---

1. We are indebted to Joan Lewin, ADTR, for this observation.

has been treated for more than eight years by a psychiatrist, a dance therapist, and an art therapist. This tripartite treatment structure has provided numerous advantages in terms of the treatment of the patient's loneliness. It has cushioned the losing danger around vacations, providing ongoing relationships within which to discuss temporary separations in other relationships. It has cushioned the fusing danger, in that it has always provided the patient a means to hear differing points of view and relate negativistically to one or another therapist by highlighting the differences. An underappreciated function of the splitting that borderline patients do is just this, namely, that it provides opportunity for negativism that protects against the fusion danger. This tripartite structure has also provided the means for exploration of different means of expression with different representational, affective, and psychomotor components.

Perhaps most importantly, it has provided a collaborative structure, which has not only served to assuage the loneliness of all three treating persons, providing succor, encouragement, and insight at dark moments in the treatment, but also served to provide for the patient quite unobtrusively and yet most consistently a model for ways of relating that mitigate loneliness. The pleasure that the three therapists took in their collaboration and the professional growth and learning it made possible for them was not lost on the patient. Nor did she fail to notice and appreciate their mutual respect.

About five years after discharge from the hospital, this same borderline patient happened to call her psychiatrist in distress one morning when he could not talk to her because he had his small, wet, crying daughter in his arms. When her therapist expressed his concern about this incident a few days later, the patient became irritated. "Why," she asked, "do you always want me to be so envious? What do I have to gain by indulging in all these vicious and envious feelings the way you all want me to?'' Here the ''all'' referred to the consortium of the three therapists, illustrating the patient's sense that the envy she felt was too great to be contained simply in one relationship.

She went on to tell her therapist about the conversation she had had with her cat, Niobe, after the difficult telephone call. ''Well, Niobe,'' she told the cat, holding it in her arms, ''I am the center of the world and so are you, Niobe, and you're a beautiful cat, and one of these days you're going to make me a million dollars posing for cat chow ads, so that you'll be able to take care of me and let me live in the style to which I wish to become accustomed.'' As she finished her story, she laughed, seeming to relish her own wit. Yet the laugh was rueful, too, not far from a sob. She knew Niobe was not going to make a million dollars in the near future.

The identification with her therapist was clear, as was her hurt over being left on her own and her sense of the enormity of her own need. The cat served to carry her own sense of vulnerability as well as her sense of omnipotence. In holding her cat, she also held herself. This already represented a major step toward resolving a part of the dilemma of loneliness. She was now able not only to do something other than fall apart in the face of being left alone, but to talk, after a surge of negativism, with her therapist about having done something else. This approximates an experience of being alone in the presence of an other.

THE FAILURE OF ILLUSION AND THE ILLUSION OF FAILURE

Loneliness may rest in the failure of illusion and the illusion of failure. Many lonely patients have gotten annealed to their internal objects, really internal objects they have made up out of whole (or should we say "hole") cloth because of the desperate failings they have experienced in their primary love and hate objects. They have both taken these failures in and been taken in by them. Illusion has failed them because they have been forced to rely on it too early, too extensively, and under too great pressure. They have had to ask it to do too much, which has distorted it as a faculty. Their illusion of having failed protects them against the deeper helplessness and hurt of having been failed. So much borderline blaming masks the most desperate idealizations.

Another very lonely patient said to her therapist that she could accept nothing less than perfection in herself or in her parents. Her therapist had the sense that he had been left out in this discussion of the requirement to be perfect. After some further discussion, he asked her, "What about me?" She looked up very casually, as if his question was hardly worthy of notice, and said, "Oh, you. You're reliable enough so you don't have to be perfect." The response represented the most baffling mixture of compliment and dismissal, indicating just how difficult a different attachment was for this patient.

It is the force with which these patients have had to glue themselves to their internal illusory and improved objects that ties them up so terribly, making it so difficult for them to separate and gain access to more satisfying forms of relationship. At the separation point, there is the bursting forth of enormous amounts of disappointment, disillusionment, and rage. Again, there is a progression–regression dilemma. The threat to the self is great in proportion as the object is diminished. When these patients lose the idealized object, they feel as if they have lost themselves.

Treating lonely patients is particularly difficult now

because the environment is peculiarly and often perversely inimical to forms of treatment based on actual human relationships that have any degree of intimacy, as if aloofness were being prescribed as the approved societal mode. Recently the reviewing psychiatrist for an insurance company was trying to bully a resident into discharging a borderline patient at a time when the resident felt the patient very much needed to be in the hospital. He said to her on the telephone, "I know what the patient needs. Get her a cat. She'll be able to relate to a cat. That's what these patients can do."

Ah, but a cat like Niobe, the living Rosetta Stone that makes possible the translation of a purely private realm into more accessible and expressible illusion, cannot be so simply gotten. Before a trip to the pound or the accepting of a gift of a kitten from a friend or relative is possible, an enormous creative project fraught with the dangers of grief, envy, rage, and disappointment must be undertaken. The cat, as a dynamic function, must be created inside so that the cat, as a live animal, can be found outside. We recapitulate here the paradox of whether the transitional object is found or created. The resolution of the problem of loneliness depends on meetings between inside and outside.

There is no quick fix for loneliness. Impositions only deepen it. There is no recipe for moving from the dreadful illusion of isolation to the kinder and more life-promoting illusions of tactful contacts. What we have never had is what is hardest to give up because the disappointment that must be accepted is so massive and so threatening.

The following dream-like sequence recounted by another young, terribly lonely, suicidal borderline patient may provide a fitting close to our discussion of loneliness. One day she was driving in her car with a friend who was voicing quite mildly the criticisms of the patient's mother that the patient felt most intensely, bitterly, and shamefully. The patient slammed on the brakes of her car and told her friend to get out and walk, despite the fact that they were miles from the neighborhood where they both lived. This incident represented the external enactment of the drama that the patient repeated with herself so many times each day, when she would have feelings about her mother that she considered so unacceptable that she would slam on the mental brakes and tell herself to get out of her own mind and walk. No wonder she was lonely.

9

Chronic
Suicidality

Chronically suicidal patients with serious personality disorders present their therapists with clinical problems that are subtle, intense, and complicated. Therapists need to tolerate a great deal of uncertainty, recognize both the interpersonal and the intrapsychic complexities of the functions and meanings of suicidality, and, above all, keep in view the fact that the suicidality is both a hindrance and a help to the patient. Suicidality, in fact, may be central to a patient's search for a degree of dignity and autonomy as well as connectedness worth staying alive to enjoy. That is, it has transitional value for patients whose transitional processes have been frustrated, arrested, and distorted in the process of development.

SUICIDALITY IS NOT SUICIDE

Especially with patients who have made repeated serious suicide attempts, often of such lethality that they are in
the "alive by accident" category, the boundary between
what is fantasy and what is an action plan about to be
implemented can be very blurred. Often such patients are,
throughout the range of their functioning, unclear as to the
distinction between fantasy and impulse to action. "I can't
talk about it," said one such patient, "because, if I talk about
it, I'll do it. Thinking about it doesn't help. It makes it
happen."

Patients who say this sort of thing are reporting the
subjective truth of their experience. What they say is not to
be taken lightly. Yet, it is true that the fantasy is not
tantamount to the act and that a major therapeutic task is to
assist in the construction of a boundary between feeling and
fantasy on the one hand and impulsive action on the other.
This construction of a dimension of reliable symbolic representation and containment is commonly the work of many
years. It has to do with the whole realm of transitional
experience.

The desperate intensity of the patient's suicidal feeling
and the patient's lack of any subjective security about the
boundary between feeling and action put tremendous pressure on the therapist to take what the patient says literally as
an action plan and to focus his own attention at the level of,
"What shall I do?" What gets lost is the focus on, "What
does this mean?" and "How does it work for and against
the patient both interpersonally and intrapsychically?" The
therapist who develops a tough approach and insists that the
patient will not really kill himself, so that the correct course
is to call the patient's bluff, has also been captured, only
under the sign of negation, by his own sense that fantasies
are tantamount to action. Otherwise the distancing certainty
would not be necessary. Where the patient appears most

certain with driven intensity is the place where the therapist must struggle to remain truly uncertain.

Suicidality is a complex affective state, quite different in different patients and at different times in the same patient. While there is a radical difference between suicidal feeling and fantasy and suicidal action, our conclusion from working with especially the very disturbed personality disordered patients is that we cannot know with any certainty and reliability when suicidal feeling and fantasy will pass over to action. We need the patient's help in trying to gauge this, recognizing all the while that, when the patient claims to be quite as much in the dark about it as we are, this is often a frank report. Therapist and patient sometimes have to misjudge the transition points together a few times (or in some cases more than a few times) before greater reliability is achieved. Hospitalization is definitely indicated at some points, especially after a seriously self-injurious act. Each therapist must find his own thresholds for utilizing hospitalization, which may be different with different patients and also different depending on the therapist's own experience and personal circumstances.

In deciding when to intervene actively and concretely, a therapist must pay attention to the inner cues he gets from his own affective experience as well as all the information he receives from his and the patient's social surround. A danger of being thought adept at treating this kind of patient is that others who have information about the patient that is of crucial importance may not convey it because they have the fantasy that the adept one already knows. This can reflect the projective power of the patient's idealization as well as hostile vectors both from the patient and from the holding environment.

Long-term hospitalization, now increasingly unavailable, has been very helpful to many chronically suicidal patients by providing them and their therapists a laboratory where this boundary could be mapped (Lewin and Sharfstein 1990). The patients identified with and imitated the staff's capacity to observe, name, and respond to danger signs. This provided a model for joint observational processes that could be elaborated upon in outpatient work. In the changed economic climate, halfway houses, quarter-way houses, and day hospitals will have to be called upon to perform the same sort of function. It is not helpful to patients to abandon the exploration of meaning and psychological function and join them in an agitated focus on action possibilities in an indefinitely prolonged atmosphere of impending doom. Suicidality is much more than the search for the doorway to death.

RESPONSIBILITY MEANS RESPONSE, NOT CONTROL

So many personality disordered patients hunger for response, abominate being controlled, and deny their primitive dependency needs, which drive much of their thinking, feeling, and action. They cannot know or ask for what they need, yet have a genius for producing interpersonal atmospheres fraught with imperious demand. If the therapist realistically disillusions, he may be experienced as murderously rejecting. If the therapist realistically provides support and gratification, he may be experienced as intolerably alluring, with the patient feeling like an iron filing in the presence of a magnet. The therapist's problem is how to maintain the relationship, without withdrawing in frustration or taking over too much as his own province and problem. The middle ground of providing responses that are intended to be useful—and therefore depend on the patient's activity in using them, often in the long run, not immediately—is exquisitely uncomfortable.

The temptation to act—to prescribe, interpret, refer, hospitalize, not to mention call the police—to alleviate this discomfort is great, particularly when the patient, often in the service of avoiding awareness of intense dependency conflicts, is very devaluing and very threatening. In great distress, a colleague yelled at a patient, "I'm the doctor. You're the patient. If you don't take the medication I prescribe, there is nothing I can do to help you." Apparent in this outburst were: (1) the blurring of self-object representation boundaries ("I'm the doctor. You're the patient."); (2) the struggle over control ("you don't take . . . I prescribe"); (3) helpless despair ("nothing I can do to help you"); and (4) anger as the predominant affect, probably as a negativistic defense.

One can easily find analogous examples centered around insistence on the acceptance of an interpretation, a particular life decision, eating, and so forth. The point is the shared psychological and interpersonal predicament of the patient and the doctor. The outburst *stands for* so much that has not been recognized, admitted, contained, and openly discussed between them, just as so much of the personality disordered patient's action *stands for* what he cannot remember, recognize, admit, contain, own, say, or feel.

In working with these patients, the question is not whether the therapist will be angry with them. He will. What is important is what he does with his anger. How can he experience and express it and, keeping in view the interpersonal context, convey acceptance of anger, too, as a manageable and energizing part of human life, not some split-off destructive force with a will and a way of its own? So many of these patients experience their anger as having a life and will of its own, much as very young children do. To see someone managing anger differently provides the basis for important learning through imitation.

Chronically suicidal patients are as likely to be relieved by an expression of anger as they are to be hurt and further agitated. When someone is angry with such a patient, there is the consolation for the patient of not being the only angry one. Indeed, a contained expression of anger from a therapist can sometimes bring a life sustaining sense of contact without engulfment: "I suppose I don't like it when you get mad at me, but at least I know that you're there and that you care, which is more than I can say at other times." Anger can be essential in the creation of warmth through friction.

SUICIDALITY AND SEPARATION

Don't worry. When you get back from vacation, I won't be here. I'll be dead.

How would you feel if you got a telephone call telling you I was dead and that you would never see me again?

These kinds of communications from chronically suicidal patients with personality disorders are common, dispiriting, and effective in putting the therapist in touch with a sense of his helplessness and the limitations of his efforts. Often used as exit lines, they turn the tables, threatening the therapist with a separation over which he has no control, which will be of infinite duration. "Don't worry" is a ferocious injunction to worry. It reflects not only the patient's tenuous sense of his therapist's investment in him but also the fragility of the patient's own ongoing investment in himself. Object constancy, like self-constancy, whether in patient or therapist, is at best only a relative developmental achievement, subject to perturbation by a variety of life stresses, both internally and externally generated.

How a therapist feels in response to these threats will depend on his previous experience with separations and his habitual methods for dealing with loss. Repetitive interactions with a chronically suicidal patient mobilize aspects of a therapist's previous experience with separations and losses that are largely unmastered, if not beyond the reach of explicit memory. He is likely to feel himself being carried into a world that is more unstable and unpredictable than the one to which he has become accustomed. The developmental analogue is the world of the very young child, with its intensity and rapid affective and cognitive shifts. Such experience is at once the major reward for undertaking and sustaining the work and the major impetus for avoiding it.

One way out of the dilemma for the therapist is to decrease his investment in the treatment. The theory is that by abstaining from or minimizing attachment, you protect yourself from both engulfment and loss. This is what chronically suicidal personality disordered patients urge at great length. "It took me years," said one patient, "to realize that when I won't let myself get involved because I don't want to lose anyone, I take everyone away from me." From the therapist's side, technical assurance, interpretive confidence, rigid boundaries derived from theories of the need for "neutrality" are often part and parcel of a withdrawal that deprives not only the patient but the therapist of more than he may realize. It is all too easy to create a withholding environment instead of a holding environment.

Ends of sessions, weekends, holidays, vacations, and intermittent illnesses, not to mention serious lapses of attention in sessions, are all facts of therapeutic life. The chronically suicidal personality disordered patient's struggle with the repetitive sequence—(1) attachment, (2) loss, (3) reunion—needs to be reflected in the therapeutic sequence:

1. *Identification*, by allowing the inner resonance of what is projected from the patient toward the therapist.
2. *Differentiation*, through the formulation of the therapist's own experience—including how the present mobilizes his past—in contained symbolic terms.
3. *Communication*, concerning what is being experienced. This challenges symbiotic enmeshment with limited reunion mediated by specific symbolic formulations allowing for feelingful responses.

A therapist might respond, "I certainly do worry when I go on vacation and the worry is uncomfortable. I know that, for you, it is almost as if I ceased to exist, or the only good excuse for my not being here would be if I had ceased to exist. You wonder if you can exist without me and your anger at me frightens you a great deal. In our separate ways, we both have uncomfortable feelings to bear.'' This is a composite example of what might be communicated, hesitantly and step-by-step over years. With these persons, so much has to be lived and shared before it can be discussed. A point often neglected is that reunions are every bit as agitating as separations as they can highlight serious fusing dangers. Silence at the beginning of a session, the lack of an entrance line, can be every bit as telling as the more celebrated exit lines.

The emotional atmosphere surrounding many chronically suicidal personality disordered patients' threats is confused. The compression of three strategies for dealing with the tension of separation—merger, homicide, and suicide—into a single rapidly reverberating state of what might be termed *mergicidality* may account for some of the confusion. Merger denies loss through dedifferentiation and carries the danger of another loss, the loss of self. Homicide eliminates the offending object at the risk of losing the prized object on which the self depends. Suicide gets at the hating hurting self at the price of losing the loving and loved self. These feelings, affect bridges between self and object representations that are not stabilized, reverberate and change rapidly, because none works. Each carries a danger to be avoided. In the course of time, each must be dealt with.

SUICIDALITY AND SPOILING

I'm not going to stay alive just in order to have some trashy relationship with some trashy man.

You might enjoy life and other people might, too. But I don't and I won't put up with it.

Some seem to use their suicidality as a veto power deployed against pleasure, success, and intimacy, just what they claim to crave above all else. Pleasure, success, intimacy, and the like all have in common that they call for the loosing of internal moorings to make possible new experience. New always calls old into question. Just as new must be evaluated in terms of old, so new experience may reveal old experience as not quite what we thought it was. Unless pleasure, success, and intimacy are absolutely sterotyped, in which case they are parodies, they ask for a reorganization to a lesser or greater degree of self-representations, as of the modes of experiencing and relating to the self as object.

It is a real internal saying good-bye that calls for real grieving, which is an everyday task. To say good-bye, we have to be able to remember, that is, to comfort ourselves with illusions toward which we have vivid feelings in a way that does not disturb our sense of reality and its frustrations. Pleasure, success, intimacy—the "goods" of life—are monumental tasks. There are few, if any, enduring satistfactions that do not call for the acceptance of a measure of pain.

The patient's veto of the "goods" of life is often delivered with a sneer that expresses triumph over the therapist's efforts: "You think so well of yourself. I'll fix you." Here the verb "fix" is polyvalent, because not only destruction but a repair of the therapist's implicit grandiosity may be surreptitiously intended. This triumph in spoiling, for all its vigor, is a substitute satisfaction, thin stuff that brings desolation in its wake. From the therapist's side, it can be extremely wounding. To deny the hurt, to fail to notice that the dynamic is directed to hurting, is to offer the patient more evidence of his insignificance. "I can't even make contact with you by hurting you," said one patient, "because it makes no difference to you."

However, it is also true that the issue is joined internally between two parts of the patient, one with grandiose and magical expectations and standards, the other with very little ability to adapt and cope. "Nothing in my life works

out, because I don't know how to make it work out," said a
patient. On closer examination, what the patient meant by
"knowing how to make something work out" had nothing
to do with any step-by-step effort involving accepting frustration and reassessing means and ends in an ongoing way.
The patient's idea was that special intensities of wishing,
magical effects of inborn qualities and outside interventions,
get you what you want, just as you want it.

A therapist, quite appropriately, was trying to speak to
her patient's grandiose expectations of herself: "You have to
learn to crawl, before you learn to walk." The patient shot
back: "This has nothing to do with learning to crawl before
you learn to walk. This is about a baby's learning to roll over
from its back onto its tummy."[2] What was confusing for the
therapist was that she began to talk with one part of the
patient—the grandiose part—and then found herself hearing
from another complementary part—the inadequate, overwhelmed part, which correctly recognized an ally in the
therapist and, equally correctly, cautioned this ally not to
overestimate what the patient could do.

Therapeutic zeal and hopefulness, for example, seeing
the patient as a "high functioning borderline" because of
impressive splinter competencies that are not well integrated, can be very toxic to these patients. Spoiling, using
the all-or-nothing formula, "I'll kill myself," or even acting
it out, may represent a desperate effort by the part of the
patient that knows it is overwhelmed to get across the
message that it needs more shoring up than has been recognized. Spoiling is often a way of saying, "I can't," under
conditions where a grandiose part of the self cannot bear
either to hear "I can't" or to participate in investigating
what the troubles are. "I won't" masks the deeper ache of "I
can't." Again, this can be thought of as a deficit in grieving.
Inability to accept what seems a huge narcissistic blow
makes adaptation impossible. The patient who uses suici-

---

2. We are indebted to Dr. Beth Wadman for this vignette.

dality to spoil is often telling us that much more is rotten in Denmark than we—either one of us—have yet been able to face. We should not forget that Hamlet's "To be or not to be" is the anguished question of a son who has terrible troubles in relationship with a mother who has no firm grasp either of who she is or of who he is.

THE CASE FOR SUICIDALITY

Once we have found some clarity that suicidality is not suicide and that responsibility means thoughtful and fee-lingful response, not control or rescue, we are in a position to look at how suicidality can be helpful to a patient. "Living this way is unbearable," runs the refrain of the chronically suicidal personality disordered patient, "so I won't live at all." Acquaintance with how most of these patients have lived and are living makes acquiescence with the first part come easily. "I wouldn't have any respect for myself if I didn't want to die," said one patient. The problem is the plunge of despair that leads from the first part to the second part. The therapeutic struggle is joined around the question, "Is it possible to transform the legitimate impulse to revolt into a sustained and detailed project for reconstruction?" Personality reconstruction is a long, lonely, and uncertain process.

When a patient like this protests, "You're just trying to stuff me into a mold," there is a nostalgic wish for comfort alloyed with genuine terror. Among other things, the patient is confessing ignorance both as to what he wants to be and what he feels he can come to be. The patient's wish to be molded is in conflict with his inexorable wish to be free. The two need to enter into a lengthy negotiation, in which each can cite a litany of bitter wrongs suffered at the hands of the other.

A woman who had made a number of serious suicide attempts claimed continually that her numerous young children would be better off without her. She fantasized that, once she was dead, she would be able to observe their growing up without in any way interfering with them. As she described this fantasy, she would develop an expression of satisfaction and relief that was strikingly different from her normal distress. She recounted that her friends marveled that she tried to "treat each one of her children as if they were an only child." Her own dependency needs were intense, primitive, and denied.

With her therapist, as with her children, she tried to shut out the rest of the world, sometimes achieving a degree of attunement that was remarkable. Along the same lines, her husband's infidelity was absolutely intolerable to her, even though she said, "He's no help." The transference implications, namely that her therapist was no help and also unfaithful, were clear. She obliterated whatever was limited or frustrating in her mind on an ongoing basis, producing an inner world that was remarkably unstable.

This woman's suicidal fantasy expressed her sense of her own stymied developmental project. "I had no idea I was so fed up," she said. The only way to be separate and ongoing, she felt, was to enlist the magical assistance of death to remove frustration and the attendant rage that she found so terrifying. Her goals were legitimate: to find a less consuming way to be with her children, to be able to maintain more differentiated, consistent, and realistic awareness of her needs and theirs, and, above all, to develop an experience of herself as securely individual with a full complement of affects, including rage and grief. Death, as she imagined it, was a distorted department of life in which what was now left out would be let in.

Her preoccupation with self-destruction contained so much self-constructive material that it could be seen as a scaffolding. It had the flavor of a maternal preoccupation directed back at herself. She was, as the object of her suicidality, the helpless infant awaiting perfect succor from outside. Death, like a dark and soft breast, appeared as a liberation from a set of unbearable internal tension states. She got suicidal both in the face of separations and in the face of pleasures and successes. "I don't think about my needs," she half boasted and half lamented.

These patients do not give up their suicidality until they no longer need it. Like teddy bears for small children, suicidality seems more to fade away than to be actively renounced. "I can get mad at you only after I get suicidal," said one patient. Here the suicidality is perceived by the patient as an aid to the integration and expression of a conflicted affect. No doubt suicidality is frightening. However, small children regularly experience their transitional objects as frightening when they are in the throes of aggressive feelings. The stuffed animal functions as an overflow reservoir, holding what cannot yet be held within. Imagine the child's distress and desolation should we take the stuffed animal away on the grounds that it is frightening.

Suicidality, the reservoir for so much hurt, despair, anger, and aspiration, can be life-giving if both its threat and its promise are simultaneously kept in view by both patient and doctor. It is a complicated system of illusions with enormous communicative as well as alienating force. It is possible to get beyond exasperation to appreciation, although this is no guarantee against passages of terror. How could it be, given how overwhelmed the chronically suicidal personality disordered patient has been for how long? Nietzsche remarked, "The thought of suicide is a great consolation: by means of it one gets successfully through many a bad night" (1954, p. 468).[3]

ON CONTRACTS PROSCRIBING SUICIDE

A peculiar locution often heard in clinical discussion provides a clue to trying to understand the strengths and weaknesses of the approach to suicidal intent and action based on making contracts. "I made a suicide contract with the patient and I believe that she is going to keep it," said one psychiatrist, quite oblivious to the fact that he was saying, in effect, that he and the patient had made a pact to suicide together. In this phrasing, it is not clear whether the therapist is saying that he believes the patient will suicide or will not suicide. The clarifying device, the contract, seems to have become infected with unclarity, perhaps for the better, given the borderline patient's all-or-nothing drive for exclusionary pseudoclarity.

A contract, however elaborate and however imposing its language or the solemnity of the social rituals surrounding it, is basically a good faith undertaking. This is especially clear about contracts to stay alive, since, once the undertaker has hold of the deceased, efforts at enforcement or recovery of damages are moot. All this is to suggest the limits of usefulness of the contracting device, rather than to suggest that it is useless. Contracting provides a way to provide certain kinds of structure and concrete support for illusions that may be life sustaining.

A contract gives both therapist and patient a concrete way to focus on certain aspects of the situation surrounding the suicidal patient's distress. A sense of being accompanied into a danger zone can be created this way. A negativistic tension that provides support for the illusion of the thera-

---

3. We are indebted to Robert King, M.D., for calling this aphorism to our attention.

pist's internal presence prohibiting suicidal action can also be generated in this way. It is also true that the contract can become a goad to action, being seen by the patient as an intolerable threat to his own autonomy. For this reason, while helpful limit setting can sometimes be achieved with the delineation of consequences if the patient makes suicide attempts or gestures, the contract, in its concreteness, can also provide both parties with a way to sabotage their work together.

"When I'm afraid enough of something then I have to do it immediately," said one patient. "If I'm afraid of losing you, then I have to go try to kill myself. It doesn't make any difference what I promised or what I said I was going to do. I know the staff hates me and I hate myself for that, too. I hate other people who break their word."

The notorious legalism of borderline patients with their ferocious, extravagant, and often whimsical discoveries of escape hatches from any promise of collaboration expresses their pervasive need for negativistic support of their separateness. They are driven to drive a therapist to ever more concrete and specific provisions in a contract and then to try to defeat these, perhaps out of a frustrated appetite for a more abstract and continuous internal guidance system. It is even possible that these dynamics, which have their paranoid aspect (e.g., "You can't trust anyone, especially not yourself"), have something to teach us not just about borderline patients' difficulties with fusing and losing, separateness and separation experiences, but also about what drives our ever-ramifying legal system. It is hard to avoid the fantasy of a borderline patient who stays alive in order to get a 900-page suicide prevention contract exactly correct so that he can have the exquisite pleasure of transgressing it.

We have tended to avoid the concrete device of the

suicide prevention contract, pointing out to the patient instead that therapeutic work would be impossible if the patient were dead and that this would represent a loss both for the therapist and for the patient. Every therapy is based on an agreement to collaborate, however negativistically understood and expressed. "I looked at the pills last Thursday and I thought of you," said one patient. "I was going to take them all, but thinking of you made me so mad that I didn't do it." Here is an example of a suicide prevention contact that makes use of a transitional process centered around prescribed medications.

For us, the issue is the provision of relational conditions that help the patient to move from more concrete, literal, and external props for transitional processes to transitional object relations that are more abstract, internal, and metaphorical. Suicide proscription contracts can be both helpful and inimical to this process, depending how they are conceived and used by both the therapist and the patient.

10

Understanding and Using Countertransference

THE COMPLEXITY OF COUNTERTRANSFERENCE

Any ongoing treatment of a borderline patient produces a situation of extraordinary potential intimacy between the persons involved. It is true of psychotherapy in general that it makes possible a brand of intimacy that is specific to this situation. Hour after hour after hour, season after season, often year after year, the regularity of the contact can establish the conditions for a near hypnotic collaboration in which both parties are extremely suggestible, linked at levels too numerous for naming and committed to each other in a way that is identical with no other relationship. In the relationship, an illusory "interperson" comes into being that is supported by intrapsychic conditions and interpersonal contributions from both sides.

To be with a patient and to listen to a patient is to take

on a new realm of experience *within ourselves*. We understand by personalizing. We listen to feelings with our feelings. We put the flesh of our own experience onto the skeleton of the patient's narration, producing a peculiar composite creature, which is neither just the patient's nor just our own. Or to put it another way, it is our own internal cinema production company that undertakes the enormous job of bringing the patient's script to life for the internal screen we watch. Nor are we unmoved movie goers. Each patient brings us new interests, new aversions, new versions of our old interests and our old aversions. We may be shocked and enlightened by new perspectives that patients bring us. When this happens, we find ourselves freshly aware of the reality of the psychotherapeutic experience and its attendant terrors, sometimes most present when the work is most rewarding and fruitful.

We also misunderstand by personalizing. We inflect what we hear in ways of which we are never completely aware, just as we are inflected (if not infected) by what we hear in ways of which we are never completely aware. It is this peculiar mixture of understanding by personalizing and misunderstanding by personalizing that represents the conundrum of countertransference, the ways in which the therapist both reveals to himself and conceals from himself the newness and distinctness of what he hears by assimilating it to the body of his previous experience and understanding. We approximate by personalizing. The problem is to continue the process while gauging the error. Of course, the same errors, the same wanderings, attend the process of trying to gauge the error.

When we listen to another we create that other for ourselves out of ourselves and in ourselves and, in so doing, we find ourselves always recreating ourselves, always in the currency of illusion, the *now* of it. We are always on a middle ground of that which is neither utterly so nor utterly not so. We are always in a realm of successive approximations. It is for this reason, the decisive, liberating, and fateful uncertainty of the process of illusion making, that dialogue is so important. Dialogue mediates the process of collaborative approximation toward lived and liveable truth that is psychotherapy's healing hope. Psychotherapy, for all the buzz of complicated theoretical talk that often surrounds it, is a supremely practical undertaking. If it does not bear practically on the patient's plight in life, then it has lost its bearings. "Practical" does not mean either "quick" or "simple" or "easy."

The terrain of countertransference experience is not simple, either at a theoretical or at a practical level. The following celebrated lines from "The Man with the Blue Guitar" by Wallace Stevens (1973) refer to a set of problems that may usefully be regarded as similar:

> They said, 'You have a blue guitar.
> You do not play things as they are.'

> The man replied, 'Things as they are
> Are changed upon the blue guitar.'

> And they said then, 'But play, you must,
> A tune beyond us, yet ourselves.

> A tune upon the blue guitar
> Of things exactly as they are.'

In describing the problem of this poem, Stevens compared it to the "painter's problem of realization" and wrote, "I have been trying to see the world about me both as I see it and as it is" (pp. 252–253). The tension between illusion and the idea of the real is apparent. Or should we say that it is both apparent and real?

In wrestling with the question of the problems and opportunities posed by countertransference experience, we are in the realm of double or even triple vision. We want always to see two or three ways at once, without giving one necessarily a priority over the other. We want to see what we see while at the same time keeping an eye on how what we see is influenced by our own habitual biases in seeing as they are brought into play by particular stimuli.

If we break this last notion down, we can see that three kinds of seeing are involved: (1) We want to see what we see. That is to say, we want to let ourselves experience what we experience in the face of the patient rather directly and immediately. We want to be able to feel first and to ask questions later. Otherwise we are in danger of letting our theories shut off just the experience that is most likely to call them into question. We are withholding ourselves in a way that is likely to be experienced by the patient as aloofness. (2) We want to see how what we see is influenced by our habitual biases. Previous experience, the raw material out of which we compose our present impression, imposes a set of biases. To the extent that we have already questioned this experience, we may have a good bit of knowledge of its principles of composition and how they make both our attention and our inattention selective. If we are not aware of our own biases and areas of special comfort and discomfort, we may have trouble making a place for the patient as a person in his own right. (3) We want to see how stimuli from outside ourselves, that is, from the patient, evoke our biases. Our experience can serve as a sensitive instrument for detecting what surrounds us in much the way that, when we hear certain resonances set into play in the strings of a piano, we know that certain waves are being propagated in the air. What our experience tells us about ourselves can tell us a great deal about the patient. Such awareness is essential to being able to contain projections from the patient in such a way as to be able to return to the patient a modified version that might be of use.

A CASE EXAMPLE

We want to use the example of an extremely difficult and tumultuous inpatient treatment to bring to life our ideas about two extremes of countertransference reactions, *over-involvement* and *rejection*. Rather than viewing these extreme polarities as simply undesirable and so being moved to issue immoderate injunctions to moderation, we see these extremes as entry ramps. They are forms of relatedness that can lead to more optimal forms of participant-observation with the patient and so to a more optimistic prognosis for the treatment and the patient. These extremes are places to start or to pass through, not places to stop.

We do not believe there should be any difficulty in applying the concepts we propose both to inpatient and to outpatient work. The advantage of a case example taken from the hospital setting is that the hospital, with its different "real" figures with their different personalities and propensities, provides a reaction vessel that produces illustrations of extraordinary clarity and vividity. We have seen similar material not just in outpatient treatments but also in the dreams of both patients and therapists. What we are after, as in the discussion of holding, is the illustration of pervasive developmental processes that have both interpersonal and intrapsychic ramifications.

Our account of this case is excerpted to focus on the range of countertransference reactions Ms. E. evoked. A 21-year-old single woman, Ms. E. was admitted twice to the hospital, the first time for five months and then the second time for sixteen months. Between the two was a four-week period outside the hospital after she ran away. She was followed for nine months as an outpatient following her discharge.

Ms. E.'s symptoms began approximately five years prior to admission to our hospital. When she went away to college, she was depressed, had crying spells, and overate. She began stealing clothes and smoking marijuana. She tried attending a number of different colleges, but was unable to settle down anywhere. She failed school courses, was sexually promiscuous, and used LSD. Eventually, she adopted a hippie life-style, travelling about the country, but no place was the right place.

She began therapy two years prior to the hospital events on which we will focus. She was described as depressed, beating herself, suicidal, and indulging in eating orgies. She had a stormy course involving a series of therapists, hospitalization, and eventual transfer to our hospital.

The patient's father was a brilliant professor who was a study in contrast to the mother. He came across as reasonable, stable, and rational, so much so that a disagreement with him was almost impossible. He would simply go on being calm, serene, and honest. In many ways, he paid little attention to the patient in her early years. He was quite tolerant of her deviant personal life-style. Overall, he was hard to engage affectively, his stability being perhaps just a bit too stable, as if there were dangers just across the frontier that he did not care to admit. Ms. E.'s mother was attractive, if a bit garishly adorned. She easily became involved in friendly conversation with a steady flow of charming speech and smiles. She showed marked upset when she talked about her own father's murder in a gangland slaying. She spoke positively and supportively of the patient's intelligence and strength, giving a variety of examples of Ms. E.'s competent performance.

Ms. E.'s mother had a history of becoming abusive or disorganized in times of crisis. Ms. E. once was pushing her younger brother on his scooter when he fell and cut himself. Hysterical, Ms. E.'s mother screamed at her, "You bitch!" A year later, this brother pushed the patient through a window. The result for Ms. E. was a cut face and a broken tooth. Frantic, the mother started howling in such an upset fashion that Ms. E. herself had to call the doctor and the dentist. She had to perform the holding function for her mother at a moment when she herself was in enormous distress. By the time Ms. E. was sixteen she and her mother were so embroiled in bitter arguments about television watching and room cleaning that her father, demonstrating again his propensity for emotional strategies based on disengagement, decided that she should go away to college. Here the extremes of rejection and overinvolvement were present in the family, personified in the patient's mother and father.

The therapist at the previous hospital sketched Ms. E.'s presentation as follows:

> [Patient was a] dark-skinned and voluptuous beauty with arresting light green eyes and long dark hair, either bound firmly back or loosely curtaining her cheeks. She dresses usually in midthigh miniskirts and hot colors, varying her garb daily, often changing during the day. She has not missed an hour, usually arriving early in the waiting room. She enters the room quickly and looks at me with an expectant intensity as a preamble to whatever mood she is in, whether confused, furious, content, seductive, sad, humiliated, or methodically rational. Her careless leg crossing is only minimally diverting compared to her double-whammy steady intense stare. . . . When I put words to what I sense she is transmitting, a frantic and furiously urgent yearning for affection, she (thankfully) eases up on her gaze.

Such a description gives ample testimony to Ms. E.'s appeal and the fascination and discomfort Ms. E. could elicit in a therapist.

When the patient was transferred to Sheppard, she was violent, destructive, self-mutilating, and quite impulsive. After five months in the hospital that can only be characterized as chaotic, she ran away to continue with a doctor on the outside. Chaos continued and she was readmitted a month later. At that time, she was excitable, easily annoyed and angered. She complained that she could not relate to her therapist. She cut herself superficially with small pieces of glass and was started on trifluoperazine. She professed to be unable to understand why her outside therapist had recommended readmission because, in a phrase that beautifully expresses the borderline patient's trouble telling a fantasy from an action plan, she said she was only "play acting" when she threatened suicide.

She repeatedly asked for a change in therapist. After eight weeks, she was transferred to the care of a female resident. Ms. E. made persistent efforts to be seen by this new doctor for daily sessions. She cried constantly and complained about the staff and the system, about how people hated her and neglected her to the point where they would leave her to die. As she experienced them, each and every one was unfair to her.

Her new therapist was scheduled to go on vacation for five weeks two months after she started with Ms. E. Upon learning of this, Ms. E. went out of control and was placed in seclusion. This occurred after she had achieved a high responsibility level in the hospital, worked for two weeks in a local department store, and was doing volunteer work with children. This illustrated in dramatic fashion her separation sensitivity. The idea of the separation in itself evoked an inner storm.

After her therapist's return, Ms. E. settled down again. She did reasonably well for several months. When her therapist told her that she would be leaving in two months at the end of her residency rotation, all hell broke loose. Ms. E.'s disturbance increased as the date of this separation approached. She started to cut her wrists, became suicidal and disorganized. She was taking drugs surreptitiously without telling the staff or her therapist, as if she needed that degree of secret, magical control. She ran away and returned after two days. During a briefer vacation of her therapist, she was in a seclusion room for much of the time. She cut her wrists, swallowed razor blades, and tried to suffocate herself. She had to be watched constantly.

Again, when her therapist returned, Ms. E. seemed to settle down. A family visit to the hospital went well. About three weeks before the date of termination with this second therapist at Sheppard, the patient's self-destructiveness again intensified. In the final session with her doctor, Ms. E.

began to cut her wrists and to bang her head. The doctor felt compelled to restrain her physically in order to keep her from hurting herself. In the ensuing struggle between the two of them the patient's capped tooth was knocked out. The therapist became so murderously angry that she felt like allowing the patient to bleed to death. Here we have an example of a dramatic countertransference experience that, fortunately, went no further in action. It was as if the patient needed to bring to life her fantasy that she would be left to die.

In an expression of the hospital's commitment to sustaining work with difficult patients, Ms. E. was transferred to the care of a senior psychiatrist, who became her third therapist at Sheppard. His diagnosis of her was cyclothymic borderline personality disorder. Neuroleptics offered little benefit to Ms. E. At the time of the treatment we describe here, the use of lithium was narrowly confined to cases of manic depressive psychosis. Intensive and comprehensive psychotherapeutic treatment with special attention to the holding function of the inpatient milieu seemed the treatment of choice.

At the time she was transferred to the care of this senior psychiatrist, Ms. E. had managed to achieve a position of virtual isolation on the hall. Her previous therapist seemed not to have been alone in entertaining the fantasy of completely disowning her. She and her fellow patients were so angry at each other that there was very little contact. She was living in a seclusion room and was recessed out into the main part of the unit only when the other patients were off the hall for meals or activities. This in itself represented a powerful social communication that was probably troubling not just to the patient but to everyone who participated.

Ms. E. had recently broken the glass covering a picture and threatened the charge nurse with it. This nurse responded by breaking off all contact with her. Other members of the staff were quite angry. Some of the doctors were recommending electro-convulsive therapy to break what they saw as a hopeless cycle. ECT is still used in inpatient milieu in this way today, often as much to treat hopelessness and despair in the holders and helpers as to treat the patient. Her therapist, mindful of the need to repair the milieu, if the patient was to have a chance of getting the treatment she needed, met regularly for three sessions a week with Ms. E. and devoted a fourth hour to a combined meeting of the day- and evening-shifts of nursing personnel, in this way promoting contact and communication not just with him but between the shifts. Incidentally, we have seen many cases where shift changes represent times of special vulnerability for borderline patients, as if the discontinuity in the holding environment was sufficient to shake, if not shatter, their tenuous sense of their own internal ongoingness. It does not take much change to shatter a very fragile sense of security.

The patient objected to this arrangement, arguing that all of her therapist's time should be devoted to her. Simultaneously, illustrating her all-or-nothing approach, she questioned whether she was really worth any attention from her therapist. The double bind message that he was spending both too little and too much time with her was clear.

One early initiative aimed at restoring channels of communication was to have the patient placed in a cold wet sheet pack and wheeled into a community meeting. Her new therapist was assistant medical director of the hospital at this time. Anticipating that the staff might feel that they would have to put up with the patient "come hell or high water," he told the staff that they could blow the whistle at any time and she would be transferred out. The patient and her family were informed of this plan, which had an enormously relieving effect on the nursing staff.

Her therapist also told Ms. E. that he was in no position to scuffle or physically grapple with her. He told her that her feelings would all have to be put into words since he had only recently recovered from a lumbar disc problem. This therapist's only physical intervention was in the very first session. He put up his hand when she started to bang her head against the wall. As he did so, he asked her to tell him what she was feeling that made her bang her head.

The staff were intensely divided in their attitudes about the treatment. The charge nurse, having broken off all contact with Ms. E., was not in a position to exercise effective leadership. The therapist's goal at the time was not one of trying to mediate among staff to try to bring about a consensus of attitudes toward the patient. Rather, he operated on the assumption that all the diverse emotional responses had their validity, so that a more reasonable goal was simply to help the different staff members return to and remain in communication with each other.

A standoff crisis situation in which the staff is in the position of assuming total responsibility to protect a patient who is equally adamant in harming himself is one of the most paralyzing situations in the psychiatric milieu, one also that occurs with a fair degree of frequency. The task is to redistribute the responsibility so that it is shared by the treatment team, the patient, and the patient's relatives, who have a specially important function as representatives of the past, the world outside the hospital, and the patient's future. If this sharing of responsibility cannot be achieved, chances are the holding environment will rupture and the staff will extrude the patient. This has unfortunate consequences not only for the patient but for the staff, not just for the difficult instance at hand but for those that follow, as it sets a precedent that can exert a remarkable, pervasive, and long-lasting influence. A "getting rid of" dynamic can be established that threatens not just difficult patients but also members of the staff, so many of whom cherish the basic human fantasy, at one level or another, that they are, themselves, "difficult."

The threat need not be overt. Covertly it can establish an interpersonally restrictive environment that leaches much of the kindness and the firmness out of the atmosphere. While no milieu can work with everyone, extrusion should be a very last resort, not a rash response that appears to indulge aggressive fantasies in action.

It is an untenable position for staff to feel totally accountable in a situation that they cannot possibly control. Nor should we ever underestimate how seriously nursing personnel take their responsibilities for patients' welfare. Recognizing just how serious the bind was for nursing staff, the therapist's allowing the staff an option, namely, to say that they had had enough and could not go on with Ms. E., relieved them enough so that they could resume communication among themselves and with the patient.

Later on, after her recovery, when she and her therapist were reviewing her treatment, Ms. E. pointed out a parallel between the option the therapist offered to the staff and a response he had made to her. She emphasized a difference that she regarded as crucial between his response to her expression of an urgent wish to leave the hospital and the one she had grown accustomed to receiving from others.

Most people met these wishes with a tone of urgency that mirrored the patient's own agitation, trying to tell her why she could not leave the hospital and putting pressure on her, as she saw it, to admit she was sick rather than to deny her illness. Instead, this therapist agreed with her that she should leave the hospital. The problem, he said, was simply to find out how they could accomplish this. She said this gave her a sense of the possibility of finding a way out of the hopelessness and endlessness, analogous to the option of a way out that had been given to the staff.

These two interventions, both bounding in nature, challenged the all-or-nothing construction of the therapeutic situation, by shifting from a contentious mode to one that emphasized collaboration and expressed trust without abandoning realism. The establishment of bounds that were not overspecific, which did not goad the patient to concrete acting out, had a liberating effect on the participants in the treatment, one astutely recognized by Ms. E. herself.

Because of her doctor's position in the hierarchical structure of the hospital, Ms. E. was a "special patient," a role that always has its advantages and its disadvantages. Two means were used to try to combat the pitfalls in this situation. Ms. E.'s doctor arranged for another senior psychiatrist to make major decisions about changes in the treatment program. Also, the regular meeting with the nursing staff provided a means of keeping in focus any obstacles posed by the patient's being seen as "special." This power sharing and communicative access, very different than the conditions that obtained in the patient's family, helped repair a holding environment that had been extremely stressed and distressed by Ms. E.'s treatment. Just as these factors helped to promote communication instead of covert disagreements erupting into actions founded in polarized factionalism, Ms. E.'s doctor's setting of limits on possible physical struggles fostered thought and discussion of feelings in the sessions. Limits provide channeling devices that open up new freedoms.

Limits of this kind are often more simply arrived at if there are "reality" factors impinging on the therapist. For example, it is easier for a therapist not to extend sessions beyond a specified time if he has to catch a bus or a train or to pick a child up from nursery school. Similarly, Ms. E.'s therapist's use of a physical limitation to explain his demurral from struggling with her may have made its sense more tangible and more palatable to her. Certainly, it avoided blaming her for the past instances where things had escalated so dangerously. Borderline patients may be reassured by the concreteness of an explanation that appeals to set factors in the outside world because this provides a prop for their transitional process. More abstract explanations may be disorganizing.

Reality factors can have a transitional function, helping to contain intense affects. However, there is also a risk that these reality factors may be drawn into the situation to obscure the countertransference conflict around simultaneously being attracted to the patient and wanting to avoid being with the patient.

As Ms. E. and her therapist were able to detect counter-transference manifestations during the sessions, they made use of them by connecting them to patterns in the patient's history. For example, they found themselves competing with each other in discovering interpretations and saw this as a reenactment of the complicated situation in which the patient and her mother competed like sisters for the father's attention. When the patient was telling how she was having sexual relations without contraception, she noticed the distressed look on her therapist's face, hastening to reassure him that everything was perfectly all right because this was occurring exactly in the middle between two periods. Here the therapist's response, neither so aloof as the father's nor so hysterical as the mother's, and the patient's response to that response disclosed an important gap in her under-standing and made possible some essential education.

A year after starting work with this third therapist, Ms. E. was an outpatient attending college. She had recently had a paper accepted for publication. One day she described an episode in which, acting upon the recommendation of a professor, she went to the registrar's office seeking an increased number of credits for a course. Apparently, this request came through as a demand. After an interchange, the clerk at the registrar's office became angry and threw a pencil at Ms. E., telling her to shut her mouth. The clerk called her supervisor who, quite predictably, supported the employee. Ms. E. prevented any further escalation by re-maining calm enough to suggest that they meet again the next day to discuss the matter further.

Her doctor was reminded of several interactions with the nurses on the hall during her inpatient stay. When he tried to link these different incidents together so that he and Ms. E. could look at the pattern, she became tearful and angry at him for reminding her of those epsiodes. She wanted to keep these experiences compartmentalized. However, she was able to master her anger and hurt enough to listen to the following formulation. While she had objections, she was eventually able to take these ideas in and work with them.

At the core are conflicts over experiencing dependency needs. Ms. E. disapproved enormously of needing anything because it made her too vulnerable. Because of the power of the counterdependent trends in her, she could not express dependency needs in any simple and direct way. She could not make requests. Instead her needs gained expression through cutting herself, the act of cutting serving simultaneously to elicit care and closeness from others and to elicit disapproval and distance. Or, along similar lines, she presented her needs in such a demanding way that she provoked anger from the other. The other's angry and punitive reply again served both to provide some closeness and gratification and some punishment and disapproval. It expressed her own disapproval of her dependency.

In the treatment situation, she regularly denied her neediness. This took a variety of forms, including wanting to decrease the number of sessions or to transfer to another doctor. As she moved to decrease what she was getting from her doctor, she regularly complained that she was not getting enough. When a professor singled her out for special praise or suggested that a specially good paper of hers be published, the resultant sense of being a special person partially and temporarily offset the continuing barrage of internal self-disapproval.

Self-disapproval was a prominent theme in two dreams she reported in this same session. In one she described how she and a girlfriend were running away from some man and then saw another and felt trapped. Ms. E. felt as though she were going to be attacked or killed. She was threatened and frightened. In the other dream, Ms. E. stood accused of the murder of a man. She thought she might best take the arsenic herself, since she was accused of giving this man arsenic. In working with the themes contained in the dreams, it became apparent that this patient was now able to process much of the material through thinking instead of through action. Whereas before, action had been often an experimental groping toward thinking about a problem, one that did not work because the chaos it unleashed produced a whole new set of problems that were enormously distracting, now thought experiments carried some conviction for her. Ms. E. had a capacity to delay action, although the possibility of action as impulsive expression was constantly with her.

This new capacity to delay, opening up horizons of thought, choice, and combination that were not there before, was the crucial difference between her state at this phase in treatment and her state when she lived on the inpatient unit. The same problems occurred, but along with these old problems were new possibilities for dealing with them.

A brief vignette from the inpatient phase illustrates the change well. After she began work with her third therapist at Sheppard, Ms. E. had calmed down enough so she could begin to go to meals in the cafeteria. One day, the assistant director of nursing greeted the patient in the dining room and expressed her pleasure that Ms. E. was able to get there. She also said she would stop by to see Ms. E. on the unit. A few weeks later, Ms. E. was attending a tea on the ward when she happened to see this nurse. Ms. E. thought, "She promised to come up to see me and she didn't—I'll make her notice me. I'll break some windows out so she will have to pay attention." Instead of doing that immediately, she was able to pause long enough to think, "Oh, hell, why don't I just go up and say 'Hi.'" As she approached, the nurse said, "Hello there, I'm sorry I missed you. I have been up to see you twice. Once you were asleep and the other time you were having a session." The patient was quite impressed by her erroneous assumption about this other person. The delay between impulse and action made possible a zone of uncertainty in which new possibilities for understanding emerged.

EVOLUTION OF COUNTERTRANSFERENCE CONCEPTS

We began with a discussion of the complexity of counter-transference as a clinical concept, then proceeded to provide a case example in which countertransference phenomena played a central role. After a brief discussion of some features of the historical development of counter-transference concepts, we will present a method of broadly categorizing countertransference attitudes that we believe may be of practical value in work with borderline patients.

Freud (1910b) wrote of the physician's emotional reaction to his patient in the following terms:

> We have become aware of the "counter-transference" which arises in him as a result of the patient's influence on his unconscious feelings, and we are almost inclined to insist that he shall recognize this counter-transference in himself and overcome it. Now that a considerable number of people are practicing psychoanalysis and exchanging their observations with another, we have noticed that no psychoanalyst goes further than his own complexes and internal resistances permit; and we consequently require that he shall begin his activity with a self-analysis and continually carry it deeper while he is making his observations on his patients. [pp. 144–145]

From this initial rather all-or-none view of countertransference as an interference the notion developed that it could be a helpful tool by way of indicating what might be taking place in the patient. A new ambivalence about counter-transference emerged, with the idea that it could be either helpful or harmful in the treatment, but that in any case it was an essential component of the treatment experience.

A current of thinking has suggested that counter-transference reactions are especially prominent in contact with borderline and psychotic patients. Kernberg (1965), for example, has provided the following perspective:

> One can describe a broad range of counter-transference reactions ranging from that related to the symptomatic neuroses on the one extreme to psychotic reactions at the other, a continuum in which the different reality and transference manifestations become increasingly predominant in the patient's contribution to the counter-transference reaction, displacing the importance of those counter-transference aspects which arise from the therapist's past. When dealing with borderline or severely regressed patients, as contrasted to those presenting symptomatic neuroses and many character disorders, the therapist tends to experience rather soon in the treatment intensive emotional reactions having more to do with the patient's premature, intense and chaotic transference, and with the therapist's capacity to withstand psychological stress and anxiety, than with any particular, specific, problem of the therapist's past. In other words, given reasonably well-adjusted therapists, all hypothetically dealing with the same severely regressed and disorganized patient, their counter-transference reactions will be somewhat similar, reflecting the patient's problems much more than any specific problem of the analyst's past. [p. 42–43]

Here Kernberg is arguing the case for countertransference experience as being about the patient, by downplaying how it is about the analyst when the patient is borderline or psychotic. It is as if the onus of countertransference had to be distributed, so much going to the patient for provoking it and so much to the doctor for providing a fertile ground in which it can arise.

While we agree on the importance of the countertransference experience as a guide to what is going on in the patient, we think the difficulty of countertransference experience with borderline patients may have to do with how it gets hold of specific experience in the analyst's past that is not so easily representable in clear, distinct verbal form. These transferences with their "premature, intense and chaotic" flavor speak to the analyst's preoedipal experience, much of which has been excluded from awareness in the service of structuralization of the personality. After all, it is before the oedipal phase, with its heightened capacity for clear representation, that the development that is decisive for a person's capacity to bear "psychological stress and anxiety" has taken place. In many cases, work with a borderline patient awakens intense and chaotic experiences that the therapist would just as soon not know about.

Searles, who has been known to joke that he is, if not the best adjusted analyst, then at least the most adjusted analyst, has been the foremost proponent of viewing the therapist's experience as the primary source of data regarding the patient. His book (1979d) is an exhaustive account of the varieties of clinical usefulness of countertransference in therapy. He emphasizes that it is precisely because the therapist shares vulnerabilities with the patient that countertransference can be useful as a mode of understanding the patient.

The concept of projective identification, a bridging concept that relates not just emotional states in one person to emotional states in another, but the intrapsychic to the interpersonal, provides a basis for understanding the back and forth of transference and countertransference experience as a communicative flow offering new potentials for containment and clarification. While we have previously quoted Ogden's (1982) definition at some length, it is worth repeating at least the first part again in this context: "Projective identification is a concept that addresses the way in which feeling-states corresponding to the unconscious fantasies of one person (the projector) are engendered in and processed by another person (the recipient)" (p. 1).

Probably a great deal of healing and maturing takes place in and out of therapy through the back-and-forth processes of projective identification. We have stressed them already in our account of hospital treatment and pointed out how they can operate internally between self and object representations. It is as though a person's unintegrated part aspects are flung out as pieces of a jigsaw puzzle to be stuck selectively on others who contain and alter the fragments. Once the puzzle pieces have been modified in this way, they can be taken back in, making it possible to put the puzzle together in a different way than before. The opportunity of reworking latent feelings and conflicts within us that are activated by patients' projections accounts for both the fascination and the troublesomeness of the work.

As one astute patient with extensive experience as a helper put it, "I don't know why I wrote these three words down on a piece of paper. I just woke up and heard it this way. I think this is how it goes: Scare, care, hear. I think when you're scared of things in yourself, you start taking care of others. Then when you are not quite so scared, you can start to hear."

COUNTERTRANSFERENCE MONITORING CHART

Table 10–1 represents an effort to summarize a great deal about the experience of working with borderline patients in a concise way that provides a means for observing the therapist's own reactions and links them to processes in the patient. It may be thought of as a design concept for a clinical navigation system—for staying with borderline patients while countering the opposed and complementary dangers of rejecting them and being engulfed by them.

This chart categorizes the responses of those working with borderline patients in a field situated between the two poles of overidentification with the patient and rejection of the patient. The idea is to move from these extremes toward a middle integrated category of observation and utilization of participation in countertransference.

These two categories—overidentification and rejection or distancing—are precisely the identical processes that are so prominent in our borderline patients. We have postulated that developmentally these patients have not formed the relatively ongoing sense of self-constancy for which the prerequisite is the differentiation of self representation and object representation. Hence, they are specially vulnerable to fusion and engulfment when becoming intimate with another and to loss or abandonment when parting from another. This is the familiar dual cycle of the fusing and losing dangers on which we have placed so much emphasis. Each of us retains the same potential within us even though we may not be as vulnerable to the regressive reactivation of these processes to quite the same degree.

To paraphrase Sullivan's (1953, p. 16) celebrated maxim, we may all be in certain deeper strata more simply borderline than otherwise. If we were not so susceptible to the fusing and losing dangers, we could not find our way to that middle ground that makes the back and forth of a rich relational social life possible.

In our contact with these patients we have activated within us both identification and distancing responses. To treat borderline patients is to get a chance to contemplate aspects of oneself in a mirror whose truth and relevance may be hard to bear, but, if borne, are quite enriching of the capacity to contain, to create, and to feel. Or should we simply say to create feelingfully? Working with borderline patients provides a different, possibly deeper perspective, not only for working with patients who are generally regarded as less deeply troubled, but also for working with oneself. The issues of fusing and losing are ubiquitous and endlessly intriguing in their ramifications for being human.

Table 10–1 lists a slightly modified version of symptoms found associated with the borderline patient as diagnosed in *DSM-III-R* (1987) in the left-hand column. We have

TABLE 10–1. Treatment Team Positions with the Borderline Patient

Symptoms (*DSM-III-R*)—Modified	Therapist/Staff Responses Including Countertransference		
	Overidentification with Patient	Observation and Utilization of Participation	Nonempathic Rejection of Patient
Item 1 Unstable intense relationships; all/none, splitting; idealization/devaluation; stable instability; projection and proj. identification	Sides with a split aspect; accepts as reality	Keeps split components communicating; retains and contains projections	Insists on pseudofront in response to split staff; views patient as manipulating staff against each other; defensive denial
Item 2 Impulsiveness; impulsivity; substance abuse; acting out; violence	Vicariously enjoys behavior; overly controls environment; fosters acting out	Curbs behavior that precludes treatment; interpretation; provides holding situation (predictable environment); views acting out as communication; provides model of thoughtful exploration	Obliterates or eliminates behavior vs. using to patient's advantage; extrudes patient from treatment or laissez-faire approach; punishes acting out
Item 3 Affective instability; anxiety/panic; depression, despair	Joins patient in frantic overidentification or insists on medication	Empathy with confidence of ultimate resolution	Premature use of medication; insists on reality assessment; ridicules patient's feelings

Item			
Item 4 Intense anger; rage/anger; negative transference	Seeks justification in patient's anger and sides with patient	Sensitive to actual precipitants in treatment relationship	Retaliates or untouched by anger; interprets negative transference as related to previous figures
Item 5 Recurrent suicidal threat; mutilation; suicide attempt	Overly anxious response; assumes total responsibility	Responds with support and explores function	Ignores threats or terminates treatment
Item 6 Identity disturbance; negativism; seeking external guidance; identity diffusion	Pleads with patient, feels rejected by patient; decides too much for patient bypassing patient's participation	Optimal distance with engagement; explores behavior	Rejects or opposes patient
Item 7 Emptiness, boredom; lack of creativity/zest	Tries to entertain patient	Views attitude as defensive against affects or anxiety attended by achievement and initiative	Sees it as patient's problem
Item 8 Avoidance of abandonment; dependency (infantile); erotic transference; vulnerability to separation (object loss)	Infantile dependent gratification	Fosters mature dependency with selective autonomy	Insists on complete pseudoautonomous functioning

used the *DSM-III-R* not because we specially endorse this way of looking at borderline patients, but because it may provide a point of reference that helps the reader bridge from behavioral observations to the more abstract and dynamic point of view and way of working that we advocate. In effect, we are trying to provide support for a movement from a more concrete to a more abstract form of transitional process in the therapist.

In the second column are some responses typical of overidentification in relation to each symptom cluster. In the fourth column are some responses typical of nonempathic rejection of the patient. The third column represents what one works toward after entering from either of the extreme modes of overidentification or rejection.

We want to emphasize that it should not be construed that the second and fourth column of responses are to be avoided. Rather they should be recognized in order to move toward the approach of observation and utilization of participation. It is not uncommon to find oneself stuck nearer one extreme than the other not just with a particular patient but with a range of patients. Movement toward the center may involve the dual task of linking this position with previous aspects of the patient's experience and previous aspects of one's own experience. This can be a large task, one in which ongoing collegial discussion and consultation both have their parts to play. Self-disclosure, sometimes to the patient, can be a helpful step in dealing with some countertransference difficulties.

It is of interest that these polarities were observed in an early Freud (1915) writing on transference love:

> It is, therefore, just as disastrous for the analysis if the patient's craving for love is gratified as if it is suppressed. The course the analyst must pursue is neither of these: it is one for which there is no model in real life. He must take care not to steer away from the transference love, or to

repulse it or to make it distasteful to the patient; but he must just as resolutely withold any response to it. [p. 166]

In 1915, Freud sees the polarities as "disastrous." This is a distancing response, which itself expresses a polarity. The later development of the sense of therapeutic possibilities as described by Kernberg, Searles, and Ogden provides a movement toward a more moderate view in which it is recognized that an empathic middle ground can exist where response, not concrete, not in action, but in symbolic and contained terms is allowed and used. Of course, the real world model for this is the good enough and bad enough mother.

We can examine our case example, Ms. E., in relation to the chart. The doctor who, caught up in a physical struggle with the patient, became murderously angry with her and had the urge to let her bleed to death showed a response to the patient's anger that fits under the category of non-empathic rejection of the patient. This would be found on the chart under Item 4 in the far right column. The problem was not that the therapist became murderously angry at the patient. This, in itself, is not an uncommon experience in working with these patients. Rather, the problem was the therapist's inability to contain her own anger and to use it as an example of an affect precipitated by the patient. For example, it may have been that, at a moment when the losing danger was heightened, the therapist was enacting a projective identification originating from her identification with the patient's projected anger. The patient had had significant experiences with losses and also with being extruded from different settings, including her own family. A contained linking of the patient's current rage and fear to past losses might have been a great help to her in achieving more control.

The outpatient doctor who took care of the patient between hospitalizations accepted her in treatment out of ambition to rescue her and to prove the hospital wrong. He overidentified with what is often termed the patient's "good self" as split off from what is often called her "bad self." Again, the issue is not that he wished the best for her or wanted to help her function better, but that the over-identification with a split-off aspect blinded him to so much else in her. His response would be categorized in the chart in the second column under Item 1. The patient then brought what was left out forcefully to his attention with her suicidal threats at the same time that she professed not to understand why he was so bothered by them.

The charge nurse had broken off all contact with the patient, who was exiled to the seclusion room and isolated from the remaining patients. The charge nurse *acted* on her fear instead of being able to notice how frightened she was and to wonder whether this provided a guide to terror in the patient. The element of repetition of events in the family is quite prominent, broken glass appearing again as a virtual leitmotif. The charge nurse's response would be located under Item 2 in the extreme right column, again, a non-empathic rejection of the patient. The resultant impasse was modified by arranging a meeting with the nurse and then bringing the patient into the day room in a cold wet sheet pack to discuss the situation with staff and the other patients. This was more a middle approach than ECT would have been.

When the senior psychiatrist told the patient of his physical limitations, he was using self-disclosure to spare himself the need to become impossibily heroic on the one hand or resign from the treatment on the other. This avowing of limitations may also have had the effect of reassuring the patient that she was not the only one with limitations and also that she was not powerless. In a sense, it could be seen as a use of a reality factor to convey a sense of empathic identification with the patient's own sense of injury and limitation.

When he put up his hand when Ms. E. started to bang her head during their first session and then asked her what she was experiencing, he shifted the focus from mere behavioral limit setting to inviting her to search for the cause and meaning of the behavior. This represented a movement toward the middle position under Item 2. He made the confidence-building assumption that she could stop and think.

An advantage of the model as presented in this chart is its wide applicability to all who work with borderline patients, not just to the patient's psychotherapist. These dynamics emerge in work settings, family settings, day treatment centers, halfway houses, and all other holding environment components. If an attitude can be fostered that these strong countertransference feelings and responses are a natural part of the experience of working with and living with these kinds of patients, it is much more likely that those involved will be able to be at least relatively open in the exploration and communication of their feelings, rather than becoming isolated and captured by partial aspects.

It would be a mistake to regard countertransference as something that can be resolved for the duration of the patient's treatment. Rather, it is an ongoing process that recurs in various forms. A continual focus of therapeutic attention is how to turn countertransference experience into an asset for the treatment, how to find the range of enough but not too much in responding. This highlights the need for holding for the holders. Collegial collaboration, which may take many forms, is essential to the effort of turning countertransference response into a tool of therapy.

We have observed how merely the idea of having a consultation in a situation that is stuck and polarized can make it possible for the participants to develop new ideas. That is to say, the process of consultation may be much more important than the content. It recognizes limitation and provides a more open horizon. We have also noticed that, in the course of supervising residents on difficult patients, aspects of our own countertransference difficulties with patients have come into much clearer focus, so that it could be said that we were receiving effective supervision from our supervisees. Here again, processes of projective identification play an important part.

11

The Therapist's Dependence

Conflicts around attachment and dependency lie at the core of borderline pathology and, not surprisingly, also appear at the core of the therapeutic struggle. So much is enacted and conveyed through complex interpersonal pressures in the treatment of borderline patients that sustained work with these patients requires of the therapist a capacity to struggle with his own dependency and attachment conflicts.

This is a subject that is regularly neglected for defensive purposes. A projective cycle in which the therapist disavows his own dependency needs and then focuses harshly on the patient's is common. The therapist's capacity to understand and discuss his own internal responses in the area of dependency conflicts can provide an important therapeutic tool. It can help him in containing projected elements from the patient, in clarifying his own countertransference positions, and in maintaining an atmosphere conducive to the exploration of feelings.

THE PATIENT–THERAPIST DUAL UNIT

Winnicott (1959) made provocative statements to the effect that there is no such thing as a baby without care, that is, without a mother. Conversely, from such a perspective, there is no such thing as a mother without a baby. Baby and mother form a dual unit, each one depending upon the other in myriad ways. Similarly, there is no such thing as a patient without a doctor, and no such thing as a doctor without a patient. Mapping the forms of the interdependence between patients and doctors is a fundamental part of understanding the psychological dimensions of any treatment process. This mapping is of central importance in fathoming the dynamics of treating borderline patients.

DEPENDENCY CONFLICTS
IN BORDERLINE PATIENTS

A patient slipped one day. Where she meant to say "ax murderer," she said instead "ask murderer." For her, the whole enterprise of expressing a need was fraught with enormous danger. Even as she contemplated asking for the least thing, she fantasized the rejection of her request with such force and fervor that the fantasy took on the solidity of a reality. The illusion of being refused without even a hearing had strong foundations in her experience. Within herself, then, she responded to the rejection with rage that was of murderous proportions. All this stood in the way of her expression of her own deep and genuine warmth toward others and toward herself. Through her own efforts she had achieved a remarkable amount. Her trouble was in appreciating herself.

In her day-to-day functioning and in her self-presentation in therapy, she used a reliability that was scrupulous to the point of punctiliousness to avoid engaging on the terrain of need, disappointment, rage, and grief. Her interpersonal technique came close to making a fetish of a kind of "neutrality." Her "technique" put her therapist's to shame. The strain she imposed on herself in this way was palpable. Even as she hungered for connection, the ferocity of her appetite was such that she disconnected not only from others but within herself from herself, out of fear of her need's devouring and destructive character.

A lifetime of prolonged disappointment at the hands of capricious caretakers, in whom she nonetheless remained highly invested, waited in the wings to be enacted as a transference drama. Short bursts of intense rage at her therapist alternated with longer periods of more constricted interchange of an apparently more cooperative nature in which fear and resentment were present as undercurrents. It seemed as if, in these times, she and her therapist both feared that small missteps, which both knew to be inevitable, might have the most dire consequences for their relationship. They both walked on eggshells, knowing full well that this was no way to make an omelette.

Intense conflicts about dependency are the rule in the treatment of borderline patients, not the exception. Borderline patients can career back and forth with dizzying rapidity between needing someone totally and an aloofness that declares that they need no one. What they cannot do over long periods of time, except with tremendous struggle, is settle down into the middle zone of attached interdependence, with a collaborative striving toward greater articulation of needs and a wider adaptive repertoire for meeting them both inside and outside therapy.

"I want you to marry me," said one borderline patient, "so that I won't ever have to have anything to do with men." This statement beautifully and unwittingly encapsulated both the drive to depend and the urge to take flight from any of the experiences actually involved in dependence. Marriage appeared as a dreadful refuge. This patient said shortly after, "Whenever I'm actually aware of something being out of my control, I panic. It's like trying to think about eternity. I just can't grasp it."

Another patient became acutely suicidal whenever there was an interruption in therapy, all the while maintaining that her therapist meant nothing to her. With tremendous fervor, she attributed the suggestion that her falling apart had something to do with her therapist's absences to a conceit on his part, which illustrated how self-centered he was and how little he cared about her. His suggestion that this "falling apart" was how she experienced his being away met with a haughty disregard that was unconsciously eloquent, not only of how devastatingly disregarded she felt by him but of how devastating her disregard for her own feeling was.

A great deal more is written about dependency conflicts in borderline patients than about conflicts around depending and being dependable in the therapists of borderline patients. Why is this so? What purpose is served?

THE THERAPIST NEEDS THE PATIENT
TO BE A THERAPIST

The ambiguity in this heading's phrasing reflects a fundamental complementarity within the dual unit of the therapist–patient. The therapist needs the patient so that the therapist can be a therapist. Moreover, the therapist needs the patient to be able to imagine and identify with the therapist and the therapist's concerns, ways of thinking and feeling, broad attitudes, and orientation. This imagination and identification are essential to any further project of differentiation. A prior accord is the prerequisite for any differentiation that has content. The therapist needs for the patient to be able to construct an illusion of the therapist that can be useful to the patient. The patient has to make up the therapist out of what is in the patient. The patient's creation or discovery of the therapist in this way is on the way to a therapeutic posture in the patient toward himself.

In the sixth year of a very productive therapy, a young patient made a time line in which he placed his first meeting with his therapist a month prior to the brief hospitalization after which he had been referred to this therapist. In discussing this slip in sequence, it became clear to both the therapist and the patient that the patient had invented the role that the therapist later came to fill in his mind prior to the first meeting. His longing for help was already part of a creative project that he brought with him to therapy.

In the fifth year of an intensive treatment, a patient said to her therapist, in a tone of aggrieved resignation, that she did not think she would ever be able to live without him. Her therapist replied that, while he had full confidence that some day she would be able to stop therapy when other life tasks and commitments seemed more promising, he very much doubted that he would ever be unavailable to her as an internal presence. He also said that he thought she experienced him some-times as a persecutory and constricting inner presence, so that the angry wish to be rid of him brought in its wake the frustrated sense that she never would achieve what she longed for.

The borderline patient, with his devastated lack of self-esteem and compensatory competitive, even annihilatory grandiosity, can represent a serious threat to the therapist's sense of identity as a "healer" and bring into question many of his own concerns in regard to his ideals. He is likely to experience extended passages when he feels more heel than healer. Sullivan (1953) observed that our view of others is but our self-regard broadcast over a wider field. Certainly, borderline patients have a gift for devastating the self-esteem of those who work with them. In supervising talented psychiatric residents who encounter seriously ill borderline patients, we have been impressed with the intensity and depth of their reactions to the borderline patient's distress and its projected intensity.

"All this anger," one gifted resident said, "it just isn't me. I had no idea there was so much anger inside me. This year hasn't been at all what I expected. I could never have imagined it, not in a million years. Do we really do them any good? I'm not sure." An ongoing question in working with borderline patients is what we mean to accomplish. The resident's lack of certainty about whether she was helping her patients was a step forward. If the patients must learn to trade in a magical all-or-none view of treatment's potential efficacy, the therapist must find ways to manage his wishes to rescue (which can often have the valence of annihilating what is frustrating) and the attending senses of desperation and grandiosity, so that these impulses can be put in the service of limited projects of partial and collaborative reconstruction. Part of working with seriously ill borderline patients is a sustained questioning of why in the world one would choose to take this on. The flavor of these treatments often has much more in common with the atmosphere of the cancer ward than is commonly recognized. Often psychotherapy, like chemotherapy, can seem to be about poisoning the patient as much as about helping him.

The questioning of the meaning of doing the work does not confine itself to the years of residency and early practice.

It goes on and on, taking on with each new phase in the therapist's development the particular cast of that new developmental moment and, particularly, that moment's opportunities for disappointment and despair. Disastrous regressions in patients, repeated impasses, not to mention tragic outcomes—suicides or even homicides, for example—darken the colors with which the therapist paints for himself the portrait of his own working life.

Loss and disappointment knock over and over again and demand to be included without being exaggerated to the exclusion of all that is good. The work on splitting operations and the reconciliation of apparent emotional opposites through more complex internal psychological figures is never finished. These struggles can move the therapist closer to the terrain on which the borderline patient finds himself writhing and protesting and declaring his settled intent to give it up once and for all. Or, if the therapist's pain is too much or his internal capacity to grow and accommodate it too limited, such struggles can push him to such great distances that he simply cannot work with this kind of patient.

An extremely experienced therapist with a record of real effectiveness in working with borderline patients said, "Sometimes I sit there and think, 'Why don't they enjoy the things about life that I enjoy?' I can't understand it. It's like not liking chocolate. But they don't." His tone was marked by sadness. He clearly considered the patients candidates for pleasure in life, and recognized and accepted their frustration.

THE PATIENT TAKES CARE OF THE
THERAPIST BY PAYING

The most concrete token of the patient's care for the therapist is the money paid for therapy. Unless the therapist is independently wealthy, he is actually dependent on the patient for the provision of his livelihood. Even if the therapist is independently wealthy, the patient's payment may provide needed reassurance that he could earn a livelihood should this become necessary. The specific meanings attached to the monetary transaction depend not only on the backgrounds and personal circumstances of the therapist and the patient, but on the phase of treatment and the specific quandaries being worked out and played out at specific times.

Much can stand in the way of the recognition of the therapist's actual dependence, which is real even if the therapist is salaried and paid by an institution, if the cost of therapy is borne primarily by insurance, or if therapy is paid for by a family member other than the patient. Reduced fee arrangements can represent not only an actual aid to the patient but a defense on the therapist's part against his own conflicts around being dependent. The patient and the therapist can each have powerful motives for neglecting the monetary dependency of the therapist.

For example, it may embarrass the therapist to realize that he requires help from the patient. In the service of his own grandiosity, he may enjoy the fantasy that he provides but is not provided for, a fantasy that is reinforced by rigid role boundaries. This fantasy may also protect him from awareness of his own greed, at the same time that he may have a heightened awareness of greed in the patient. This can be particularly important when the therapist feels blocked or dissatisfied in other major areas of his own life, a not unusual human circumstance. Also, it may protect him from the awareness of separation vulnerability, again at the same time that he has a heightened awareness of such vulnerability in the patient. He may not wish to know how much he would feel he lost if he lost the patient. This represents a limitation on the capacity to understand what the patient means. Neglect of this dependency can also involve important dynamics around fusion.

Every role boundary emphasizes certain qualities at the expense of others. The healer's sadism, for example, is downplayed in the definition of the healing role, even though healers have their fair share, if not more, of sadistic impulses. Similarly, the healer's social representation as caretaker downplays his own needs for care and compensation. When the social role boundaries downplay a particular quality, this creates what amounts to socially sanctioned avenues for projective identification. What is not sanctioned within the role boundary must find a place outside the border. The healer's dependent need to have people depend on him may be very difficult to reclaim.

The patient may be only too pleased, sometimes even consciously as well as unconsciously, to participate in playing down what he gives and the therapist receives. Seeing the therapist as a person with actual needs, including the need for payment, threatens the notion that it is possible to escape from need. The patient's minimizing what he provides may be in the service of an idealization of the therapist with which the most disturbed part of the patient identifies. This identification with a fantasied triumph over need may be much to the detriment of the patient's capacity to engage with himself on more complicated realistic middle grounds in which he is both provider and provided for, both active and passive, and both entitled and obligated. The therapist who colludes with this may be setting up a stalemate. Why should the patient come to grips with his own needs when he can cherish the belief that his therapist has found the key to getting rid of the therapist's needs? A borderline patient once said to his therapist in absolute earnest, "I never realized that therapists had feelings or that they needed anything. I never thought we had a thing in common."

We have made it a practice wherever possible to expect some portion of the fee to be paid through the efforts of the person being treated, however small that portion may be. This has the advantage of adjusting the balance of helpfulness and helplessness, not only between the patient and the therapist but also between the patient and the person who is assisting in supporting the therapy. We have been impressed with how often patients have denied that they pay anything at all. Their discomfort with the middle ground of paying some but not all themselves has had myriad determinants, from a feeling that they have nothing to offer, through intense shame about not being able to do everything for themselves, to a sense, often with considerable justification, that they have already given so much care to caretakers that it represents theft for anyone to expect anything more of them.

The capacity to take care entails a recognition of destructive potential. The power to feed is, as mothers and small children know, the power to starve. If a patient recognizes in himself a capacity to take care of a therapist, then the patient must also come to grips with his capacity to withhold the care. If the recognition of a caretaking potential is empowering, then the power can bring in its wake enormous conflicts over how it might be employed, specifically for various projects of vengeance carried on in unconscious identification with those who have been the most hurtful to the patient. Needless to say these conflicts are alive in the therapist as well as the patient.

Most borderline patients feel that thoughts and urges are tantamount to deeds. From the standpoint of inner representation there is a considerable weight to this notion. To think of something, to rehearse or to plot it, changes the internal simulations that make up the inner sense of emotional reality. Not only borderline patients but their therapists react feelingfully to what is fantasized. The acknowledgment of mutual interdependence can be terribly difficult because of all the memories of failed interdependence, betrayals, deliberate hurts, and periods of intolerable chaos that these unlock. Yet it is in the actuality of the therapeutic situation that the stimulus to reexamine and rework is to be found. To avoid the difficult question of the current reality of mutual interdependence is to avoid not only storm and stress but therapeutic opportunity. It is a disconnection which may be defensively inescapable for long periods but eventually must come under scrutiny if reliable communication and differentiation are to be achieved.

A CASE EXAMPLE

A young borderline woman who shared the cost of her treatment with her parents had been paying her bill at the very end of the allotted thirty days for several months. For a number of years she had had a pattern of arriving late at sessions, which she wrestled with on and off, conveying the expectation that her therapist should be reproving or solve her problem for her. The month after her therapist's summer vacation, she put the bill in the glove compartment of her car and "forgot about it." Eventually, she brought this up and said that forgetting the bill had to do with how angry she was about her therapist's going away just when she needed him so much, and how angry she was that she needed him so much. She paid the bill shortly after the beginning of the next month.

She did not pay the next bill until the allotted thirty days had elapsed. When her therapist gave her the bill for the following month, he asked her if she was aware that she had not paid. This happened on a Monday. She became immediately enraged and stated that her therapist was deliberately trying to persecute her by rubbing salt in her wounds. She said that she had done her duty in talking about how angry she was about his leaving during the summer and did not appreciate his subjecting her to repeated humiliation when she had so much else that she needed to discuss with him.

She stated that she would reduce the frequency of her therapy and declared that it would make much more sense for her to talk with someone else besides him. She also indignantly made the correct observation that it was not like him to bring up the matter of a late bill so soon; ordinarily, he tended to wait for her to bring it up, which she pointed out that she regularly did. She felt insulted that he was bringing a responsibility of hers to her attention and, although she would have been able to understand this if she were not working in therapy, she was working very hard. Her therapist's bringing it up made her feel that he minimized her efforts and she had enough trouble believing that she could do anything without further devaluation from him. She also included in her tirade a lengthy and stinging attack to the effect that all therapists are infatuated with themselves and enjoy making people grovel, a quality she could not understand at all. That is, she had no inkling of trying to use money to make her therapist grovel.

She cancelled her session for the next day. She and her therapist had a telephone conversation in which he expressed the hope that she would be able to discuss how angry she was with him. She said that she had cancelled as early as possible to avoid paying. He said, angrily, that he intended to charge her anyway. He later decided that it made sense to change his position on this and brought up the point that it sounded as if she had seriously considered not talking to him again. She said this was so, but she couldn't do it. She knew only too well what it was like to be cut off in that way, since her boyfriend had done it to her. Her therapist thought of her previous psychiatrist who had committed suicide while she was in treatment, providing neither warning nor explanation.

Not only did her therapist recognize the validity of her observation that this was not his usual way of handling delayed payment, he also recalled that he had noted the angry and tense look on her face as she entered his office that Monday morning and debated whether he should say anything about the bill. He had decided that he should say something at the beginning of the session so that he would not interrupt her at an awkward time. He wondered if he had been having a hard time listening to her talk about her struggles to believe that her relationship with her boyfriend had ever been real.

A number of factors went into the therapist's maladroit handling of the delayed payment. He was aware that he was more anxious than usual about money because, since his wife's death two years earlier, he had curtailed his working time and therefore his earnings. Recently, he had been spending more money and had begun to feel that he should expand his practice again. Given that he had not taken on a new patient in a long while, he had anxieties about how easily he could accomplish this.

Discussing the interchange around the bill in a later session, her therapist explained that he knew he had been more anxious about money recently and that he felt more vulnerable with his reduced practice. He said that he thought that previously, when he had worked more and earned more, he had been able to mask his dependence on individual patients from himself more effectively. He was able to recognize an angry component in his way of broaching the subject and a real discomfort with dependency.

The patient recognized the theme of masked dependence. In subsequent sessions she talked more freely about it with regard to her father and to other members of her family. She described relief in having been able to be so openly angry at her therapist. She pointed out that she always had a quandary about using talking about her life separate from him as a way to avoid talking about what went on between the two of them. After noting this device for masking dependence, she went on to describe how hard the death of the therapist's wife and his subsequent remarriage had been for her and how much trouble she had accepting disappointment and loss. She spoke of her longing for her mother's approval and the hopelessness of this longing. She took on in depth the theme of how much she hated it when she was not appreciated and her efforts did not receive a response. With some vigor she described how much trouble she had charging appropriately for her own work and how much she resented it when she was not paid or got paid late, even if she did collude in not getting paid. She had, she said, counselled a friend to simply withdraw his services if payment were late. Wryly, she noted it was easier to advise it than to do it.

If they can be understood and brought into open discussion, most countertransference errors are actually errands in the sense that they point to material that is, although very difficult, ripe or even overripe for discussion. In this vignette, the therapist's dependency anxieties prompted an ill-timed inquiry about payment that precipitated a crisis that proved to be extremely fruitful, once he was able to avow his own dependency needs and conflicts around them. Self-disclosure in this area provided increased containment and led to a much broader and more open discussion of difficult dependency issues both within the therapeutic dyad and in other areas of the patient's life, both past and present.

DEEPER STRATA OF DEPENDENCY

The therapist's need for the patient to consolidate, confirm, and maintain his own professional identity as a therapist, with all its personal meanings for him, and the therapist's actual dependence on the patient's payments for his livelihood are features that are built into the treatment relationship. These features serve as organizing foci for a variety of meanings and conflicts that are different from treatment to treatment, depending on the individual participants and what they need to express. In a sense, they are screens on which a variety of different contents and images can be projected. It is important to keep them in view in order to discern the deeper and more idiosyncratic forms of dependency dialogue. It is a regular and recurring observation about therapy that the deepest difficulties have a way of showing up in surface features whose profound importance is difficult to appreciate except through long engagement with them.

What characterizes the deeper and more idiosyncratic forms of dependency dialogue is the re-creation within the therapist–patient dual unit of old situations, possibly ones that have long been exiled from conscious memory. The particular flavors of the individuals' experiences color the dialogue, which often contains feelings that are hard to represent adequately in words.

What follows is a brief and relatively unsubtle example of an aspect of deeper dependency dialogue.

A very stubborn, obstinate, and denying borderline patient had long periods of ferocious silence. She made continual threats of self-destruction, sometimes coming to therapy intoxicated on drugs and promising to leave immediately and kill herself. As the silences became deeper and darker, her therapist found them harder to bear.

One day he had the fantasy that he had a sledge-hammer in his hands and that he was beating her over the head with it as hard as he could. The only result was the sound of metal ringing on metal and a stinging pain in his hands. He realized that he felt desperately cut off from her and also so enraged that he was inhibited not only in communicating but in thinking. He was not able to say anything to her about this fantasy, but he did find his attention directed to aspects of his own feelings of maternal deprivation that he had long denied. He began to think about how important it was to him that this patient listen to him and how much trouble he had with her difficulty in hearing him. He began to suspect that these feelings echoed his own early childhood and that they had a fundamental bearing on his decision to be a therapist, with its crucial confrontation with issues of hearing and being heard.

He realized that, in working with her, he had assumed the posture of a small child whose appeals go unheard and whose rage is at once terrifyingly out of control and in no way practically effective. He suspected that she had similar feelings and found it more possible to bear with the silence. Within a few days, she ventured into a discussion of severe beatings she had received as a child. He had not heard about this in any detail before.

The difficulties in communicating with this patient did not resolve, but rather ebbed and advanced, assuming over and over again the characteristic of being overwhelming. The therapist's own sense of the play of his own dependency needs in the therapy helped him to tolerate the situation without needing to become too active or too confronting. He was able to focus a good deal of his urge to be active and understanding and clarifying within himself on himself, and to wait for what was forthcoming from the patient. He also was able to see the patient as being a help to him in coming to grips with features of his own experience that he liked to ignore.

In the past, this patient had been seen as terribly difficult and demanding, with next to nothing to offer, and had been extruded from a number of treatments. The therapist's own trouble with facing his pain provided him more empathy for her difficulties in facing her own experience.

A colleague was bemoaning the difficulties of working with borderline patients. An extremely perceptive person who often aroused envy for his seemingly effortless acumen in characterizing people and situations, he declared that he envied the borderline patients the purity and intensity of their affects. He said they often made him feel like he lived his life in shades of gray, watered-down tones with very little conviction. He wondered what had impelled him to renounce the kind of intensity that so appealed to him. In his attitudes towards psychiatry as well as in his relationships, alternating idealizing and devaluing trends of considerable intensity vied for primacy.

It seemed fairly clear that one of the functions that borderline patients filled for him was to provide him a vicarious opportunity to participate in intense feeling, thus compensating for a lack he felt within while allowing him at the same time to keep a safe distance from emotional issues that troubled him more than he was comfortable in granting. He was dependent on his patients to bring him to life, unconsciously employing them as stimulants to counter inward depressive feelings.

The envy that this colleague aroused was not unlike the envy that he reported was aroused in him by borderline patients. We all enjoy some of the borderline maneuvering at the limit in the way that one could enjoy a roller coaster at an amusement park. We envy it in colleagues and friends as well as in borderline patients. We may even discover that one part of us, more sober and responsible, envies another part internally. The acceptance of limitation is not a once-and-for-all process. When one looks beneath the surface, sorrow intrudes, but it is precisely the sorrow that adds depth and a lustre that is richer than simple excitement, intensity, or facility.

McCormack (1989) has described a marriage constellation involving one borderline spouse who provides intensity and a pull toward involvement and one schizoid spouse who provides an opposing pull in the direction of lower intensity and rigid boundaries. Each complements the other, projecting important parts onto the spouse and utilizing identifications to remain in touch outside with what cannot be tolerated inside. A similar coupling mechanism may bind together a therapist with a defensive style that steers away from substantial affective involvement and a borderline patient. It is even possible that a therapist will need the urgency of a patient's suicidality to permit a response at an emotional level, thus supporting the patient's suicidality.

ON THERAPEUTIC INGRATITUDE
AND REPARATION

"How sharper than a serpent's tooth it is to have a thankless child," bemoans Shakespeare's King Lear, in one of the best known expressions of a common theme. What is much less common is any discussion of parents' ingratitude towards their children. The Ten Commandments enjoin respect for parents but do not carry an injunction regarding respect for children. Development of this theme comes later in the history of Jewish law.

MacLean (1985) has made the point that the command-ment, "Thou shalt not eat thy children," intended quite literally, stands prior to the Ten Commandments and marks a crucial watershed between reptilian and mammalian lines of development. The emotional analogue of this command-ment, "Thou shalt not use thy children to meet thine own needs without acknowledging this, bearing responsibility for it and expressing gratitude where it is realistically indi-cated," is still the focus of an enormously complicated developmental struggle in human parenting.

As the therapist's dependence on the patient is played down, the occasions for appropriate recognitions of what the patient has given and appropriate expressions of real gratitude pass in silence. This imposes a large strain on the patient's struggle for realistic regulation of self-esteem. Can he learn to appreciate himself without being appreciated? Most borderline patients have been the object of such intru-sive projections and such extensive neglect that this question has already been answered in the negative in their develop-ment. It imposes a strain of secret guilt on the therapist as well, for at some level he is aware of having committed a form of theft, quite possibly with resonances from his past as well as the patient's.

Searles (1979b, c) has had the courage and creativity to challenge the rigid boundaries of the therapist's role along two related fronts. He has emphasized the role that hostility can play in the therapist's dedication, advocating an ambivalence toward therapeutic zeal. Winnicott (1949) has taken up a related topic in discussing the place of countertransference hate and its expression in treatment. Searles has also attacked another set of implicit splitting operations by discussing the capacity of extremely sick patients to take up a therapeutic posture toward the sickest part of their therapists. He has pointed out that the healer is not an all-powerful source of goodness any more than the sickest patient is a totally incapacitated source of unalloyed ruination. In this way, he has suggested two lines of response that open up wider capacities for communication, feeling, and mutual recognition of shared humanity between patient and therapist.

Gratitude presupposes the recognition of neediness on the part of the one receiving and of generosity on the part of the one giving. Much filial ingratitude probably originates in parental ingratitude and neglect. A good deal of ill feeling on the part of patients toward therapists may be related to the therapists' difficulty in relating both to themselves and to their patients as people with a full range of human capacities and needs.

Therapists' recognition of their own needs and expressions of gratitude for what they have received from their patients can play an important part in reclaiming projections that have a fundamentally debilitating effect on the therapeutic process by confining both patient and therapist within stereotyped positions that have little to do with them as real people. This does involve self-disclosure on the therapist's part. If the therapist is comfortable with self-disclosure to himself of his own needs, the acknowledgement of the patient represents much less difficulty. Even at the level of acknowledging what we have learned from patients, it has been our impression that we, as therapists, talk much more about this to each other than to the patients. Are we afraid that we will frighten them by showing clearly that we share in the tasks and troubles of learning?

The therapist's recognition of his own needs and appropriate expression of gratitude for what the patient has really offered him represent the opposite of exploitation of the patient. The patient can identify with the therapist's capacity to appreciate and allow for his own needs, to accept imperfections, even to apologize when a need of his own has produced what he has come to be able to recognize as a strain or interference in the therapy. All these issues are at the core of the borderline syndrome. Certainly, there is an ethical obligation to conduct therapy for the benefit of the patient, but, if therapy is to be truly a collaboration, something done *with* and not *to*, then there is as well an ethical obligation to recognize how the patient benefits the therapist—by promoting the therapist's growth and understanding and even by providing some maturational supplies that the therapist did not realize he needed until he received them.

The capacity to care for oneself is rooted in the care one receives from others and in the care one gives to others. The failure to recognize how much they care can deform people beyond recognition. Is it possible that we are, at some levels, as guilty of ingratitude toward borderline patients as we accuse them so often—if not out loud then in our hearts and subtle gestures—of being toward us? If this is so, then we not only have an obligation to make amends but are likely to discover that the amendments made are of significant benefit to ourselves, not just in our work but across the range of our living.

12

On Self-Disclosure in Treatment

This chapter is presented in a slightly different format than the previous ones. A discussion of self-disclosure in treatment by one of us (Lewin) is followed by a discussion by the other (Schulz). We have elected this format for two reasons. The first is that we practice differently. The second is that this essay, as originally written, had a highly personal dimension that it did not seem useful to disguise. This book arose out of a sustained discussion between the two of us about issues in treating patients. In this chapter, the compound narrative voice of this book resolves into its component parts. This, too, represents self-disclosure.

ON SELF-DISCLOSURE

The first question is what we might mean by the term *self-disclosure.* In discussing the history of the usage of the term *disclosure*, the *Oxford English Dictionary* brings together two important currents of meaning, one having to do with revelation and discovery, the other having to do with growth and development, specifically, hatching and the emergence of an insect from the pupa. Is disclosure about releasing or revealing what was already there, that is, discovering it to the light of day? Or is it about a stage in a process of creation in which what is coming to be takes a definitive step toward a discoverable form? Is revelation in itself an act of creation?

Rather than trying to choose between these two tributary currents of meaning, we would do well to bear the tension of keeping them both in mind. The form of this paradox will be familiar to readers of Winnicott (1953), who discusses it in terms of the nature of the child's activity in regard to the transitional object: "Of the transitional object it can be said that it is a matter of agreement between us and the baby that we will never ask the question: 'Did you conceive of this or was it presented to you from without?' The important point is that no decision on this point is expected. The question is not to be formulated" (p. 95).

No doubt self-disclosure involves a description of what was found to be there, as, for example, a space probe beams back information regarding a planet that was already there. However, it is a characteristic of the worlds of inner space that self-disclosure is not simply about the revelation of the self as an object to be discerned and described, but about constituting it as a more or less valid illusion. What is so often neglected about self-disclosure is its practical, active, and creative movement. We may say that self-disclosure is "self*ing*-disclosure."

"Words," sang Pablo Neruda (1975) in one of his great crystalline and yet deeply shadowed lyrics, "give glass quality to glass, blood to blood, and life to life itself" (p. 9). We become ourselves in the process of saying what we are. The words Neruda is referring to are what I like to call connected words, by which I mean that they relate to the actual inner world of the person using them. They are not idle words because they give shape to the interior. They are not the dull words of vain scholarship or of bureaucratic process for the sake of an institutionalized utilitarian numbness, but words that are the vessels of passion and experience. These are the words that have some hope of healing in psychotherapy, for they possess a mundane magic that reaches far beyond the literal. They have the power to change even that aspect of presence we call the past and that so often seems, wrongly, to be both utterly finished and unutterably tyrannical.

A young patient complained, "Do you know the trouble with my father? He keeps trying to reduce the size of his mind. He makes walls and then more walls and then more walls. It's so sad. He's always afraid that he's going to drown in there. I think most of us are doing that most of the time. We are all so big inside that we terrify ourselves." Self-disclosure is about an inner openness, not just about making room, but about learning to inhabit it.

SELF-SELF DISCLOSURE AND SELF-OTHER DISCLOSURE

In conventional usage we overlook the ambiguity of the term self-disclosure. We assume that it means the disclosure of the self to an other. It can also mean disclosure to oneself. And it can refer to the disclosure of one part of the self to another in an internal dialogue in which each is to the other an other. This kind of dialogue, which is much more common and enriching than is normally assumed, is an essential part of all creative activity, including psychotherapy. It has to do with the capacity to be alone in the presence of yourself, the developmental consolidation of the capacity to be alone in the presence of an other.

Being with patients is a form of psychological potential

space for the therapist. The therapist who spends hours listening to patients is simultaneously engaged in listening to himself, hearing, at least intermittently, things that are interesting and stimulating.

A. Szalita (1981) told a story about Erich Fromm some years ago at Chestnut Lodge. Fromm was complaining that his analysis and his analyst were useless and that he was getting nothing out of them. "Come now," Dr. Szalita asked him, "you are a bright and interesting man. How can you say that you get nothing out of an hour of listening to yourself?" (This is a close paraphrase rather than an actual quotation.) Fromm's inability to attend to himself is the kind of blockage that in the essence makes life a draining and drained experience for so many people. The therapeutic question, one that Dr. Szalita left aside, is how to go about resolving this kind of blockage.

When, for example, the borderline patients express and enact their voracious demands for response of the most concrete kinds, providing hair-raising and offensive demonstrations to the effect that nothing could ever be enough, what is most sad and dispiriting is the picture of inner deafness and aloofness, if not deadness, that emerges. The problem is the one highlighted by Dr. Szalita for Erich Fromm, only carried to the extreme, namely, that these patients lack the most rudimentary faculties for responding to themselves. Their emotionality and excitements, their faculties for putting themselves in extremity, once understood, seem like the most pathetic and desperate efforts to produce some tiny flicker of inner life. The issue is not so much affect containment as affect attainment, if by affect we mean a symbolically organized and related performance of an *inner* experience that has any variety at all in tonality and intensity and carries a sense of conviction. Often, these can be very feelingful people, very sensitive, who have turned to stone inside over the years.

By now, I hope I have managed to sneak up on the practical clinical question, how can we usefully conceive of the relationships between self-self disclosure and self-other disclosure in treatment? This chapter's title leaves it deliberately unclear whose self-disclosure to whom we are to discuss. We expect self-disclosure from the patient to us in the hope that this will facilitate the patient's increased understanding. We expect self-disclosure from ourselves to ourselves so that we will be able to understand and utilize our countertransference responses to benefit the patient.

I think it is striking that, not only are we terribly uncomfortable about any explicit and personal self-disclosures on our part to the patient, but we also minimize the very considerable amount of self-disclosure that we actually are making about ourselves all the time simply by being there as we are. What makes us most uncomfortable—positive feelings about ourselves, negative feelings about ourselves, or positive or negative feelings about the patient? Are we simply uncomfortable with any real vividity of feeling, that is to say, any real feeling? Maybe, like my patient's father, we hold back because there is an inner "oceanic" feeling, a sense of potential dissolution of the self, that we fear if we let ourselves connect. When we worry about being too "self-absorbed," perhaps we are alluding to an inner fusing danger of which we are too little aware. Perhaps we are afraid of soaking ourselves up like sponges so that we have nothing left of ourselves.

A resident was feeling irritated with and estranged from her very difficult patient, a feeling that showed in her body carriage and posture as she described the situation in a continuing case conference. She had had the desire to say something quite irreverent to the patient. When she was asked what had stopped her, she visibly stiffened and referred to what she felt was the general impropriety of this level of self-disclosure, especially where negative or critical feelings were concerned. This led to a discussion of the wider question of self-disclosure. Another one of the residents said that whenever he told a patient something about himself or what he was feeling, it seemed to him that he was stepping into quicksand. What would the patient ask next? What would he say next? What would the patient think about him? Where would it lead? He described a discomfiture that was tantamount to a sense of loss of identity as a doctor with a patient.

The thought that came last to me in the ensuing consideration of the resident's quicksand image was perhaps the one that should have come first. His being able to use the image represented an important piece of self-disclosure, one that opened up important lines of discussion. Was he not tuning in to a way that patients often feel, that self-revelation is dangerous, because they have no idea what others will think of them, what they will think of themselves, what their new sense of themselves will demand of them? That is, paradoxically, self-disclosure leads to a heightened awareness of the incompleteness and complexity of the self. Self-disclosure makes the self less finished by replacing constriction with chances for construction.[1]

It has not, in fact, been my experience that self-disclosure leads to anything so dangerous as being mired in quicksand, but rather often to productive collaborative work with patients. Unlike this resident, many therapists are quite unaware and, unfortunately, quite unconflicted about the extent to which they, as real people, have walled themselves off from their patients as real people. They accept a rigid construction of the boundary between personal and professional, as if the two were antithetical rather than complementary modes. Characterological predilection and theoretical conceptions have become alloyed in many cases to produce the impenetrable and terribly constricting armor of an authoritative professional identity. This is only too likely to represent an inflexible defensive compromise that forecloses the developmental struggle toward modu-

---

1. We are indebted to Drs. Laurie Orgel, Kathleen Lyon, Susan Wait, and Michael Fulop for this material from an ongoing case conference.

lated responsiveness over a wider experiential range because the fear of internal chaos in the therapist is too great.

The one who is in terror of his "personal" primitivity can not risk the complementarity of a personal/professional identity because it would remind him too much of what he finds most dangerous in himself. The flight into professional identity is so often a flight from the self, especially from those aspects of the helper's self that need help so desparately. Striving to turn Sullivan's famous dictum, "We are all more simply human than otherwise," (1953, p. 16) on its head, many of us do try to present ourselves as therapists who are more "otherwise" than "simply human." I do not think that it is possible to exaggerate the inhibiting and shaming action of this kind of attitude on patients.

Certainly, the "biologizing" of treatment reinforces this trend, with so many of us picturing ourselves in dialogue with patients' molecules, not with them as suffering persons. I do not mean by this statement to deny the usefulness of the biological perspective, but rather to insist on its grounding in a more profound sense of the biological. This sense is that which pertains to the *logos* of a life, to what fills a life with meaning for the one who lives it.

ROLE SANCTIONED SELF-DISCLOSURE

We should not neglect the particular forms of self-disclosure that the role of psychotherapist sanctions. We are allowed to admit, even to display prominently and with pride, our curiosity concerning the feelings and innermost mental processes of other persons. We can put on display our insistent concerns with connections of the most peculiar and counterintuitive kind. As one patient put it after she had just come up with an arresting new idea about herself, "If there is one thing that I have learned from you and that I really believe, it's that there is no theory too weird for serious consideration.'' The kind of curiosity that is openly present in psychotherapy, with all its possibilities for intimacy and dangers of voyeuristic fascination, probably exceeds that which can be comfortably accommodated in most spousal relationships, parent–child relationships, and friendships. We stand revealed to our patients as people with very powerful needs to know and urges to mastery through understanding. The farther we advance as psychotherapists, the more intrigued we become with the personal determinants in the areas of aggression and intimacy that have stimulated our interests.

I have become more and more aware how my own loneliness as a child, my sense of my parents' remoteness and preoccupation, my troubles with sudden unannounced and prolonged separations, and my fears of my own rage served to promote a premature structuralization emphasizing curiosity and mastery through fantasy and understanding of what seemed most overwhelming to me. Thinking about this, I have observed, has been of considerable use in trying to explain to patients why I am so interested and what I am interested in. That is to say, my internal avowal of the personal dimension of what is role sanctioned has helped me to be able to respond more fully and flexibly to patients' concerns in these areas. It has also helped them feel that it is legitimate for them to be curious about me. In a sense, it has made me usefully available to receive a certain kind of projection, for patients, like all of us, are not curious about what does not concern them inwardly.

To some degree, the difference between a job and a vocation is the extent to which one has identified and been able to listen to and understand the voice that calls one from within to the work one does. If the personal dimension of the ''vocational'' choice involved in being a therapist is not available for examination, then the question of who is called to do what by what from inside may be rendered more inaccessible than need be. This would be an example of using a too concrete reality orientation to shut off consideration of the deeper reality of illusion and personal experience.

UNAVOWED SELF-DISCLOSURE

As she leaves, one young patient performs an unconscious ritual that says more than words. She pauses just through the door, takes a deep breath, stiffens, closes the door almost all the way, grips the knob just a bit more tightly, and then, without looking, pushes it fully and definitively shut, as if she were sealing me in my office until her next appointment. This is how she discloses the pervasiveness of her worries about separations and the way in which they are bodily occupying, determining her rigidity of posture, the constriction in breathing, and a host of psychophysiological symptoms.

Patients are not the only ones who disclose everything in this manner. Stories of the sensitivity of psychotic patients to the deepest levels of their therapists' characters and disavowed feelings are clinical commonplaces. The dedicated analyst's abstinent aloofness endows his telltale cough with a seductive eloquence of enormous impact. A shift in the pace of breathing or in posture can be enough to warn a patient away from a line of self inquiry that occasions distress and discomfort in the therapist, just as such cues from mother are what shape and define the boundaries of what is accepted in an infant's and toddler's internal repertoire.

Describing the differing natures of the presences within his mind of his mother and father, a patient said, "My father is a voice. I can hear him inside me and even sometimes disagree. My mother is an action that happens in me." This patient's material makes the point more eloquently than any theoretical discussion. When we do not avow our presence as a potent influence, full of prejudice, premature judgment, and unfortunate foreclosure of options, we deprive our patients and ourselves of a realm of interactive liberty. This deprivation works to the disadvantage of both of us. We are still influencing, but irresponsible about our influences because we deny them.

I worked for a bit more than two years with a borderline woman of 50 who had had a considerable amount of previous treatment, including an extended hospitalization twenty years earlier. She came to me because of a bewildering array of physical symptoms that only got worse the more she was medicated. Within the past few years, her mother-in-law, who had made her life miserable and whom she hated, had died and been cremated. The ashes were still in the back of this woman's car and she seemed powerless to get rid of them. She described herself as powerless in so many other areas as well. She had enormous worries about her husband's health, serious and realistic ones magnified by the force of her own hostile wishes that defended her against both the deeper merger dangers and the deeper loss dangers.

Midway through our work together, she presented me with a drawing in pastels that she had made of the two of us in my office. The perspective was from behind her, so that she was rendered as the relatively impersonal back of a head, a vague figure shrouded in a chair of the kind doctors have in their offices. It was uncanny the extent to which she had caught my posture, the attitude of my body, the tilt of my head. I was reduced to a teddy bear sitting in a chair with an expression that was at once wistful, whimsical, and, so it seemed to me, profoundly lost and sad. Tellingly, my feet did not come close to reaching the ground.

I was very grateful to her for the drawing, because it seemed to me that it showed me to myself with a new clarity and fullness both. I was aware, too, that she had made me up out of herself, that is, that her drawing of me was part of her internal repertoire. I talked with her about how small and sad and lost, yet wistful and whimsical her representation of me seemed to me. I said that what most struck me was the gentleness portrayed because, internally, I tended more often to experience myself as ferocious and dangerous. She talked about how scared she got of her own anger, too. I remarked in passing that I had noticed how left out she was in the drawing, appearing only as a head that melds into the chair. She said her life had always been that way.

I still have this drawing in my office. It surpised me with how openly and completely I was on display to my patients without my being aware of it. In view of this drawing, the subsequent course of therapy was interesting. With time, the patient began to worry more and more about the expense. She became involved in a church different than the one her husband was involved in and experienced what she described as a spiritual rebirth. Although she provided me with numerous invitations to denigrate her conversion, I was careful to state my respect for faith and religious community. She made it clear to me that "Jesus and religion are much bigger than any psychiatrist and psychiatry." With her physical symptoms having receded into the background, she quite amicably, but with considerable undertones of sadness and longing, left my care, bringing me a bottle of red wine as a farewell present. My association was to communion wine.

USES OF THE THERAPIST'S
SELF-DISCLOSURE

A very insecure and tentative young woman who had been hospitalized for a year because she was despondent and suicidal pointed out to me one day that every time she complimented me I flinched. We discussed this interaction for years, starting while she was in the hospital and continuing through five years of outpatient treatment. My initial reaction was that she was so effusive in her compliments as to border on being assaultive. I saw myself being sent aloft on a cloud that could fail at any time to bear my weight, sending me crashing to the ground. I granted that, while I had not been aware of it, her observation that I flinched in the face of her compliments was probably accurate. I also told her that I was aware that, when I flinched, she felt rejected and hurt. I said that I was very sorry to be hurting her feelings in this repetitive way and that I hoped we could work together on it.

As time went on, it became clear to me that, not just her compliments, but compliments in general were threatening to me. They made me feel I might melt. I told her about this, going on to say that I was aware as well that I desperately craved compliments and that, perhaps, this craving was part of what made me so uncomfortable with them. She responded that it seemed very sad that I could not accept compliments, because to her I really seemed just as wonderful as she said. She also said that she knew just what it is like to want compliments and to want to make everything better for everyone, but also to know that you did not deserve them and could not do it. She said it was sad, too, that, even though she knew all this, she could not stop trying, as if she really could be a fairy godmother if she just tried hard enough. She also said that no one in her life had ever been able to bear her compliments.

As I started to look at this kind of interaction from her point of view, I found myself thinking about my own father. I realized that my trouble with compliments was a fairly accurate copy of his. I also remembered being very injured by his diffidence and his deflating of my efforts to compliment him when I was a little boy. How was I to protect myself through identification with someone very powerful and perfect if he refused to grant his own power and perfection?

When I discussed this new layer of my understanding with her, my patient responded that she often felt she was hurting her father when she complimented him. She said she didn't think that it would ever be possible for him to acknowledge her feelings for him, because it was just too dangerous. This led into a discussion not only of the oedipal problem, but also of her experience of her older sisters and mother as dangerously envious in the most primitive ways.

We were able to discuss her fear of the envy of my other patients and her worry about my capacity to acknowledge her affectionate feelings. Sometimes this terrified her. My self-disclosure had not inhibited her development of a robust transference relationship with me. Actually, I think the idea that self-disclosure on the doctor's part will distort the transference developed by the patient is not unlike believing that it is possible to divert the Amazon from its course with a canoe paddle. Paradoxically, those who insist on a distant, "neutral" technique in the name of not diluting or distorting the transference relationship seem to be expressing their doubts about the reality and power of the transference process.

Over the next two years, as she began to be able to develop the theme of her own rage and efforts to avoid knowledge of it, the patient spoke about how each compliment she received felt like an injunction coupled with a threat. If she were complimented on a performance, or even on any everyday action, or even on the way she looked, that meant to her that she had to do that well each and every time. If she failed to live up to the standard, then she would be entitled to no self-respect or self-recognition. Every success or chance of success seemed to her a great danger, ardently desired and ardently feared. In a way, we had come full circle. My flinching at compliments enabled her to begin to look at an important feature in herself, how compliments, success, and any self-liking made her flinch.

The theoretical point here may be that self-disclosure on the therapist's part is essential to the back and forth of the metabolism of projections. We may need to project our difficulties onto others in order to get a glimpse of them. This is the positive, contact-making feature of projections. If we are to be able to reclaim them, the other must be able to show us that part of himself that the projection fits, as well as how he is able to do something a bit different with the projection.

The personal detail provided may be important from the point of view not only of validating the patient's perceptions and experiences, but also in providing substantive clues as to how we manage to do something different. Showing, if it is properly timed and fitted to the patient's emerging understanding, can be substantively enriching, not overwhelming or depriving. Far from threatening emerging autonomy, it can serve to confirm it and extend its potential scope.

From my point of view, this patient helped me reexamine an important aspect of my relationship with my father. I acknowledged this help to her. Of special interest is the fact that this patient came from a family where there were only daughters and no sons, that she had been assigned the impossible role of compensating the parents for not having a male child. As we worked, she talked about how deprived she felt because she could hardly imagine what it was like to be a boy and found it very hard to develop any rapport with men. This was part of what made dating so frightening for her.

HOW MUCH SHOULD WE DISCLOSE?

A senior colleague, a man in his late 60s, was talking with a schizophrenic patient whom he had been seeing for years. The patient seemed more bothered and agitated than usual. The doctor found himself wondering whether it was time for a medication change and thinking about whether he had been able to keep up adequately in the area of psychopharmacology. As he was considering various strategems for trying to make sure that he was up to date, he asked himself whether all this inner consideration about possible inadequacies might relate to what the patient was experiencing. He asked the patient whether he felt that he was having trouble keeping up at work. The patient responded with an audible sigh of relief that this was, indeed, an area where he had a lot of worries at the present time.

This is an example of how introspection can guide the therapist in the identification of a projectively stimulated affect within himself, thus making it possible for him to help the patient take up an affective experience that is at the limit of his capacity for containment. The question that I want to raise has to do with how much to disclose. In the example given, the patient has no way of knowing how the therapist came to ask the question about the possibility of trouble at work. He has no way of knowing that the therapist may have aspects of adequacy worry that are analogous to his own.

When we disclose more of ourselves to patients, we may burden them, we may interfere with their idealizations of us, and we may threaten their sense of separateness. However, we may also broaden and deepen the area of contact between us. We may indicate an acknowledgment of their capacity to help us think, search, and struggle that is very helpful to them in dealing with shamed feelings that have been activated in treatment. I told my colleague that I would have been tempted to talk with the patient about how I came to ask the question and to share my own worries about keeping up or being outmoded. The clinical issue may be to gauge the relative strength of the losing and the fusing dangers at that particular moment in time.

In working with an abused borderline patient with

dissociative features, who was initially seen as schizoid and unable to make human contact, I did a considerable amount of talking about my own reactions, telling her a good bit about my own childhood. The patient had moved every year of her growing up and had attended more than twelve different schools all over the world, although she claimed that this childhood experience had made no difference in her life. After a year of treatment, she told me that I was the first doctor who had ever given her the idea that he had any feelings at all like the ones that she had. She had assumed that doctors did not feel anything, were never upset, and had no interest in their patients' inner emergencies. My self-disclosure supported hers.

Levi-Strauss (1963) made the point that, just as the analyst aims to heal by purporting to listen for the patient, the shaman's healing strategy rests on the claim to speak for the patient. A patient of mine said one day, "I figured out that the way to talk to my girlfriend was to listen to her." I then toyed with the notion that the way to listen to him was to talk with him. Within a few sessions, he was discussing how he had the worst time talking and listening to himself. He had diagnosed the blockage within himself that represented the residue of so much of the trauma and conflict that he had struggled for so long to allow himself to notice.

I do not think the question is so much what we can do *for* the patient, but what we can do *with* the patient. If therapy is to move in the direction of creative collaboration, then we must be able to speak for ourselves and to listen for ourselves. We must recognize the complementarity of listening and talking and promote both as modes that inform and deepen dialogue. The issue is not so much whether behaviorally we talk out loud or to ourselves and to the patient within ourselves, but whether we can allow ourselves a flexibility of choice that does not back us needlessly into corners because we take an all-or-nothing view of who is to do what in treatment.

Returning to the anecdote concerning Eric Fromm, I

think it is possible that Fromm had a legitimate complaint about his analyst and his analysis, namely, that the analyst's activity and the structure of the analysis may not have been as helpful as possible in terms of noticing and resolving the inner blockage as they could have been. Similarly, I think there is an increased place for self-disclosure on the therapist's part in the treatment of seriously character-disordered patients who can manage so little of themselves within themselves. To disclose one's own feelings and reactions is very different than requiring someone else to share them or accept them. I say this because so many of the seriously character-disordered patients have grown up under intense projective pressures and have never heard an avowal of feeling that was not coercive. As a result many live in an interpersonal isolation that is almost inconceivable.

A SELF-DISCLOSURE

Another reason to explore technique that recognizes and makes room for self-disclosure is that there are real events in life that make self-disclosure necessary. These often have to do with sudden and important changes in a therapist's life circumstances, often involving loss and illness. They make it perfectly clear that vulnerability is a shared human condition and that therapists are not immune. It is fanciful to believe that such major changes can be concealed from patients and, in my view, cruel to attempt to do so. When a major life event changes a therapist's being, his demeanor and attention cannot remain the same.

A few years ago, my first wife collapsed into a coma and died two and one half weeks later without regaining consciousness. I was left with an 18-month-old daughter. I did not work for most of the next month and had to rearrange my entire schedule so that I could spend much more time with my daughter. Even after I returned to work, I was deeply grieved, overwhelmed, and in a state of shock. In my practice, I had a woman whose mother was mortally ill at the time, a young man who had lost his mother at the age of 4, and a young woman whose previous psychiatrist had suicided, who had received no subsequent care regarding the traumatic effect of this loss. No one in my practice was without deep experiences of loss.

I have been able to continue work and have received a good deal of succor from my patients. We have been able, I believe, to discuss in some depth how the events that disrupted the course of our work together were not new events for them, but a new mold into which old experience was cast. We have also been able to discuss how I was different after this loss and the advantages and disadvantages of the ways in which I was different. Each patient had worries about his responsibilites for my loss and, in every case, these worries had roots in early experience.

I have struggled, often painfully, with the new limitations of what I have to offer. I have discussed these struggles with the patients as they have become relevant. Without going into detail, I think I can say that my previous experiments with a wider range of self-disclosure served me well in adapting through this difficult period. One seriously disturbed character-disordered patient said to me in the midst of this process, "I think that I've learned more by watching you go through this than anything else. I guess I can stand to listen to what you say to me because you're not telling me anything different than what you have to tell yourself."

DISCUSSION

Dr. Lewin's presentation on self-disclosure in treatment has been preceded by the chapter on the therapist's dependence. There we see the logical introduction to locating strivings, needs, and yearnings not just within the patient but also in the therapist. These shared experiences are not merely "pathological" elements in common, rendering the caretaker and patient both human, but opportunities for illumination of the therapeutic process itself. Instead of featuring the therapist as a person who expertly tells patients the meaning of their communication, therapy rests on the therapist's ability to pay attention to thoughts of one's self and of the patient's self.

When we can rid "dependency" of its pejorative connotations, we can allow it to surface in a way that facilitates examination of both the therapist (staff) and the patient. We continue to grow psychologically as we explore our inner world in the process of making sense of our experiences as related to our patients. Thus, a partial answer to the fascination of intensive and extensive therapy with borderline patients can be found in the injunction, "Physician, heal thyself!" which is applicable at all stages of one's professional life. I experienced it later in my career, when I no longer had pressing financial needs, just as vividly as when I was a neophyte therapist, and of course, such healing continues interminably.

It is my impression that monitoring one's self-experience in detail, during the therapy, will become a step equal in importance to the advance of psychotherapy technique as the formulations of transference, countertransference, self psychology, and object relations. Dr. Lewin's exposition coincides with the arrival of a new book by Natterson (1991), who describes what he calls the *intersubjectivity* of the therapeutic process. He outlines the preceding historical roots of this concept, including the work of Ferenczi and the self psychologists. However, he does not mention Searles's (1979) pioneering contributions of the use of his own reactions to patients' communications—both verbal and nonverbal. Natterson writes:

> Because it involves all aspects of a relationship between two people, such as intense emotions, questions of values

and morals, and other unconscious psychological factors, interpretation addresses the whole person of the patient, and the psychological world he or she inhabits. And it draws from the counterparts in the therapist. Effective understanding of this exquisitely human experience requires involvement of the whole person of the therapist. The adoption of this approach by the therapist inexorably, and usually implicitly, conveys to the patient that all aspects of a person's life are enriched by exploration of a wide range of intersubjective experiences. As a result, the patient more exuberantly faces his or her intricate and contradictory feelings, images and wishes. After all, the therapist has, in an essential way, communicated that he or she is continuously in the same kind of experience as the patient—and so is everyone. [p. 206]

Self-disclosure as advocated here is not that of a therapist unloading on the patient. No doubt under some circumstances self-disclosure can be a step toward the acting out of sexual involvement with a patient. Jorgenson (1991) states, "There is usually a role reversal. The therapist begins telling lots of information about himself to the patient, about his house and family" (p. 13).

The issue then must not be whether to disclose or not to disclose, but to what purpose and to what ends. Can the therapist use his self-monitoring capacities and disclose his observations in order to facilitate the patient's understanding of his own internal world? In the identification process, the therapist begins to pay more attention to the way his thoughts match the experience of therapist with that of the patient. In addition, one begins to trust the relevance of one's associations and then ventures to formulate an inquiry or observation to offer the patient.

In this context we can return to the countertransference polarities previously postulated and discussed in Chapter 10. As stated, we would see our therapist possibly experiencing overidentification with the patient or withdrawn underinvolvement. In either entry, we would expect that paying attention to his experience would provide clues as to what was going on with his patient and help him in securing the patient's assistance in exploring the genesis of his reaction. Here we see another dimension to Sullivan's (1953) concept of the therapist as "participant observer." One need not fear the "quicksand" of intimacy if one uses the "searchlight" of participant observation. The more fully one can explore oneself, the greater the guarantee that one will not go overboard in this process. The freedom to explore would replace a rigidity of proscriptive technique, thus enabling a rich experience for both patient and therapist.

My association with Dr. Lewin over the past ten years, culminating in this book, has influenced the way I practice with my patients. This observation was validated by a patient who returned to analysis after an absence of four years. He noted both the change in me and the consequent change in his feelings about himself along the lines of greater self-acceptance and the sense of collaboration in the resumed analysis.

A Self-Relations Approach with Borderline Patients

WORTH OF THE SUBJECTIVE WORLD

Our goal has been to write a book that would be of practical value to those who are grappling with the arduous clinical task of how to be of use to borderline patients. We take the subjective experience of the patient and the therapist as the foundation of the work. We regard it as substantive and significant. For us it is a central true measure of the "real."

Although we are open to investigation at the molecular and cellular levels and make extensive use of such therapeutic initiatives as psychopharmacological interventions, which draw their inspiration from conceptualizations of molecular and cellular processes, we give the person's experience the central place. In psychiatry, the measure of a medicine is its effect on the person's experience, which we can know only by listening. What we hear often depends on how well we listen, how well we are able to help our patients speak with us and with themselves.

It is vital to remember that molecules and cells exist for the sake of the experiencing human person, not the other way around. Once this is forgotten, which is all too easy to do, the way to a humane practice of medicine, psychiatric or otherwise, is barred. It is the individual, specific, historical, vulnerable person who holds the drama and destiny of the therapeutic enterprise. No matter how we take the person apart, concentrating on units of behavior, cognition, feeling, physiology, or whatever, the person as a whole and the role of complex integration in constituting the person as a whole will still command our attention.

While classification is a central human faculty for attempting to gain a measure of mastery—and we can all be thought of, at least partially and intermittently, as instances of one or another disease—at the core of the clinical enterprise n remains always equal to one. The category never subsumes the individual. As clinicians, we are interested in this particular patient with this particular set of taxing problems, at this particular time.

Our comparisons and contrasts are for the sake of the patient, although it is tempting to see patients for the sake of our fascination with comparisons and contrasts. This is not to minimize the importance of research, but simply to emphasize that, as clinicians, we are interested in peril not generically, but specifically. This illuminates the common experience that, while we may find help or succor in one or another book or article, from one or another "authority," we never find anything so simple, concrete, or definite as "the answer."

Responses are generated in the space of clinical encounter and remain always provisional, moments in the flux of experience. Too much clinical discussion leaves out the uniqueness of the encounter between each doctor and each patient, the existential matter not just at hand but at heart. When the doctor values above all else his ingenuity and is internally reduced to the status of a technician, much of the worth of his own living as well as of the living of his patient is placed at risk.

A SELF-RELATIONS APPROACH WITH BORDERLINE PATIENTS

Our approach might be termed a *self-relations approach with borderline patients*. We look at the borderline syndromes as core disorders of affective self-identity. We place the focus on what the patient can and cannot bear to feel, on the way in which feeling is experienced as disruptive, overly intense, and a threat to any sense of orderly and discrete ongoingness. Arrest in the development of transitional process significantly hampers the capacity to make transitions, to feel and to deal with feeling, to relate one state of the self to another. In our view, what the borderline patient aspires to in therapy is a transformation in the forms of his relationship to himself. The therapeutic relationship mediates the change, which is, like all revaluations, neither all loss nor all gain.

Borderline patients know a great deal about what is most difficult in life and have a long and sad journey to go in coming to terms with their hurt and what it means not only about themselves but about their companions on life's journey. Most treatments of borderline patients lead to nothing so simple as triumph, but rather onto the terrain of loss, grief, reparation, and, in some measure, that resignation that is part and parcel of acceptance, an inherently ambivalent act.

Self-relations are different than object relations in that they emphasize the "self" pole in the creation of the world of internal relations. They emphasize how our experience of others is made up out of our experience of ourselves. They emphasize the complexity of the self, how it is not necessarily all of one piece, free of deep contradictions, every-where connected and communicating, and static, but rather always endowed with a dynamic potential that represents at least a potential challenge to existing order and ardors, or lack thereof. It is of the very essence of the self that it regularly takes itself as its object, complementing itself through subtle and supple inner division, and, in so doing, continually changes its form. How the self responds to itself is the crucial dimension of responsiveness.

A borderline patient was running in a large city one early morning when she saw a man exposing himself to a little girl. The patient was shocked and overwhelmed. She continued to run and saw some police officers, who were drinking coffee and talking to each other. As she described it, she almost kept on running, but was able to tell herself that there were police officers right there and they *might* be able to help. She was not at all sure they would, a state of uncertainty that showed clearly in the way she phrased what she said to them. She was all shy diffidence, worried that she might be disturbing them. She was shocked when they quickly thanked her, broke up their colloquium, and headed around the corner to see what they could do to help.

The patient continued to run, but spent the rest of the day at work in a state of shock, located not in the present but in the past. She remembered a day when she was less than 5 years old when she took her younger sister to the beach near their home and, on the way home, they passed a man who exposed himself to them. She could not recall having done or said anything about it at the time. "I suppose," she said sadly, "I must have told my mother about it and that was the end of it right there." Her therapist was not at all sure that she had told anyone, as she had been so accustomed to suppressing her communicative urges.

She went on to describe her struggle to decide whether to tell her boyfriend about what had happened to her during the day. She was not convinced that he would be interested any more than she had been convinced that the police would take any interest in what she said. After considerable back and forth and with considerable discomfort, she was able to break the shame barrier and tell her boyfriend not only about that morning's experience but about what it brought up from the past. In therapy, she wondered whether perhaps she was making too much of it all.

We can think of this patient as struggling to resolve a self-transference, that is to say, to gain a certain distance from and perspective on an old attitude toward herself that no longer fit the current reality of the self and closed off avenues for adaptation, mastery, and enjoyment. This borderline patient saw herself as simultaneously totally responsible and powerless. She became passive and shamed in the face of any encounter with difficult material that called up conflicted feelings inside herself. In the course of her recounting of the day's struggle with a profoundly troubling experience that resonated deeply within, we could see her struggling to adjust the passivity–activity balance, adjusting her all-or-nothing attitude toward actions, taking a more realistic and current attitude toward communication and responsibility, and beginning to see herself as a member of a community with limited but real resources, not a shamed isolate.

Her therapist helped her to see that in this incident so many of her long-term struggles around how to view herself were crystallized. Eventually they discussed the change in the therapist–patient relationship that had taken place—moving in the direction of a much more collegial and collaborative interaction. They talked about the mixture of pride and pleasure and disappointment it brought, as the patient grieved her wishes to be taken care of totally and celebrated her increased capacity to take care of herself, not in isolation, but interactively.

Perhaps self-transference has always been implicit in more classical object-centered discussions of transference in the sense that the point of resolving an object transference is to change an experience in the self. Making the "self" pole explicit and central can be a help in dealing with patients, because it seems often to make more sense to them: "When you keep insisting that I miss you when you're gone, I just think that you're a self-centered megalomaniac who wants me to miss you because you need to think you're so damned important," said one patient. This patient took much more readily to a discussion of how badly she felt when she was forced to notice that situations were out of her control and that she was not consulted about events that made a significant impact on her. In a sense, this diluted the helplessness and vulnerability by helping her to stay a bit more removed from the overwhelming question of her feelings for another person.

With borderline patients, *approach* is no simple matter, for the regulation of interpersonal distance is a vexed issue. There is virtually no zone of comfort, but instead an agitated oscillation between being *too near* and *too far*. We have highlighted what we have called the *fusing* and the *losing dangers*. The borderline patient, ill-equipped to handle either one of these dangers, is often faced with a war on two simultaneous fronts. Efforts to shore up defenses against the fusing danger by increasing interpersonal distance with devices such as negativism increase vulnerability to the losing danger. Conversely, movements close to the other to protect against the losing danger threaten the self with the fusing danger. We have suggested that it is because of the dynamics of the fusing–losing double danger that treatments of borderline patients can seem so consistently unstable, continuing only by virtue of being about to be broken off.

What, we have asked, are borderline patients missing that makes it so difficult for them to deal with the fusing–losing dangers? These, after all, as we have tried to suggest with our Sunburst Diagram, Figure 2–4, are built in at the core of the human attachment experience. We have focused on the difficulty that borderline patients have in generating and utilizing appropriately self-soothing and self-animating illusions. Borderline patients, as we know them in clinical practice, tend to be stuck at a developmental level where their illusions require a great deal of concrete, literal, and external support. As one patient put it, "My world is just too bulky, too difficult to rearrange."

We have emphasized a relative arrest in the development in borderline patients of transitional object relations and transitional process. The use of the patients' own bodies as transitional objects is prominent, as is reliance on the actual physical presence of a concrete external transitional object, such as a doll, food, or alcohol. The cutting, burning, overexercising, binging, purging, drinking, and drugging that are prominent features of borderline syndromes all have important transitional functions. In however compromising a way, they help protect the highly threatened self by toning down affective experience until it is in a more manageable range: "I don't know what I'd do without razor blades. I can't imagine it. I don't know how I'd get through the day."

We have pointed out how intrinsically transitional process is involved in stabilizing the self against the fusing–losing danger. We have emphasized that the function of transitional process is to do two things at once, to link and to wedge apart. To underscore the simultaneity of the two, we have coined the term *mortar factor*, invoking an analogy to mortar, which, by interposing itself between them, also joins the bricks together. We have extended the analogy to point out that this mortar factor makes possible a good bit of construction. Stabilizing the shifting intensities of pre-oedipal experience depends crucially on transitional process.

We have suggested that a central therapeutic task in working with borderline patients is to support the development of a more reliable, flexible, abstract, and internalized transitional process. We have pointed to the borderline patient's difficulty in sustaining a fantasy life because of the threat of the impulse's breaking loose from the fantasy and literally wreaking havoc. The concrete, literal, external transitional object helps keep the borderline patient off terrain that is too dangerous, given the resources at his command.

Pain can make an edge, a border, a discrete presence, where otherwise merger is simply too great a danger. If borderline patients are simultaneously sticky and thorny, it is because the arrest in the bloom of their transitional processes has left them no alternative. They maintain themselves in states of virtual starvation, sometimes literally as well as metaphorically, because they so fear being devoured by the response that they hunger for.

For all the reasons outlined to this point, achieving a state of working *with* a borderline patient is no simple task. Not only in transitional object relations, but in any kind of relating, negativism is enormously prominent. A common clinical observation with our patients has been that the atmosphere of agitation and antagonism peaks just when a hidden feeling of closeness or affection is about to emerge. Often the fury can be seen to shore up a border that has been in the process of construction, but is not yet far enough along to bear this kind of traffic in affection or closeness.

We have emphasized the need for the therapist not only to tolerate the patient's negativism, but to appreciate it, using the phrase "warmth by friction" as one device for calling attention to what is positive about the negativism. We therapists may rely more on negativism to shore up our boundaries than we are commonly willing to admit. This may play an important part not only in generating professional controversies, but also in the rigid construing of professional identities, with the emphasis on what we are not, what we do not do, and how unlike others we are by reason of being "expert." Our position is not that we should stop being negativistic, but that we should own our negativism and be able both to enjoy and to moderate it, so that we are not prone to make aggressive, hostile, and ultimately self-defeating responses to negativistic overtures from the patient.

Getting to the point where we can work *with* a borderline patient is an arduous crossing, because therapy, like the person of the therapist—like the hidden and unintegrated aspects of the patient's personality—is an exquisite mesh of threat and promise. By the time a therapist is able to work reasonably securely and comfortably with a borderline patient, the major goal of therapy has probably been achieved. A place has been made in the room for two interdependent, mutually respectful human beings who are linked through symbolic communication rather than symbiotic enmeshment. Therapy with borderline patients has to take on the task of constructing what are often regarded, erroneously, as its preconditions. That is to say, it has to pay serious attention to the deeper foundations of therapy, relatedness, and symbolic communication and affect attainment.

Our approach emphasizes from the outset the collaborative features of therapy, giving an important place to successive approximations along the road to thinking and feeling with the patient, rather than for the patient. Therapy depends on joint authorship rather than authority; on a play, back and forth, of feeling and ideas, including antagonisms and antipathies; on the shared trepidation of discovery and repeated revaluation of premises, rather than the application of an algorithm. We emphasize the patient's not knowing and the therapist's not knowing. Instead of decision-making trees, we think in terms of branching points with nodes of creative indecision that make possible new interrogations of developmental possibilities. We emphasize the patient's capacity to have an idea—a new vision—and the therapist's capacity to have an idea, which is only a glimpse of the possible, open to refinement or refutation. We emphasize the capacity of both the therapist and the patient to err, to wander and to wonder, often under conditions of extreme discomfort. And we emphasize the sharing of responsibility and responsiveness between therapist and patient, the joint surveying of the patient's and therapist's actual capabilities and limitations.

We try to build a therapeutic space that makes room for playful seriousness and serious playfulness, for gladness and a new grasp of old predicaments, as well as rage, sorrow, vulnerability, and appropriate deep resignation to what of the unfortunate cannot be changed. We emphasize the therapist as a person with ongoing developmental struggles of his own, lest, by failing to do this, we provide unwitting and destructive hope to that grandiose part of the patient that cherishes the project of a once-and-for-all escape from the human predicament. We try to work with the borderline patient in a style of participant-observation that models such a style for the patient's internal use and leaves him enough room to develop his own. The goal is to help the patient be with himself within himself.

HAZARDS OF CHANGE AND HOLDING

After discussing the borderline patient's core difficulty—their unstable affective self-identity and their defective transitional process, which makes them so vulnerable to the paired fusing–losing dangers—we turned our attention to providing a framework for understanding the hazards of change in borderline patients. Why are borderline syndromes so intractable? Why is forward developmental movement so charged with risk, so fragile, and so likely to entrain massive regression? Why is it so hard to consolidate gains? Our response was in terms of what we called the *progression–regression dilemma*. We proposed a more general concept of splitting, one that involved all-or-none attitudes in all spheres of mental functioning, excluding the middle grounds of modulation, flexibility, negotiation, compromise, forgiveness, and repair. All-or-none attitudes are also a major inhibition in the development of play, which depends so crucially on shifting frames of reference, shifting levels of abstraction, and shifting intensities of intention. Limiting as the all-or-none style may seem, we underscored that, for many patients, this represents a major developmental achievement, providing some bulwarks against inner chaos, confusion, and an overwhelming sense of helplessness, vulnerability, and futility.

The essence of the progression–regression dilemma is that, to the borderline patient whose preoedipal foundations are so flawed, moving forward may seem indistinguishable from moving back into the world of chaos, confusion, and vulnerability. Any uncertainty opens the door to terror. Doubt devastates rather than intrigues. Life outside the ramparts of borderline defenses may seem more frightening than life within. Hence, once the rear view and the forward view become confounded, the door can slam shut on prospects for change with rapidity and force.

Negative therapeutic reactions in these patients, their getting worse when it seems they should be getting better, testify to profound weaknesses in psychological infrastructure that it is easy for therapists to underestimate. With these patients, a settled guardedness against the allure of therapeutic optimism, often a veil for defensive idealization of the patient, is wise policy. Excessive hopefulness on the therapist's part, like an excessive pessimism that masks defensive devaluation of the patient, excludes from view crucial parts of the patient's predicament. Illness itself often represents a precious transitional object tie, one that should not be prematurely severed, but rather helped to mature.

When a part of the patient seems ready to move forward, the question always is, given the fundamentally unintegrated nature of these patients, what is the status of the rest of the patient?

Taking our cue from Winnicott (1953), who underscored the environmental dependence of development, usefully effecting a rapprochement between ideas about intrapsychic and interpersonal processes, we moved to a consideration of the broad question of "holding" as a convenient rubric under which to group the provision of a wide variety of developmental supplies in individualized sequences and styles. We focused on the way in which holding moves from the concrete to the abstract, the literal to the symbolic, the external to the internal, the symbiotic to the communicative. Holding is a frame, part of whose function is to reframe itself. We highlighted the way in which their arrest at the level of the more concrete, external, and literal makes it hard for the borderline patients to get hold of holding, which always has an illusory feature. We emphasized that before, beneath, and beyond interpretation, treatment involves an intermingling, a psychological involvement that underlies words and rests on such processes as repeated cycles of projection and introjection, imitation along a whole variety of channels.

We used the discussion of a single patient treated in the hospital for an extended period to delineate a series of stages in the development of the holding environment and function. Changes in the patient were illustrated using her own art work. This provided a means to emphasize the usefulness of expressive modalities, such as art and dance therapy, in the treatment of borderline patients. Exit from symbiotic enmeshment and blurred boundaries between self and object representations depends crucially on internal form giving symbolic capacity. Art and dance can provide privileged access to aspects of feeling embodied in figure and motion, rhythm, and line and color. We pointed out that expressive therapies are "receptive" therapies as well, in that they can help patients become more receptive to what they have been trying to disown through projective processes.

We discussed the way in which what we had outlined in terms of inpatient treatment also applied in conceptualizing outpatient treatments, where the holding environment is of equal importance, but the therapist's access to it is at a more abstract, symbolic, and metaphorical level. What goes on outside of therapy is vital for what goes on inside, just as what goes on in therapy is vital for what can go on outside. Striking in a followup interview with Mrs. D., after more than ten years, was the constancy of her need for concrete propping up of her transitional illusion-making capacities. Her recovery from alcoholism depended on the reconstitution of a holding environment outside the hospital that provided the equivalent of what she had gotten from the nursing staff in the hospital. While she described herself as having "been born" as a person with awareness of feelings at Sheppard Pratt, there was a great deal of ongoing work to be done after this psychological "birth."

EMPTINESS, LONELINESS, SUICIDALITY

After discussing "holding" at considerable length, we took up three important clinical topics in working with borderline patients. These were the patients' sense of being empty and insignificant, their agonizing sense of loneliness, and their chronic suicidality. In approaching these topics, we kept the focus on the borderline patients' struggles to attain and contain feeling, the relative arrest in their transitional processes, and their struggles with and against very early developmental dangers constellated around fusing and losing.

We pointed out that integration of experience can bring enrichment only if the self is strong and supple enough to maintain its essential form and functioning under the strain of feeling. Self-observation, crucial in making transitions from one state of feeling to another, is a transitional faculty that depends on a capacity to step back from the self inside the self, to change perspective without losing context and content. Sublimation, like psychosis, depends on the investment of illusion, but in the service of the ego and in continuity with important ego functions, not to their detriment. Our capacity for creative illusion making and symbolic orchestration determines the vividity, vitality, and reach of our capacity to participate in the experience of the self.

Loneliness is a halfway position, agonizing because it carries with it an awareness of dangers on all sides. Loneliness involves a longing to relate that feels itself checkmated, without any hope of a different kind of meeting or mating. Again, the losing and the fusing dangers play an important part in the generation of the lonely position. To move beyond it requires a change in the faculties of illusion, so as to provide more liberty in moving closer without losing the self, and more liberty in moving farther away without losing the object with catastrophic consequences for the self. We discussed how states of emergency stress, often quite prolonged, may have compromised the borderline patient's capacity to use illusion flexibly, so that the illusion of pervasive failure derives from the failure of illusion *in extremis*. Loneliness is a serious predicament.

Chronic suicidality involves chronically abolitionist fervors, threatening to get rid of problems that seem overwhelming by abolishing treatment and patient at a single blow. States of chronic suicidality are complicated affective and effective maneuvers. They highlight both the connection with the therapist and its defects by providing a horizon of catastrophe against which to view the relationship. Chronic suicidality can be a mortifying mortar that yet has a constructive potential as well as its destructive one. We emphasize again a style of managing and living with chronic suicidality that uses symbolic communications and partial responses to help the patient with the fusing–losing danger, so that more feeling and more nuanced feeling can be attained and sustained.

THE THERAPIST'S SELF IN THE SERVICE OF THERAPY

If we are interested in the patient's forms of self-relations, his style of accommodating and excluding feelings, the quality and flexibility of his participation in himself, we have a similar interest in the self-relations of the therapist. Therapy is an *involvement* between people. Engagement is the precondition for influence. We expect that treating borderline patients will involve the therapist in strong feelings, which often will have sufficient strength to challenge, at least in relative measure, and sometimes more than that, the security and stability of the therapist's self. This is both a danger and an opportunity. Creative reorganization always involves a measure of instability.

We presented a sketch of a way of thinking about the therapist's experience in treatment as lying between the two poles—between urges toward defensive overinvolvement with the patient on the one hand and urges toward a defensive rejection of the patient on the other hand. The goal for the therapist is to move from these extremes, corresponding respectively to the fusing danger and the losing danger, toward a more modulated middle position of participant observation where he has a wide range of affective experience of the treatment and is able to use it as a guide to enrich his knowledge and appreciation of the treatment dynamics, rather than being had by it. A case example illustrated a range of countertransference reactions. A treatment that had been reduced to havoc found a more even keel when a therapist, able to contain his own reactions, introduced more latitude for feeling, observation, and

communication, even in the face of significant clinical disagreements.

Next, we considered the way in which the therapist's
own dependency experiences can come into play with
borderline patients. We were concerned to explore this area
because of another common implicit polarization of the field
of therapeutic encounter, namely, the one that represents
the patient as pathologically or excessively dependent and
the therapist as someone who has no active and visible
dependency needs. We pointed to the fee as a concrete
representation of the therapist's dependence on the patient.
We also emphasized that it is only because of the patient that
the therapist can be a therapist. We wondered to what
degree the restriction of discussion to the patient's dependency needs skewed and limited the therapeutic discussion,
presenting case material in which the therapist's dependency needs also received scrutiny. The subsequent dialogue
brought broadened access to quandaries that the patient felt
in regard to her dependency needs.

We proceeded to discussion of the role of self-
disclosure in treatment, arguing that there was room for a
good bit more of this on the therapist's part than is commonly acknowledged in formal discussions. We made the
point that self-disclosure on the therapist's part may be
essential to helping the patient understand the therapist's
responses, construct a fuller picture of the therapist's animating concerns and how these impact the therapy, and
learn to question what animates his own responses. The
question is one of measure. Just as participation can be
overwhelming, a retreat to observation can be distancing
and destructive in the extreme. Therapy demands a set of
rules of sustenance, not just a set of rules of abstinence. The
issue is to be able to move back and forth between observation and participation, reserve and disclosure, in a rhythm
and with appropriate modulation of intensity to respond to
the borderline patient's need for security and support along
his tenuous borders. Transference processes are so powerful

and so inclusive that self-disclosure on the therapist's part will be drawn into these processes, rather than distorting them beyond recognition. Often, the therapist's self-disclosure can lead to developments that help clarify the patient's transference and self-transference paradigms.

ENGAGEMENT IN THE SERVICE OF DEVELOPMENT

We have attempted to answer, or at least to sketch lines of response, to two intertwined and essentially related questions: What do borderline patients need? What do those who treat borderline patients need?

Borderline patients need sustained involvement with others, if they are to be able to achieve a greater capacity to sustain feeling. They need help with mastering the threats to the self posed by the fusing and losing dangers. They need help in furthering the development of their transitional processes in the direction of the more abstract, the more internal, and the more metaphorical. They need help in distinguishing forward movement that allows them more degrees of freedom in feeling, valuing, and choosing from regressive movement that submerges them in primitive confusion, chaos, and vulnerability. They need holding—environmental responses that provide stability, succor, and modeling of symbolic communicative processes to replace symbiotic enmeshments where self-object boundaries are blurred and projective identification is the major form of dealing with disavowed potential emotional contents of the self. They need help in the form of a set of relationships with responsive, responsible others that survive the intense challenges posed in the work.

Surviving rage, that is, maintaining emotional presence through this intense internal state, is an essential prerequisite for modulating it. The outer other and that inner other, the self as object, collaborate on the project of supporting containment. Relational ongoingness provides the means to build a foundation for reliable attaining, containing, and sustaining of affect. Relational ongoingness means that both separateness and involvement need to be sustained. The middle space between fusion and extrusion needs to be constructed and explored.

It is an experiential clinical fact that sustained, long-term work with borderline patients means, for the therapist, sustaining and containing long term threats to the therapeutic self. Urges to defensive and dedifferentiating fusion with the patient alternate with urges to offensive and pseudo-differentiating extrusion of the patient. Working with borderline patients requires supple firmness, a capacity to be curious not just about the patient but about oneself in relation and response to the patient.

It calls for the capacity to make authentic personal relationships in a professional context that respects the defining condition of the work, namely that it is carried on for the benefit of the patient's development as a person with an inalienable right to try, choose, value, lose, repair, and care. It calls for the capacity to tolerate a great deal of doubt, ambiguity, disagreement, and even therapeutic despair. It calls for the capacity to be neither too sure nor not sure enough, allowing oneself to feel both ways on occasion and to wonder why one visited that place in feeling when one did.

The fusing–losing dangers are implicated, too, in the therapist's relationship to his own ideas, theories, and notions about technique and therapeutic stance. Fusing with certain cherished notions and ideas may exclude the most educative and promising forms of anxiety. A therapeutic shell can replace the therapeutic self. We believe that, to a large extent, this has taken place for many who approach borderline patients with convictions, if not prejudices, that border on the mechanical and algorithmic. This mirrors the rigidity of so many borderline selves.

Losing any urge to theory and disciplined examination

of attitudes, techniques, and quandaries in working with borderline patients also involves the perils of rigidification, isolation, and loss of a larger context. Therapists who take on the hard work of "holding" borderline patients as they struggle for more reliable means of differentiation and involvement need "holding." Our picture of treatment with borderline patients involves a series of concentric holding circles with the therapist–patient couple at the center, but not isolated. What is difficult needs discussion, not just in the core circle, but rippling through the holding environment as well.

Borderline patients highlight cultural issues relating to appropriate satisfaction and limitation of dependency needs, that is, to achieving reliable differentiation and involvement in the face of the losing and the fusing dangers. Cultures, too, can be driven regressively to the more concrete, materialistic, mechanistic, literal, and external pole of transitional processes. They, too, can have troubles maintaining a stance on the more integrative, abstract ground of values. Freedom always needs redefinition so that it can bring content, sadness, and contentment, not emptiness, alienation, and, eventually, a retreat to rigidity. When we work with borderline patients, we are working not only with ourselves but also with the cultural surround. The experience we generate involves a critique that may have implications far beyond the therapeutic couple.

References

Ablon, S. L. (1990). Developmental aspects of self-esteem. *Psychoanalytic Study of the Child* 45:337–356. New Haven, CT: Yale University Press.

Bergland, C., and Gonzalez, R. M. (In Press). Art and madness: can the interface be quantified? The Sheppard Pratt art rating scale—an instrument for measuring art integration. *American Journal of Art Therapy.*

Bergland, C., Klement, M., Lewin, R., et al. (1984). *Therapeutic processes in the hospital environment.* Paper presented at Scientific Day, Sheppard Pratt, Towson, MD, June 2.

Blos, P. (1962). *On Adolescence.* New York: Free Press of Glencoe.

Bollas, C. (1982). On the relation to the self as object. *International Journal of Psycho-Analysis* 64:347–359.

Farber, L. (1966). *The Ways of the Will.* New York: Basic Books.

Fiedler, E. (1973). Personal communication.

Freud, S. (1910a). The antithetical meaning of primal words. *Standard Edition* 11:155–161.

_____ (1910b). The future prospects of psychoanalytic therapy. *Standard Edition* 11:139–151.

_____ (1915). Observations on transference love. *Standard Edition* 12:157–171.

_____ (1920). Beyond the pleasure principle. *Standard Edition* 18:1–64.

_____ (1924). Neurosis and psychosis. *Standard Edition* 19:149–153.

_____ (1927). Fetishism. *Standard Edition* 21:152–157.

Furman, E. (1991). *Toddlers and Their Mothers: A Study in Early Personality Development.* Madison, CT: International Universities Press.

Furman, R. (1984). *The seduction hypothesis: the interaction between psychic reality and objective reality; reflections from clinical child psychoanalysis.* Paper presented at panel discussion of the American Psychoanalytic Association, New York, December 23.

Goethe, J. von (1984). *Conversations with Eckerman.* Trans. John Oxenford. San Francisco: North Point Press.

Greenbaum, T. (1978). The "analyzing instrument" and the "transitional object." In *Between Reality and Fantasy*, ed. S. Grolnick and L. Barkin, pp. 191–202. New York: Jason Aronson.

Hatfield, H. (1963). *Goethe.* New York: New Directions.

Heidegger, M. (1971). *Poetry, Language, Thought.* New York: Harper & Row.

Hong, K. M. (1978). The transitional phenomenon. *Psychoanalytic Study of the Child* 33:47–79. New Haven, CT: Yale University Press.

Jorgenson, L. (1991). Avoiding misconduct charges depends on simple precautions. *Psychiatric News* 26:6, 13.

Keats, J. (1818). Letter to John Hamilton Reynolds of Sunday 3 May 1918. In *The Selected Letters of John Keats,* ed. L. Trilling, pp. 126–127. New York: Farrar, Straus and Young, 1951.

Kernberg, O. (1965). Counter-transference. *Journal of the*

American Psychoanalytic Association 13:38–56.
_____ (1987). *Borderline Conditions and Pathological Narcissism.* Northvale, NJ: Jason Aronson.
Kilgallen, R. (1972). Hydrotherapy—is it all washed up? *Journal of Psychiatric Nursing* 10:3–6.
Klein, M. (1955). The psychoanalytic play technique: its history and significance. In *New Directions in Psychoanalysis,* ed. M. Klein, P. Heimann, and R. Money-Kyrle, pp. 3–22. New York: Basic Books.
Laplanche, J., and Pontalis, J. B. (1973). *The Language of Psychoanalysis.* Trans. D. Nicholson-Smith. New York: Norton.
Lévi-Strauss, C. (1963). The effectiveness of symbols. In *Structural Anthropology,* pp. 186–206. New York: Basic Books.
Lewin, R. A. (1985). A mental health worker's vocation. *The Psychiatric Hospital* 16:79–83.
Lewin, R. A., and Sharfstein, S. (1990). Managed care and the discharge dilemma. *Psychiatry* 55:116–121.
MacClean, P. D. (1985). Brain evolution relating to family, play, and the separation call. *Archives of General Psychiatry* 42:405–417.
Masterson, J. (1989). Maintaining objectivity crucial in treating borderline patients. *Psychiatric Times* 6:1, 26–28.
McCormack, C. C. (1989). The borderline/schizoid marriage: the holding environment as an essential treatment construct. *Journal of Marital and Family Therapy* 15:299–309.
McHugh, P. R. (1989). The neuropsychiatry of basal ganglia disorders. *Neuropsychiatry, Neuropsychology and Behavioral Neurology* 2:239–247.
Modell, A. H. (1976). ''The holding environment'' and the therapeutic action of psychoanalysis. *Journal of the American Psychoanalytic Association* 24:285–305.
_____ (1984). *Psychoanalysis in a New Context.* New York: International Universities Press.
Natterson, J. (1991). *Beyond Countertransference: The Therapist's Subjectivity in the Therapeutic Process.*

Northvale, NJ: Jason Aronson.

Neruda, P. (1975). *Fully Empowered.* Trans. A. Reid. New York: Farrar, Straus and Giroux.

Nietzsche, F. (1954). Beyond good and evil. In *The Philosophy of Nietzsche,* trans. H. Zimmern, pp. 369–616. New York: Modern Library.

Ogden, T. (1982). *Projective Identification and Psychotherapeutic Technique.* New York: Jason Aronson.

_____ (1989). *The Primitive Edge of Experience.* Northvale, NJ: Jason Aronson.

Quaytman, M. (1987). Developing a holding environment during the treatment of the borderline patient. *Psychiatric Annals* 17:344–351.

Rodman, F. R., ed. (1987). *The Spontaneous Gesture, Selected Letters of D. W. Winnicott.* Cambridge, MA: Harvard University Press.

Ross, D. R., Lewin, R. A., et al. (1988). The psychiatric uses of cold wet sheet packs. *Journal of the American Psychiatric Association* 145:242–245.

Schulz, C. G. (1980). All-or-none phenomena in the psychotherapy of severe disorders. In *The Psychotherapy of Schizophrenia,* ed. J. S. Strauss, et al., pp. 181–189. New York: Plenum.

_____ (1984). The struggle toward ambivalence. *Psychiatry* 47:28–46.

_____ (1989). A discussion from an object relations view: a resilient fist in a velvet glove. *Psychoanalytic Inquiry* 9:539–553.

Schulz, C. G., and Kilgalen, R. K. (1969). *Case Studies in Schizophrenia.* New York: Basic Books.

Searles, H. F. (1979a). Identity development in Edith Jacobson's "the self and the object world." In *Countertransference and Related Subjects: Selected Papers,* ed. H. F. Searles, pp. 36–44. New York: International Universities Press.

_____ (1979b). The "dedicated physician" in the field of psychotherapy and psychoanalysis. In *Countertransference and Related Subjects: Selected Papers,* ed. H. F.

Searles, pp. 71–89. New York: International Universities Press.

———— (1979c). The patient as therapist to his analyst. In *Countertransference and Related Subjects: Selected Papers,* ed. H. F. Searles, pp. 380–460. New York: International Universities Press.

————, ed. (1979d). *Countertransference and Related Subjects: Selected Papers.* New York: International Universities Press.

Stevens, W. (1973). The man with the blue guitar. In *The Norton Anthology of Modern Poetry,* ed. R. Ellman and R. O'Clair, pp. 252–253. New York: Norton.

Sugarman, A., and Jaffe, L. A. (1989). A developmental line of transitional phenomena. In *The Facilitating Environment: Clinical Applications of Winnicott's Theory,* ed. M. Fromm and B. Smith, pp. 88–129. Madison, CT: International Universities Press.

Sullivan, H. S. (1953). Conceptions of modern psychiatry. In *Collected Works of Harry Stack Sullivan,* vol. I, ed. H. S. Perry and M. L. Gawel, pp. 3–298. New York: Norton.

———— (1965). The data of psychiatry. In *Collected Works of Harry Stack Sullivan,* vol. II, ed. H. S. Perry, M. L. Gawel, and M. Gibbon, pp. 32–55. New York: Norton.

Szalita, A. (1981). *Issues in Reanalysis.* Chestnut Lodge Symposium. Rockville, MD, October 2.

Winnicott, D. W. (1949). Hate in the countertransference. *International Journal of Psycho-Analysis* 30:69–74.

———— (1953). Transitional objects and transitional phenomena. *International Journal of Psycho-Analysis* 34:89–97.

———— (1958). The capacity to be alone. *International Journal of Psycho-Analysis* 39:416–420.

———— (1959). Nothing at the centre. In *Psychoanalytic Explorations,* ed. C. Winnicott, R. Shepherd, and M. Davis, pp. 49–52. Cambridge, MA: Harvard University Press, 1989.

Index